War on the Dream

War on the Dream

✦

How Anti-Sprawl Policy Threatens the Quality of Life

Wendell Cox

iUniverse, Inc.

New York Lincoln Shanghai

War on the Dream
How Anti-Sprawl Policy Threatens the Quality of Life

Copyright © 2006 by Wendell Cox

iUniverse books may be ordered through booksellers or by contacting:

iUniverse
2021 Pine Lake Road, Suite 100
Lincoln, NE 68512
www.iuniverse.com
1-800-Authors (1-800-288-4677)

ISBN-13: 978-0-595-39948-2 (pbk)
ISBN-13: 978-0-595-84337-4 (ebk)
ISBN-10: 0-595-39948-7 (pbk)
ISBN-10: 0-595-84337-9 (ebk)

Printed in the United States of America

For
Elden Kellar
and
Joan Krahmer

Contents

List of Illustrations

List of Tables

Preface

The principal purpose of this book is to highlight the serious consequences of currently popular land-use policies. The urban planning community is implementing—and proposes to expand—strategies that are already seriously eroding housing affordability and intensifying traffic congestion. This could result in substantial economic reverses, because home ownership is so central to the creation of middle-income wealth and because traffic congestion reduces productivity. Since World War II, low priced land on the urban fringe has made the "American Dream"—and now the "Universal Dream"—of home ownership a reality. This, combined with the superior mobility of the automobile and consequent retailing innovations has "democratized prosperity," making it possible for an unprecedented share of households to live at comfortable middle-income levels.

A secondary purpose of this book is to expose the virtually groundless arguments against suburbanization (pejoratively called "urban sprawl"). Today's urban policies are like a house built on sand, rooted in subjective feelings, impressions, ideology, incomplete research, and outright error. The ultimate "vision" is, at best, a blurry illusion, if not a delusion.

I have spent much of my life thinking about urban policy and have consulted, lectured, and served on public boards. I strongly believe that public policies must be rational. They must be based on rigorous analysis; they must be adopted only after taking account of potential consequences; and they should be as free as possible from ideological bias.

It all goes back to Mrs. Krahmer. Joan Krahmer was my high school civics teacher at Hillsboro High School in Oregon. Her "critical thinking" unit is the most influential memory from my years of education. Any proposition had to be subjected to intense and systematic questioning. It was not enough to simply parrot conventional wisdom, whether from the academy or from popular culture. Any concept that did not survive such an examination had to be discarded. Much of the analysis upon which today's urban policies are based would not have earned a passing grade.

Through the years, I have pursued an aggressive research and travel agenda. Much of this research has been posted to three large Internet Web sites, which together constitute the *Demographia* group, now approaching 5,000 documents.

Visitors download approximately 4,000,000 documents annually. The *Demographia* group sites include:

www.demographia.com focuses on demographics, principally on urban policy. In recent years, *Demographia* has published metropolitan population and domestic migration data before any other source (based upon census reports). Moreover, *Demographia* contains the only comprehensive list of urban areas in the world over 500,000 population with population, land area and density estimates. *Demographia* has been selected by Study Sphere (www.studysphere.com) as one of the best educational resources on the Internet, along with the national census agencies of Canada, the United States, Ireland, New Zealand, Norway, Bulgaria and the Philippines.

www.publicpurpose.com focuses on transportation and other public policy issues. *The Public Purpose* has been honored twice by *The National Journal* as one of the top transportation Web sites in the nation. In 2001, *The National Journal* honored *The Public Purpose,* along with the United States Department of Transportation, the United States Department of Transportation Inspector General and the Surface Transportation Policy Project. In 2003, *The National Journal* again honored *The Public Purpose.,*

www.rentalcartours.com ("Urban Tours by Rental Car") contains articles developed from travel to various urban areas (more than 75 urban areas in 25 nations).

In some respects, this book is a summary and extension of the *Demographia* group Web sites, and throughout, there are many references to additional source notes on these sites.

The book uses extensive figures (graphics), which frequently require source notes too extensive to include in the graphics themselves. Thus, source notes for graphics are contained in endnotes that correspond to the figure references in the text.

Finally, nothing in this book should be construed as advocating suburbanization itself. The urban form is not an end; it is a means. Ends, or objectives, in this debate, are principally about the quality of life and the diffusion of affluence. As Benjamin Friedman so eloquently argued in *The Economic Consequences of Economic Growth,* economic growth is more than desirable, it is a *necessity.* Many of the currently fashionable urban planning policies must be reversed to maintain economic growth and incomes. Nothing less than such a reversal will be required to facilitate the widest possible opportunity for all.

Wendell Cox
July 2006

Cover Illustrations
Upper Left: Suburban Kansas City
Upper Right: Suburban Tokyo
Middle Left: Suburban Paris
Lower Left: Suburban Brisbane
Background: Chicago Urban Area from the Air
All photographs by author

Introduction:
Policies Have Consequences

I traveled to Toronto to criticize the provincial government's plans to fight urban sprawl by requiring all new urban development to be inside a greenbelt. As I was leaving for the airport to return home, the Canadian Broadcasting Company requested an interview with me on its *Here and Now* program. In preparation, the reporter wanted a summary of what I would say. I told him that the proposed greenbelt would create a scarcity of land for home building, which would, in turn, lead to higher housing prices and less home ownership. This would have the most negative effects on low-income households, especially on the disproportionate share who are minorities and immigrants. I noted that much of middle-income wealth is in home equity and that home ownership is crucial to wealth creation. The greenbelt could reduce future economic growth by reducing future home ownership. The reporter seemed taken aback that a seemingly benign land-use policy—imposition of a greenbelt—could have such broad and negative consequences.

Around the world, governments are implementing policies to combat urban sprawl, as in the Toronto greenbelt plan. Yet, there has been little attention to the impacts of such policies. It is simply assumed that sprawl is such a heinous ill that nothing else matters. However, like policies in any field, anti-sprawl strategies must be considered both in terms of their objectives and the broader context of their consequences. This book is about those broader impacts, the most important of which are likely to lead to a lower standard of living for most households.

A quick definition is required. *Urban sprawl* is the geographical expansion of urban areas (See Appendix: Definition of Urban Terms). It is how urban areas have historically grown. Urban sprawl is nothing more than suburbanization—the spreading out of urban areas geographically as they become larger and more affluent. Urban sprawl, or suburbanization, has been the manner of urban growth virtually since the beginning of civilization. Transport has been a critical factor. Early urban areas suburbanized as far as people could walk. During the 19th and early 20th centuries, urban areas suburbanized as far as mass-transit systems would allow. More recently, some urban areas have suburbanized as far as automobiles will allow. Automobile-based suburbanization is the target of the anti-suburban (anti-sprawl) movement.

The principal thesis of the book is that anti-suburban policies threaten economic growth, by reducing home ownership, mobility, and retail innovation. The likely decline in the quality of life would be felt by all, but would be most severe for lower-income and lower-middle-income households. Fewer of these households would achieve "The Dream"—the American Dream, European Dream, Canadian Dream, Great Australian Dream, Kiwi Dream (New Zealand), or indeed the Universal Dream—of home ownership. The anti-suburban movement can be characterized as a "War on the Dream," by virtue of the inevitable consequences of its policies.

The United States is the principal focus, but there is also an international focus. There are two reasons for crossing oceans and international borders. First, American urban planners often talk of suburbanization as if it were a uniquely American phenomenon. In fact, suburbanization is virtually universal. Second, anti-suburban policies are being proposed elsewhere in the high-income world and even in the middle-and low-income worlds, with the same inattention to the consequences, or as they are called in economics, "negative externalities."

It is hoped that policy makers and open-minded urban planners will take account of the crucial issues of wealth and poverty that are so entwined with anti-suburban policies. Of course, in the "politically correct" or "group think"[1] environment of urban planning, a planner courageous enough to objectively consider the consequences of anti-suburban policies could face disapproval from colleagues and even diminished career advancement potential. However, as will be shown, much of what the anti-suburban movement claims to be wrong is not wrong at all, and much of what is characterized as threatened is not threatened at all. Anti-suburban policies are rooted in faulty or incomplete research, and the latest tastes in urban planning or architecture and are likely to be destructive. Against this is the longer-term economic well-being of the population. These are the choices.

There are some perspectives that may not be found elsewhere.

- Nearly all new, high-income world urban growth in recent decades has been automobile-oriented suburbanization.

- The anti-suburban movement is little more than rhetorical. Anti-suburban proponents are long on platitudes about transportation, community, and urban form, but have proposed no more than that to reverse automobile-oriented suburbanization. This is because such a course of action is both impractical and politically unachievable.

• The urban planning tools of urban renewal and urban freeway construction played a major role in the decline of American central cities.

• "Leapfrog" development, the non-contiguous development bugaboo of anti-suburban activists, contributes strongly to housing affordability. In fact, leapfrog development leads to the continuous urbanization the anti-suburbanites prefer, but at a pace set by buyers and sellers, not by the dictates of planners.

• Prosperity has been largely democratized in the high-income world, as objective poverty has been significantly reduced. The democratization of prosperity has been closely associated with the defining characteristics of suburbanization, such as low-cost housing on the urban fringe, low-cost transportation by automobiles throughout the urban area, and low-cost product prices from strongly competitive retailers, such as big-box stores.

• There are serious economic consequences to the present directions of anti-suburban policy and that could lead to less home ownership, a lower standard of living, and greater poverty. All of this comes at a time that many high-income nations need to maintain or increase their rates of economic growth to finance underfunded public pensions and expensive social programs.

Part I: Setting the Stage

Chapter 1 ("The Theology of Urban Sprawl") summarizes the indictment against suburbanization. Anti-suburban advocates use near-religious terms to describe suburbanization's purported ills. They believe that the American economy is in decline and that the present forms of urbanization cannot be sustained. Their plan of salvation is to turn back the clock, returning to a time when mass transit and walking were the dominant forms of transportation. They would restrict urban development by simultaneous use of densification and urban growth boundaries," at the same time trying to force people out of cars and into mass transit, as well as outlawing big-box stores. Portland, Oregon, is often cited as a model, even as its own policies—having been soundly rejected by the electorate when given the opportunity—are unraveling.

Chapter 2 ("A Bigger World") begins by noting that much of the anti-suburban debate has been conducted in a policy vacuum. The high-income world has achieved a near democratization of prosperity by allowing economic freedom. A substantial portion of the new wealth has been generated by broad home ownership. At the same time, international research indicates that America's continuing economic leadership among high-income nations is at least partly due to its low-cost housing and retail industries, both of which conflict with anti-suburban policies. Automobile use, which anti-suburban policy would restrict, has also been shown to foster greater economic growth. Because of the role economic freedom plays in economic growth, it is important that regulations, including those aimed at the suburbs, be limited to those necessary to protect the individual and common good.

Chapter 3 ("Suburban World") describes the historical background and the present situation of suburbanization, which has been occurring virtually since urban areas were first developed. Transport has been an important, driving factor in suburbanization. In the beginning, urban areas spread to the extent that walking would allow. Mass transit brought unprecedented suburban development in the 19th century. The automobile has brought further suburbanization. Many analysts think that automobile-oriented suburbanization is limited to the United States. To the contrary, all major urban areas in the high-income world are settled at automobile-oriented densities, with the exception of Hong Kong. Automobile-oriented suburbanization has also been accelerated by the unprecedented exodus of people from rural areas and small towns to larger urban areas, falling household size, the entry of women into the workforce, and the popularity of suburban living.

Chapter 4 ("Planning and the Post-War American City") describes the unique recent history of U.S. inner cities, which have generally lost more of their population than their counterparts elsewhere in the high-income world. The conventional wisdom is that these losses occurred due to "white flight," as white residents left for the suburbs in response to entry by African Americans. This is an oversimplification. In fact, urban planning itself was a major factor in driving white residents out of inner cities. Urban renewal and freeway construction displaced millions of urban residents, often low-income African Americans. These expulsions accelerated the already-strong housing demand Blockbusting—the systematic use of racial fears to "scare" people into selling their houses at steeply discounted prices—followed, generating demographic changes faster than they could be easily absorbed. Other public policies, such as the failure of law enforcement and judicial systems, real and perceived political corruption, high taxes, and perhaps most importantly, substandard educational performance that has driven away households with school-age children, has made inner cities even less attractive than urban areas in other high-income nations. The role of misguided and distorted public policies in the decline of U.S. inner cities, including urban planning, has generally been overlooked.

Part II: Demonizing the Suburbs

Chapter 5 ("Hysteria Over Land") reviews the claims of anti-suburbanists that urbanization threatens valuable farmland and open space. The data indicates exactly the opposite—there is no shortage of farmland. Moreover, urbanization has not produced a net loss in farmland. In the United States, Canada, and Australia, large amounts of farmland have been abandoned due to greater productivity. The expansion of urban land has been small by comparison. In fact, the human footprint, including urban and agricultural land, has been significantly reduced. Urbanization covers only a small part of the land area of high-income nations. In the United States, less than three percent of the land area is developed. Absent a compelling imperative, public policy should not specify minimum or maximum urban densities.

Chapter 6 ("Missing the Transportation Connections") reviews anti-suburban urban transportation claims. Generally, the anti-suburban movement claims that suburbanization makes traffic congestion worse and makes air pollution worse. To the contrary, suburbanization dilutes both traffic congestion and air pollution. It is also claimed that the automobile-based transportation system is more costly than mass transit. Again, the facts do not bear this out. As the automobile has opened opportunities for greater mobility, mass transit's market share has declined substantially throughout the high-income world, from the United States to Western Europe and Japan. The automobile is the dominant means of transportation throughout the urban areas not only of the United States, but also of Western Europe, Canada, Australia, New Zealand and most of Japan. The principal accomplishment of the automobile has been to expand mobility far beyond what would have been possible with mass transit or any other mode of transport.

Chapter 7 ("Costs, Community, Obesity, Fear, Ad Nausea") outlines additional criticisms of suburbanization. It is claimed that government costs are higher in the suburbs, but the actual data indicate otherwise. Despite claims that consumer costs are higher due to suburbanization, the data indicate otherwise. There are claims that suburbanization has destroyed community, but community has been redefined by changing demographics and technology. More frivolous, inadequately designed research blames obesity on suburbanization, for example without examining food consumption. The anti-suburban movement has gone so far as to cite fear and stress to indict suburbanization.

Part III: War on the Dream

Chapter 8 ("Rationing Land, Home Ownership and Opportunity") outlines anti-suburban land-use strategies. The principal, and most destructive, strategies are the various forms of densification, sought through urban-growth boundaries and greenbelts. These policies ban development on considerable amounts of land. This land rationing has driven up the cost of housing, which seems sure to lead to a lower rate of home ownership. The effects are most evident in Southern California, Australia, the United Kingdom, and New Zealand. Anti-suburban Portland, Oregon, experienced the worst housing-affordability loss of any major U.S. metropolitan area in the 1990s.

Anti-suburban activists have denied that their land rationing policies reduced housing affordability, contending, for example, that the California and Portland reverses are due to demand from high growth rates. In fact, faster growing urban areas have superior affordability. Three of the four fastest growing urban areas in the high-income world are Atlanta, Dallas-Fort Worth, and Houston, and each has better than average housing affordability. Housing affordability is retained in these areas because governments have resisted the land rationing policies that bid up the price of housing. In the end, the large losses in housing affordability could lead to much lower home-ownership rates, less wealth creation, and less affluent economies.

Chapter 9 ("The Cost of Neglecting Mobility") reviews the likely impacts of anti-suburban policy on urban transportation. Around the United States, metropolitan areas have been committing a disproportionate share of financial resources to mass transit, while failing to provide sufficient capacity for the ever-increasing volume of cars and trucks. These high expenditures are justified on the assumption that people should use mass transit instead of cars. However, mass transit simply does not go from where people are to where they want to go in a time that can compete with the automobile. Because mobility is important to a strong urban economy, the anti-suburban strategies that would ration mobility can be expected to lead not only to lower standards of living and more time traveling in more congested conditions, but also less economic growth and affluence.

Chapter 10 ("The High Price of Retail Restrictions") reviews the potential impacts of anti-suburban restrictions on retailing. Generally, anti-suburbanites would like to severely limit or even prohibit the development of big-box stores, such as Wal-Mart, Target, Carrefour, or Toys R Us, claiming that these highly competitive operations are a threat to smaller, older businesses. In fact, retail and commercial development has been making progress for centuries and lowering prices. At any point in history, government could have outlawed further innovation, as the anti-suburbanites would prefer now. However, the consequences would be higher prices for everyone, and a lower standard of living, especially for the low-income households who depend on the low prices offered by big-box stores.

Chapter 11 ("Anti-Suburban Dystopia") concludes, based on the previous discussion, that the anti-suburban movement has failed to identify any compelling reasons that would justify interfering with the rights of people to live and work where and how they please. Generally, the research of the anti-suburban movement is weak and many of its propositions are fallacious or misleading. The hard-won democratization of prosperity could be at-risk from anti-suburban policies. This would occur by reducing the wealth-creating incidence of home ownership, retarding mobility, and raising prices. Indeed, it seems likely that if there had been no suburbanization, living standards today would be lower and more households would live in poverty. A future under anti-suburban policies promises just that.

Part IV: Sustainable Future Tense

Chapter 12 ("The Universal Dream") considers the alternative to anti-suburban policies. The anti-suburban characterization of a declining economy could not be more wrong. Virtually all indicators show that people throughout the high-income world are living better than ever before. At least to some degree, this appears to be associated with suburbanization. There is plenty of land for urban development, without materially reducing agricultural land or open space. Automobile-oriented urban areas can be designed so that traffic growth can be adequately handled and traffic congestion kept under control, permitting ready access to large labor markets by car. Already the state of Texas is proceeding with such a plan. Retail innovations will continue, and product prices are likely to continue to fall in real terms, either due to the strategies of today's market leaders, or others that out-compete them in the future.

In this better future, more appropriate urban planning will be required. Urban planning has evolved to the point that its principal focus seems to be to tell people what they cannot do. A more appropriate approach would be to plan the public facilities needed for people to live as they choose.

The progress that has been made in the high-income world can be sustained and extended. The American Dream has become the Universal Dream throughout the high-income world. The sooner it spreads throughout the lower-and middle-income worlds, the better.

PART I
Setting The Stage

1

The Theology of Urban Sprawl

Urban Sprawl: An Inherent Evil?

Few issues have achieved such prominence in recent years as the purported imperative for curbing urban sprawl. There appears to be a strong consensus, especially in the high-income world,[2] that urban sprawl must be stopped. There has been little dissent.

The anti-sprawl movement employs near-apocalyptic terms, not unlike the rhetoric of 19th-century revivalists to decry urban sprawl. For example:

- Peter Blake declared in *God's Own Junkyard* that the suburban pattern developing in the United States is "making life there only slightly less tolerable than on tenement streets." In this early (1964) contribution to anti-sprawl dogma, Blake admits to having written in "fury."[3]

- In *Building Suburbia,* historian Dolores Hayden complains, "Even a program for one hundred million solar houses or 130 million electric cars could not make the United States sustainable." She contends that "severe limits on land use, energy, and new construction" would be required to achieve sustainability.[4]

- Italian architect Paolo Soleri, whose dense 30-year-old Arizona anti-suburban settlement has not yet attracted enough residents to fill two buses, says that "the single-family home, and suburbia with it, goes—or we go with it." (Soleri himself reportedly lives in a single-family home on a sprawling lot in an automobile-oriented Phoenix suburb).[5]

- U.S. nationally syndicated newspaper columnist Neal Pearce implied that the Columbine High School massacre in Littleton, Colorado, was caused by urban sprawl.[6]

- The role of St. John the Divine falls to James Howard Kunstler, whose writings are the anti-sprawl movement's equivalent of what Protestants call the Revelation and Catholics call the Apocalypse. His "end times" theology condemns the suburbs as a "trashy and preposterous human habitat with no future," and as "places that are not worth caring about." Kunstler further bemoans being "ashamed of my civilization."[7]

The spirit may have been best caught by a headline in an alternative Toronto newspaper, *The Eye*, to the effect that "the suburbs are killing us."[8] Granted, many anti-sprawl activists are less outrageous or hysterical in their characterization of urban sprawl and the automobile. However, they are generally no less fervent in their commitment to stop urban sprawl and seem oblivious to the fact that their solutions might have consequences worthy of consideration.

Much of the urban planning community condemns urban sprawl as an inherent evil, fulfilling a role parallel to that of sin in the medieval church. This is not to suggest that there is no debate. It is similar to novice monks who might have debated one another, competing to impress their superiors with the most clever and convincing damnation of sin. At no point is podium time granted to those with fundamental doubts. They are not even in the monastery. However, there is dissent outside the walls. The leaders know this, but airing it would threaten their theology. Such dogmatism might be defensible in a monastery, but has no place in public forums.

At the same time, there seems to be no end to the inventiveness of anti-sprawl activists. Studies have been produced to convince the public that urban sprawl causes obesity, stress, and unhappiness. It is reminiscent of the Canadian minority party leader who proclaimed that his party would blame every sparrow that falls on the government. In a field filled with such cosmic certainty, it is not surprising that anti-sprawl leaders exhibit the smug, self-assured confidence of religious zealots.

Our Enemy, the Automobile?

The automobile occupies a special place in the theology of urban sprawl. If urban sprawl is sin, then the automobile plays the role of Lucifer. The literature of urban sprawl is nearly universal in its damnation of the automobile. One of the most strident accusers is Jane Holz Kay, who, in *Asphalt Nation*, declares, "while the world perceives poverty as a result of carlessness, it is dependency on the car that is the culprit."[9] Condemnation of the automobile is the very glue that holds the anti-sprawl movement together. The automobile is portrayed as having made community a thing of the past and as threatening the very future of the world.

Things are so grim that Kunstler foresees a time when "we shall all have to give up mass automobile use"[10]

Portland, Oregon, plays the part of Nirvana in the anti-sprawl movement. Portland is widely touted for its claimed successes in anti-sprawl regional planning, its urban growth boundary, and its conscious efforts to increase traffic congestion in hopes of forcing drivers into mass transit. The reality is that trends are little different in Portland than in urban areas that have not adopted anti-suburban policies. Moreover, even in Portland those policies have begun to unravel (see Chapter 8).

America on the Decline?

Much of the anti-suburban movement believes that things are not as good as they used to be in the United States. In *The European Dream*, Jeremy Rifkin talks of the "steady downward mobility of middle and working class Americans."[11] Architect Peter Callithorpe notes, "family wealth is shrinking."[12] Dolores Hayden says that households have to spend a larger part of their income on housing and cars than before.[13]

Middle-income households are portrayed as facing an economic struggle that has been worsening for decades. Consistent with this view, the anti-sprawl movement has largely bought into "the rich are getting richer and the poor are getting poorer" assessment of the economy. Forty years ago, Peter Blake found plenty of reason to condemn suburban environments:

> The results are palpable: children play in the street; parents spend most of their time maintaining a front garden they can't use; the community has to maintain long roads and long utility lines to service its strung-out houses; and the suburbs go broke.[14]

Echoing Kunstler, Rifkin declares, "America is no longer a great country" and claims that "The American Dream…has increasingly become an object of derision" and "outmoded," and "something to fear, or abhor."[15] This entire line of reasoning is at variance with the facts, as will be shown below.

Defining Urban Sprawl

The use of semantics has been an unqualified success for the anti-sprawl movement. It begins with the term "sprawl" itself. One Merriam-Webster definition of sprawl is "to cause to spread out carelessly or awkwardly." *Careless* and *awkward* are inherently negative terms. The *American Heritage Dictionary* characterizes sprawl as spreading out in a fashion that is "straggling or disordered," terms at least as undesirable as *careless* and *awkward.*

The anti-sprawl movement itself provides the most damning characterizations of urban sprawl. For example, the Sierra Club says that sprawl is "irresponsible, often poorly-planned development that destroys green space, increases traffic and air pollution, crowds schools and drives up taxes." Surely, no one could be in favor of something that is both irresponsible and poorly planned. But, of course, words do not necessarily convey reality, and value-laden words such as *irresponsible* are particularly unreliable. What is irresponsible to the Sierra Club may be responsible to others, and what is poorly planned to the Sierra Club may be well planned to others.

A respected dictionary should rise above subjectivity and define the term in an objective way. However, this is not so, at least not for the *American Heritage Dictionary,* which defines urban sprawl as "the unplanned, uncontrolled spreading of urban development into areas adjoining the edge of a city." The terms *unplanned* and *uncontrolled* convey negative connotations to a world conditioned to believe that planned is desirable and unplanned is not. This perception, of course, flies in the face of the collapse of planned economies and the continued success of economies that are relatively unplanned.

One of the frequent "places rated" publications provides another example. *Cities Ranked and Rated* devotes an entire page to urban sprawl, parroting commentary by the Sierra Club.[16] *Cities Ranked and Rated* goes on to note that a disadvantage of living and working in Atlanta is urban sprawl. Certainly, with its low population density, Atlanta can be considered the most sprawling major urban area in the world. Yet, the "scourge" of sprawl has not deterred people from moving there. Atlanta is not only the world's most sprawling large urban area, but it is also the high-income world's fastest-growing large urban area. *Cities Ranked and Rated* goes on to rank Atlanta as the best large metropolitan area in which to live. Perhaps the publication was engaging in an all-too-frequent obligatory condemnation of urban sprawl, or perhaps it, like the people moving to Atlanta, see urban sprawl as being nothing to be terribly concerned about.

Six smaller metropolitan areas are ranked above Atlanta, but none has more than 1,000,000 residents. This means, of course, that Atlanta is rated above Portland, the urban planning Nirvana. However damning urban sprawl might be in the dogma of the anti-suburban movement, it is not a barrier to an attractive and superior quality of life.

Objective Terms

Objective discourse requires objective terminology. If urban sprawl is an undeniable scourge, then objective analysis and terminology will not prevent its diagnosis and cure. If, on the other hand, urban sprawl is not inherently evil, no amount of ideological or religious condemnation or damning terminology will make it so.

A semantically biased debate has great potential to lead to misdiagnosis and adoption of strategies that would worsen long-term outcomes. It is not necessary to venture outside the topic of urban planning for a precedent. In the 1950s and 1960s, urban planners in the United States were convinced that cities would be strengthened by urban renewal and high-rise public housing for low-income citizens. Of course, these views have been so roundly discredited that today's urban planners seem to pretend that the planners who implemented the programs were not their intellectual ancestors.

However, objective terminology is available, as provided by the *Merriam-Webster Dictionary*:[17] "the spreading of urban developments (as houses and shopping centers) on undeveloped land near a city."

In this definition, Merriam-Webster does not offer an opinion on whether *spreading of urban developments on undeveloped land on land near a city* is good or bad. As a result, the definition achieves the necessary objective.

Moreover, the *spreading of urban developments on undeveloped land on land near a city* is both simple and consistent with the perceived problems as expressed in much of the anti-sprawl literature. The anti-sprawl movement generally believes that urban areas have expanded their land area too much and that further expansion must be stopped or severely restricted. At the same time, those who do not see urban sprawl as an inherent evil will generally have no difficulty defining urban sprawl as *the spreading of urban development on undeveloped land near a city*. As used herein, *urban sprawl* will refer to the Merriam Webster definition, *the spreading of urban development on undeveloped land near a city*.

However, a problem remains. The doctrinaire connotations that accompany the term *urban sprawl* are so intense that its use in objective discussion is difficult. Thus, a synonym is needed that is not laden with the negative connotations of urban sprawl. Fortunately, there is one. *Suburbanization* is a virtual synonym of *urban sprawl*. Merriam-Webster defines *suburban* as "an outlying part of a city or town." Thus, suburbanization is the process of developing *an outlying part of a city or town*, the same as *the spreading of urban development on undeveloped land near a city*. Indeed, as will be shown (Chapter 3), contemporary urban sprawl might be thought of as urban growth, because nearly all urban population growth has been suburban (sprawling) for decades throughout the high-income world.

Suburbanization and urban growth do not convey inherently negative or positive connotations. Thus, the terms *suburbanization, suburban,* and *urban growth* will be used as objective synonyms to describe the pejorative term *urban sprawl.* Those who seek to stop or curb suburbanization will be referred to as anti-suburban.

Purported Suburbanization Ills and Smart Growth

Sustainability is at the core of transport and land-use policy around the world. Perhaps the most quoted definition comes from the Brundtland Report of the World Council on Environment and Development in 1987: "Sustainable development meets the needs of the present without compromising the ability of future generations to meet their own needs."

The anti-suburban movement generally believes that modern urbanization patterns cannot be sustained, largely because of environmental considerations.

The anti-suburban movement has also successfully employed semantics to characterize their purported solutions, calling them *smart growth.* Few would want to position themselves against something so semantically virtuous. As a result, interest groups from environmentalists to homebuilders have attempted to define the term *smart growth* to suit their own purposes.

The term *smart growth* has become little more than a mantra that means one thing to anti-suburbanites and quite another to others. Smart growth has become, in words penned by St. Paul, "all things to all men."Some smart growth strategies would place significant restrictions on development and people. Other smart growth strategies, such as liberalizing residential zoning requirements, would increase development opportunities and make more choices available to people. The focus here will be on the intrusive strategies that interfere with the pursuit of preferences by people.

The Anti-Suburban Vision

The anti-suburban vision seeks more compact urban areas, in which it is assumed there would be much greater reliance on mass transit, and much less use of cars. Planning would be focused at the regional level, and less at the local government level. People would live closer to where they worked. Retail stores would be smaller and closer to residences. It is claimed that housing would be less costly, and there would be less traffic. The more compact development would, it is claimed, reduce government costs.

This ideal is often characterized as "livable" communities. Congressman Earl Blumenauer, who represents the anti-suburbanite of Portland, is a leading proponent of anti-suburban policies. His Internet site indicates that livable communities provide transportation choices, housing choices, and have lively downtowns.[18] Blumenauer's emphasis on choice is typical of anti-suburbanites.

A nostalgic twist is the New Urbanist school of architecture, which would serve the same objectives, but do so with the façade of a romanticized, early 1900s-era, American small town. In 1900, for example, there were very few automobiles in the United States or anywhere else in the world. Unlike today, with a U.S. mass-transit market share of three percent (including school buses, which carry 65 percent more travel than mass transit on school days),[19] mass transit in 1900 represented virtually 100 percent of motorized trips in the urban areas. Houses and businesses were closer to one another. This proximity was dictated by the fact that many people walked to work and that mass transit, though faster than walking, operated considerably more slowly than the average urban automobile does today. In addition, because mass transit services principally serve downtown, a much larger share of jobs were in the urban core, which also meant that both residential and employment densities were higher there.

The romanticized American small town of 1900 also appeals to anti-suburban advocates because they perceive that a more intense sense of community existed during that time. They imagine the blacksmith living next to the college professor and surmise that they engaged in social activities together or sat rocking on the front porch together, sharing one another's work experiences. Architect Peter Callithorpe sees an alternative to suburbanization as "simple and timely: neighborhoods of housing, parks, and schools placed within walking distance of shops, civic services, jobs, and transit—a modern version of the traditional town."[20] Callithorpe also believes that "a diverse and inclusionary environment, filled with alternative ways of getting around is inherently better than a world of private enclaves dominated by the car."[21]

At the same time, there is affection for the remaining dense 19th-century European city cores, where the anti-suburban movement finds the elements of community and mixed land uses that it prefers.

Villains and Gullible Consumers

There is a perception that suburbanization has been thrust upon consumers, against their wills, by self-seeking interests. In all of this, the anti-suburbanites claim that automobile manufacturers and homebuilders have duped the consumer. Dolores Hayden attributes excessive consumption to American suburbanization, which she sees as having been the result of real-estate lobbies whose success marginalized growth other than suburban development.[22]

Suburbanization is seen as the fault of greedy developers, who, in demonstration of their self-serving, perhaps inherently evil nature, develop as much land as they can to maximize their profits. Anti-suburban activists scoff at the modest "ticky-tack" houses that the households of returning veterans moved into in early post—World War II suburbs, such as the Levittowns of New York, New Jersey, and Pennsylvania; Lakewood, California; and the thousands of suburbs around the United States. Dolores Hayden refers to the "sitcom" suburbs, mocking the early television programs that were set in the suburbs, such as *Ozzie and Harriet* and *Father Knows Best*.

Similar sentiments are expressed with respect to cars. In a preface to Wolfgang Zuckerman's *End of the Road*, Lester Brown attributes "extremely effective advertising" to popularizing the car. Zuckerman later recommends banning automobile advertisements.[23] Apparently, against their better judgments, households throughout the high-income world have been induced to purchase houses and cars that would have, if the anti-sprawl critics are to be believed, worsened their quality of life.

Intrusive Policies

The focus here will be on the more intrusive smart growth strategies that would place significant limits on where people are allowed to live, work, and shop, such as:

- Densification Policies—Densification includes land-development prohibitions, especially urban growth boundaries and greenbelts, and requires that substantial amounts of new construction be infill (in already developed areas).

- Anti-Automobile Pro-Mass Transit Policies—These strategies would limit highway capacity increases while giving priority to mass transit improvements, especially urban rail. Efforts would also be made to encourage more walking and bicycling.

- Retail Store Limitation Policies—Restrictions, or even prohibitions, would be imposed on new big-box stores, such as general merchandisers like Wal-Mart and Carrefour (Europe) and large specialty stores, such as Home Depot and LeRoy Merlin (Europe).

Understandable Concerns

At the same time, the battle against suburbanization often receives positive reactions from the public at-large. They may not like the looks of the fast-food restaurants that line the suburban streets of Phoenix or Antwerp. The Wal-Mart in Chicago suburbs or Carrefour hypermarket in French suburbs appear to many less inviting than the former Marshal Fields department store in the Chicago Loop or the Galleries Lafayette department store in the ville de Paris. However, many of the very same people, and most others, patronize them.

There is a natural human tendency to oppose change, which is best illustrated in urban policy by the widespread NIMBY (Not in My Back Yard) phenomenon. People buy new homes and property as it appears at the time of purchase. In 1993, we arranged to have our new house built on the urban fringe of St. Louis. The summer before construction started, the neighboring farmer used much of the lot to grow soybeans. For the first year or so, the farm abutted our backyard, and there were no subdivisions for at least a mile away. As late as 2000, the U.S. Census Bureau defined the St. Louis urbanized area as ending at the far boundary of the neighbor's lot. However, more people wanted houses, and construction started on adjacent lots.

As more people moved into the area, more housing was developed. There is now a new school, and urbanization extends at least a quarter of a mile further out than when we moved into the house. There is no doubt that the view was better before the new development. However, a fair society cannot allow neighbors to deny the right of young households or new residents to enjoy the same quality of life.

Nor should society allow urban policy or any other policy to be widely adopted without carefully considering all of the consequences on other issues of importance. What follows is an examination of anti-suburbanism in the broader policy context.

2

The Broader Context

The Emergence of High-Income Economies

Anti-suburban policies have been adopted without meaningful examination of the consequences in the broader context. The most important of these ignored consequences involve the quality of life and economics.

The unprecedented quality of life improvement that occurred in the high-income nations during the 20th century was associated with expanding suburbanization and automobile use, which are the very phenomena that anti-suburbanism seeks to discourage.

Even Canada's anti-suburban David Suzuki Foundation has noted, "Probably the greatest single source of wealth creation in history has been the conversion of rural land into urban land."[24] Conversion of rural land to urban use is, in fact, the very essence of suburbanization.

Economic growth and prosperity are not inevitable. A high standard of living is relatively new to the world. The history of economics and the quality of life is largely a history of poverty.

This is illustrated by the work of economist Angus Maddison[25], who estimated historical economic performance for the Organization for Economic Cooperation and Development (OECD). These inflation-adjusted estimates indicate that much of the world continues to live at levels below the 2000 poverty threshold in the United States.[26] This includes the two most populous countries in the world, China and India. In Africa, nearly all nations had income per capita below the U.S. poverty threshold, including the rich ancient nation of Egypt. In addition, most Latin American nations had incomes per capita below the U.S. poverty threshold.

However, the history of poverty is not confined to Asia, Africa, and Latin America. During the 19th century and into the early 20th century, much of the population of the now high-income world was in poverty. On the eve of World War II, much of today's high-income world lived below or near poverty rates by today's standards. In 1939, per capita income in Canada and Western Europe was barely above the 2000 U.S. poverty threshold, and well below in Japan. The United States, Australia, and New Zealand were more affluent, but far less so than they have since become (see Figure 2.1).[27]

Over the past one-half century, however, the high-income nations have become far more affluent. From 1950 to 2000, per capita economic growth has been spectacular in Japan, the United States, Western Europe, and the rest of the high-income world.

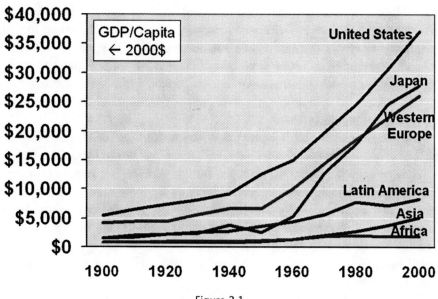

Figure 2.1

However, strong economic growth has not been universal. Less than 15 percent of the world's population lives in high-income nations, while 85 percent live in middle-income and lower-income nations. Per capita economic growth since World War II stagnated in Asia and Latin America, at less than 20 percent, and at less than 10 percent in the former Soviet Union and Africa.

Even some formerly prosperous nations have had faltering economic growth. The most obvious is Argentina, which had a higher gross domestic product per capita, than Western Europe and Japan in 1910, but has since fallen to less than one-half as prosperous.

Russia provides a further example. Russia has been well endowed with natural resources, human talent, and artistic achievement. Its people are highly educated and literate. The accomplishments of Russian authors, composers, and scientists are legendary. Yet, none of this has produced an affluent Russia.

A high standard of living cannot be achieved without a strong economy. Economics matters a great deal. Any program seeking sustainable development will need to include sustainable economic growth.

Democratizing Prosperity

Prosperity is well on the way to being democratized in the high-income economies. The overwhelming majority of households in the high-income world live well. Most people live middle-income lives, which is a new development. Indeed, Australian demographer Bernard Salt puts the matter quite squarely, suggesting that before the 1960s, there was no middle class as we know it today.[28] At the same time, the democratized economies produce enough income to provide, by world standards, comparatively generous levels of government financial assistance to low-income households.

The democratization of prosperity is different from the socialization of prosperity. In fact, socialist economies have had little or no prosperity to democratize, which is perhaps the principal reason for their general decline relative to market economies. Democratization of prosperity arises from an equality of economic opportunity, regardless of economic, ethnic, family, or hereditary status. At the same time, the democratization of prosperity is a continuing process. Even in high-income countries, it has not yet been fully achieved. However, the extent to which prosperity has been democratized in high-income nations is unprecedented in history.

Virtually all economies—high-, middle-, and low-income—have their rich. Luxury condominiums can be found on New York's Upper East Side and adjacent to the poverty of the Rocinha favela (shantytown or informal settlement) in Rio de Janeiro.

What separates high-income economies from their middle-and low-income counterparts is the extent of poverty. Virtually all economies have poverty, but high-income economies have much less. Where prosperity has been democratized, there is much less poverty and many more people live a comparatively comfortable life. The principal beneficiaries of democratized prosperity are not the rich, who prosper whatever the economic system, but rather the millions who would otherwise be poor. Similarly, when economies decline, it is the poor who experience the losses first and most intensely.

The Public Purpose of Private Property

Moreover, the democratization of prosperity depends upon private ownership, or property rights. As selfish or undesirable as it may seem, people tend to be more interested in their own well-being than that of others or of the common good. As a result, they seek to improve their own material wealth and take better care of their own property. This is not a trait shared just among the more affluent. Most college professors, urban planners, and homebuilders jealously guard their property, whether real or intellectual, and seek a better, rather than worse, future.

Sovietologist Richard Pipes notes, "no one takes proper care of objects that are not his."[29] This is a truth identified as early as Aristotle, who said that what is "common to the greatest number has the least care bestowed upon it."[30] As residents living under Eastern European communism pointed out, "what everyone owns, no one owns." Whether it conforms to the political ideology of any particular time, the fact is that people take much better care of what they own, and they use it to create the wealth without which there could be no broad prosperity.

However, as the international economic data indicate, most nations have not reached high-income status. Peruvian economist Hernando DeSoto has conducted research to find out why adoption of capitalist reforms has failed to produce prosperity in some nations. This is especially evident in former communist nations and in middle-income nations that have implemented reforms in the last two decades. Economic growth has stagnated and comparatively little progress has been made.

DeSoto's volume, *The Mystery of Capital,* describes why prosperity eludes most people in middle-and low-income economies.[31] DeSoto notes that the low-income population of these nations is not poor in terms of personal assets. It is rather that the majority of households simply do not have clear legal title to their property. As a result, they have little opportunity to convert their assets into capital, such as through sale or borrowing to start businesses. For example, in Egypt, 92 percent of household dwellings are informal—not legally protected by a property rights system. As a result, property that would contribute to wealth creation and an improved quality of life are "dead" assets. DeSoto estimates that in 1996, these "dead" assets in Cairo alone were worth nearly $80 billion. This is equal to approximately $8,000 per capita, significant in a nation with an annual GDP per capita one-half that amount."

DeSoto's conclusions are not those of an ideologue, nor is he the capitalist counterpart of Karl Marx. He does not view capitalism as a credo. Rather, he operates from a pragmatic perspective, recognizing the reality that free markets based upon secure property rights are the most effective means of broad wealth creation. It is, he says, "the only system we know that provides us with the tools required to create massive surplus value."[32]

DeSoto rejects the idea that high-income nations are rich because of culture or because their citizens work harder. There is no shortage of hard work in the middle-and low-income worlds. DeSoto says that what distinguishes high-income economies from lower-income economies is that "the firm foundations of property are in place."[33] The conditions required to democratize prosperity require a strong system of formal property rights.

Much economic and social thought is based upon this foundation. For example, Nobel Laureate Douglass C. North and Robert Paul Thomas made similar findings with respect to the advance of England and the Netherlands relative to France and Spain in the 17th century—that the key was an efficient economy based on clearly defined property rights.[34]

The importance of property rights is evident even in the literature favored by the anti-suburban movement. In *The Rise of the Creative Class,* Richard Florida argues that the more successful metropolitan areas have greater concentrations of what he calls the "creative class,"[35] a notion disputed by Urbanologist Joel Kotkin.[36] Nonetheless, a creative class requires a strong property rights system, without which it could not produce economic benefit. Artists own their work and are free to sell it in an environment of property rights.

Information technology professionals write innovative computer software, confident that the financial returns provided through the property rights system are sufficient to justify their time and effort. The very nature of creativity is to have control over what one has created, and that requires a strong property rights system. It is no different with real property, such as houses and cars.

DeSoto expresses concern that low-and middle-income economies have adopted what appear to be the characteristics of capitalism, but without the crucial elements that make it work. Without the rule of law and property rights, modern high-income economic performance cannot occur. According to North and Thomas, property is at the very heart of wealth creation; indeed, "economic growth will occur if property rights make it worthwhile to undertake socially productive activity."[37]

As DeSoto notes, the only economic system that has been able to produce substantial wealth is capitalism. The public purpose of private property is not aggrandizement of the rich; it is rather the well-being of all, from poor to rich. Perhaps the best measure would be the standard of living of the 20th percentile of income, or some similar objective measure of well-being among less affluent citizens.

Private property must be protected so that it can serve the broader interests of society by producing the wealth required to democratize prosperity. Governments around the world are committed to democratizing prosperity.

Economic freedom and property rights are inseparable. People tend to prefer freedom to the lack of it. Few would prefer to be controlled by others or to have their property controlled by others. The very idea of controlling property and using it to create wealth requires freedom.

As economic theory postulates, there is a strong connection between economic freedom and prosperity. Richard Pipes notes that one of the main reasons for the rise of the West to the position of global economic preeminence lies in the institution of property, which originated there and found there its "greatest fulfillment."[38] Further, the Fraser Institute in Canada and the Heritage Foundation and *The Wall Street Journal* in the United States publish reports each year that measure the economic competitiveness of societies.[39] Generally, these analyses conclude that societies in which people are allowed to do what they want are more prosperous and productive than societies in which people are subject to greater regulation. In *Doing Business in 2005,* The World Bank notes, "Economic growth is only one benefit of better business regulation and property protection."[40]

In addition, effective property rights are much more than a superficial matter of whose name is on the deed. Genuinely owned property, whether in Desoto's South America or in the United States, is property over which the owner has control and which the owner is generally able to use it as he or she likes. Incomplete property rights, which leave the owner with the deed but without the ability to put the property to best use, have the potential to seriously retard future wealth creation and economic growth.

Because of the nexus between property rights and economic growth, care must be taken to minimize the negative effects of constraints on the use of property.

Continuing American Leadership: Home Building and Retailing

To anti-suburbanites who perceive a declining America herded around by devious advertisers, it may be surprising that the United States continues to have the highest per-capita income of any major nation in the world.[41]

However, U.S. economic superiority took some time to achieve. As late as the early 1900s, the United Kingdom, Australia, and New Zealand had higher incomes per capita than the United States. The United States enjoyed an unprecedented economic dominance following World War II. This was because the U.S. lost virtually none of its physical productivity capacity during the War, while its major economic competitors suffered serious losses. This dominance, of course, was not sustainable. As would be expected, Western Europe and Japan made strong progress in relation to the United States and managed to close the gap to less than 25 percent by the 1980s. But, since that time, the US has generally expanded the economic gap compared to Western Europe and Japan (see Figure 2.2).[42]

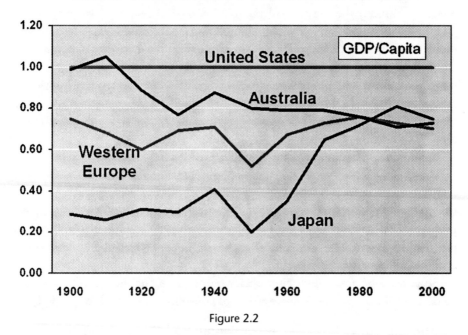

Figure 2.2

This growing U.S. economic dominance has been the subject of research by McKinsey Global Institute founder William Lewis in his book, *The Power of Productivity*. Lewis concludes that the more successful economies are characterized by more intense competition for consumer goods and services ("competitive intensity"), and less economic regulation.[43] He attributes the failure of Western Europe and Japan to close the economic gap with the United States on insufficient competitive intensity.

Moreover, the McKinsey findings place a higher priority on competitive intensiveness than on education. Lewis notes that uneducated immigrant workers quickly achieve world-class productivity in the U.S. construction industry.[44]

Lewis points to two industries as having played a particularly important role in developing the superior competitive intensity of the U.S. economy—home building and retailing.

McKinsey finds the home building industry in the United States to be significantly more productive than in Western Europe or Japan and that this is one of the principal reasons why U.S. economic dominance has continued. The principal reason is the fact that land-use regulation is far less severe in the United States. More land can be legally purchased for development of housing. The larger plots of land allow greater standardization and lower costs. The lower costs and efficiencies of this structure make it possible for smaller companies to operate in the market, with the increased competition reducing prices. Similar industry and regulatory structures were found to produce American-style productivity in the Netherlands and Australia.[45] What Lewis calls "competitive intensity" in home building is simply greater economic freedom.

At the other end of the spectrum is Japan, with home building productivity 55 percent below that of the United States, the Netherlands, and Australia. Japan's lag is due to a regulatory system that discourages large-scale housing subdivisions and an industry geared toward custom building and little standardization. If the Japanese built cars in the pre—Henry Ford way that local builders construct houses, Toyota and Honda would not have been able to compete outside their domestic market.

McKinsey also found the comparative freedom of retail development to be an important contributor to U.S. economic performance. Again, the driving factor was land-use regulation. The larger, lower-cost retailers found it much more difficult to build stores in the United Kingdom, France, Germany, and Japan. As a result, there is less retail competitive intensity, and households pay higher prices for their goods.[46]

The Public Purpose of Home Ownership

Home ownership is a principal mechanism for creating wealth, and is a principal mechanism for democratizing prosperity. There is a fundamental difference between purchasing a home and paying rent. By purchasing a home, a household adds to its wealth; part of the monthly mortgage payment is used to reduce the amount owed and becomes a part of the owner's equity in the home. In contrast, all of the money paid to rent a home that the household does not own goes to the property owner. There is no potential equity for the renter in the rented home.

In the United States, home owning households have a net worth more than 30 times greater than that of renters. Much of the net worth of middle-income households is in housing equity. A Federal Reserve Bank survey[47] found that

- House equity accounted for 65 percent of net worth among households with less than $20,000 in annual income.

- House equity accounted for more than 40 percent of net worth among households with $20,000 to $50,000 in annual income.

- House equity accounted for approximately one-third of net worth among households with $50,000 to $100,000 in annual income.

Statistics Canada data indicate that a household owning its home outright will tend to have a net worth nine times that of a renting household, while a household with a mortgage will have a net worth four times as high.

Home ownership also makes communities more stable and cohesive. Robert C. Weaver, the first U.S. Secretary of Housing and Urban Development, said, "Home ownership creates a pride of possession, engenders responsibility and stability."[48] Thus, home ownership broadens and deepens affluence. An economy is richer because of home ownership and more of its households participate in its mainstream. This recognition has been at the base of public policies intended to expand home ownership under national administrations of all political stripes, from Franklin D. Roosevelt to Ronald Reagan in the United States, Margaret Thatcher to Tony Blair in the United Kingdom, and Robert Menzies to Robert Hawke in Australia.

To the extent that anti-suburban policies reduce home ownership, they will also lead to prosperity that is less democratic, with a greater concentration of wealth and more poverty. This is the principal problem with anti-suburban strategies.

The American Dream

The American Dream of home ownership is well-known. It consists of the single-family detached house in the suburbs, the two-or three-car garage, and at least as many personal vehicles (automobiles or sport-utility vehicles) parked in the garage. With these vehicles, suburban residents can travel to jobs and shopping throughout an urban area.

Often, there is a tendency to think of an American uniqueness with respect this "dream." In his book, *On Paradise Drive, New York Times* columnist David Brooks talks of Americans living in the "future tense," and exhibiting a hopeful tendency that presumes a better life is ahead.[49] A recent Pew Foundation survey found Americans (and their nearly as affluent, but sometimes reluctant cousins, Canadians) to be the happiest people in the world.[50] This should not be surprising. It is in America that the greatest per capita affluence has been achieved and Canada has ranked near the top for much of the post—World War II period. However, living in the future tense is not limited to Americans, it is a virtually universal phenomenon (as is outlined below).

The European Dream

In *The European Dream,* Jeremy Rifkin finds Western European household aspirations to be much different than American. He suggests that there is a European Dream in which people subordinate their own interests to the common good. Rifkin foresees the coming of a virtual golden rule—based ("do unto others as you would have them to unto you") society on a foundation of European secularism. Rifkin says, "What becomes important in the new European vision of the future is the personal transformation rather than individual material accumulation."[51]

Major world religions have, of course, failed to establish such a society, despite their millennia of attempts to do so. Thus, German labor unions (like those in the United States) still put their own interests ahead of the interests of management and consumers. Moreover, they should, because this is a principal purpose of labor unions. Stockbrokers in Frankfurt and London may well seek "personal transformation," but do so while liberally pursuing their "individual material accumulation."

Nor have European businesses adopted Rifkin's interpretation of a European Dream. French-based big-box firm Carrefour, for example, is the world's second largest retailer. Carrefour has managed to earn a return on investment competitive with that of Wal-Mart (the world's largest retailer) for years. Any other result would be as unacceptable to Carrefour stockholders as substandard performance would be to holders of Wal-Mart shares. Companies compete for investors by their financial performance. The incentives that drive European companies are little different from those that drive their American cousins.

Rifkin's European Dream is an illusion, even a fantasy. The genuine European Dream can be witnessed on weekends as households visit new model houses at the Hus-Expo in suburban Stockholm or at the Dom-Expo in suburban Paris. Europeans have flocked, just like Americans, to new suburban housing in the suburbs (see Chapter 3). Despite much higher gasoline costs and far more crowded roadways, they have relied more and more on automobiles. The exploding demand for sport utility vehicles (SUVs) is no longer just an American or Canadian affair—it is occurring in Europe as well (SUVs are sometimes called "monospace" vehicles in Europe).

It is true that living in the future tense and the "Dream" are undeniably American, but they are not uniquely American. Living in the future tense is as human as it is American. This is not to suggest that there is no difference between Americans and Europeans. It is rather to suggest that the differences are far less substantial than the similarities. Throughout the world, people envision a better future and work toward a more comfortable life.

The Universal Dream

Because people live in the future tense, places that are more prosperous are magnets for people from less prosperous locales. Today, people flee the poverty of western China seeking the future tense in prosperous eastern and coastal urban areas such as Shanghai, Beijing, Guangzhou, and Shenzhen. Alternatively, some may even endure the inhumane conditions of shipping containers to reach Canada or Western Europe. Many of those who get in, often illegally, will never live as well as native Europeans or Canadians, but they will probably live better there than if they had not left the poverty of home.

Around the world, massive migrations have occurred from rural to urban areas. Millions of households have moved from the small towns and farms of the United States to urban areas. Millions of low-income African Americans pursued the future tense by moving from the American South to the Midwest, East, and California in the middle of the 20th century. A 1968 federal report echoed the sentiments David Brooks more recently expressed: "The real reason behind the migration was just plain gumption. Families with gumption got up and got out of areas where there were no longer any jobs for them."[52]

Similar migration patterns have occurred in Western Europe, Japan, Canada, Australia, and New Zealand. The "future tense" drives people from all over the world, not just Americans, to seek a better life where the jobs are and where the wealth is—in the urban areas. The history of human migration is the history of living in the future tense.

Virtually everywhere, living in the future tense means better housing and better mobility, especially in the United States. It is the American Dream that much of the world seeks to emulate, even if policy differences are sometimes considerable. The suburbs in Canada, Australia, and New Zealand have resembled their American counterparts for decades. The suburbs of Western Europe and Japan bear a much stronger resemblance to American suburbs than to the historical cores that they surround. Indeed, as former U.S. Secretary of Housing and Urban Development Jack Kemp put it, "the American Dream is a universal dream."[53]

Moreover, the Universal Dream is not limited to the high-income world. An unprecedented new housing construction boom is underway in Mexico. New suburban developments have been built near Mexico City, Guadalajara, Leon, and other urban areas. In some cases, the new houses resemble entry-level detached housing in the suburbs of the United States. More often than not, they are small row houses of one or two stories. However, they provide their new owners with a standard of living that is simply well above what was available before. There are similar trends in Eastern Europe. For example, new, comparatively large, detached suburban housing will be found in any direction from Warsaw, even Bucharest, and Istanbul.

Finally, living in the future tense is not just about moving to attractive houses in the suburbs of Cincinnati, Paris, Toronto, Tokyo, Buenos Aires, Warsaw, or Guadalajara. The Universal Dream is evident in examples that are more modest. The favelas of Brazil and shantytowns found around the world's burgeoning middle-and lower-income urban areas are manifestations of the same dream.

Mobility and Prosperity

Large urban areas provide superior opportunities, which is why people from rural and smaller urban areas have been flocking to them for centuries. According to transport consultant Alan E. Pisarski, automobile-based transportation systems have democratized mobility, which is a necessary element of democratized prosperity.[54] The automobile makes it possible to access the entire urban area and its widely dispersed employment and shopping at comparatively low cost. Without an automobile, residents must rely on walking or mass transit. It takes longer to travel by walking or mass transit and many trips cannot be made in a practical period of time. The only remaining alternatives are to not travel or to use taxicabs, which, of course, are too expensive for people who cannot afford cars.

Mobility is an important component of urban economic performance. A more efficient urban area will have a transport system that allows people to reach virtually all of the urban area in a comparatively short time, as research by Remy Prud'homme and Chang-Woon Lee of the University of Paris has shown.[55]

Nonetheless, the anti-suburban agenda would discourage automobile use and favor walking and mass transit. To the extent that any such strategies might impair mobility, there will be less prosperity and more people in poverty.

Evaluating Anti-suburban Policy: The Lone Mountain Compact

People who are allowed to do what they want will be generally happier and more productive. This means that they will create greater economic growth as well. To preserve the maximum latitude for people to act as they prefer, regulations and laws must be limited to what is genuinely important and should not be based upon flimsy research or flawed analysis.

By 2000, a number of academics and urban policy professionals had become concerned that much of the anti-suburban synthesis and agenda was based upon weak, if not erroneous analysis. As a result, a meeting was held in the mountains of Montana in 2000 to consider approaches that were better founded in the facts and likely to produce better results. The meeting produced the Lone Mountain Compact, which declared:

> ...absent a material threat to other individuals or the community, people should be allowed to live and work where and how they like.[56]

In an environment in which democratized prosperity is sought or sustained, any public policy that interferes with what people want to do must be demonstrably compelling. Policies that adhere to this principle will provide necessary environmental and societal protections while fostering a better quality of life through greater economic growth.

At the same time, nothing here should be interpreted as a brief for suburbanization (or urban sprawl). It is rather a call for policies that would broaden, maintain, and increase prosperity, while sustainably minimizing the incidence of poverty. Obviously, this can and must be accomplished consistent with other public objectives, such as environmental protection.

Legitimate environmental and community concerns must be addressed, and regulation is necessary to protect health and welfare. But urban development policies (or any other policies) must not be fashioned in a policy vacuum. Their impact on other important public policies and concerns must be assessed, and hard public policy choices must be made in light of all relevant considerations. The ultimate question is whether it is possible to maintain and extend a democratized prosperity while implementing the anti-suburban agenda.

The starting point must not be "fury" as Peter Blake put it or in "criticisms rooted in an ideological conception of the city," against which Thomas Sieverts of the University of Darmstadt (Germany) warned.[57] The policies of the future must emerge from objective, fact-based analysis.

3

Suburban World

Urban Sprawl is Suburbanization and Urban Growth

Human settlement has been expanding geographically for as long as it has been feasible. The first sprawl might be thought to have occurred when history's second household constructed its house. However, throughout most of human history, urban areas were much more dense than today, because residences and businesses needed to be within walking distance of each other. Two technological advances accelerated suburbanization. The first was mass transit and the second was the automobile, both of which made it possible to increase the geographical area that could be conveniently accessed.

Measuring Urban Sprawl: "Density Does It"

The term *urban sprawl* is used rather loosely. While most urban planners would classify a low-density urban area such as Atlanta or Kansas City as sprawling, the most dense areas are also called sprawling. For example, a Public Broadcasting System program referred to Hong Kong as sprawling a few years ago. Hong Kong has, by far, the highest density of any urban area in the high-income world and must thus be considered the *least* sprawling.[58]

The principal defining characteristic of automobile-oriented suburbanization is population density well below that of the former walking-or mass-transit-oriented urban areas. In general, suburban development is less dense than core city development and more recent development is less dense than earlier development.

This has long been understood. The Sierra Club, one of the most aggressive anti-suburban organizations, provides an extreme example. The Sierra Club published an Environmental Impacts of Sprawl Calculator on the Internet, defining an efficient urban area as one with 500 housing units per acre, which the club considered preferable to what it called sprawl, at one housing unit per acre. However, there was a problem. The "efficient urban" density of 500 housing units per

26

acre would, at average household size, result in population densities of over 750,000 residents per square mile. This is 100 times Western European urban densities and nearly 10 times the density of Hong Kong, which is the most dense urban area in the high-income world. To achieve the Sierra Club's efficient urban density would require the average U.S. urban area to crowd 300 people into the average space occupied by a single person.

Within hours of the Sierra Club release, Randal O'Toole and I pointed out on the Internet that Sierra Club's efficient urban population densities were far above the highest reached in any major urban area in the world, even the "Black Hole" of Calcutta. The Sierra Club climbed down quickly and considerably. Within three days, the population density categories were adjusted downward. Randal O'Toole and I continued our criticism. It was not long before the Sprawl Calculator disappeared altogether from the Sierra Club Web site.[59]

The Sierra Club's embarrassment may have given pause to other organizations promoting an anti-suburban agenda. There have been recent efforts to de-emphasize the role of density as a measure of suburbanization. An example is Smart Growth America's urban sprawl ratings. Besides density, Smart Growth America uses three factors to measure urban sprawl: land-use mix, centrality, and local grid street patterns, in addition to density. The implication is that sprawl is principally defined by the internal composition of an urban area, not by the land that it covers.

The three additional measures used by Smart Growth America produce curious results. Los Angeles, with an urban population density of over 7,000 persons per square mile, is considered to sprawl more than Providence, Rhode Island, with a population density of 2,300 per square mile, which is rated as the least sprawling metropolitan area by Smart Growth America.[60] This means that if Los Angeles were to double in its land area, but at the same time replicated the internal land-use composition of Providence, it would sprawl less than today. Of course, this is absurd. If Los Angeles doubled its land area, it would sprawl more than today, regardless of its land-use composition.

The Smart Growth America approach to defining sprawl undermines the most fundamental strategy of anti-suburbanism—densification. If sprawl is measured by factors such as grid street patterns and where facilities are in relation to one another, then combating it does not require densification strategies, such as Portland-style urban growth boundaries, Sydney-style urban consolidation, or greenbelts as in London, Seoul, or Toronto.

There is no avoiding the fact that the principal measure of urban sprawl is population density. This is consistent with much of the anti-suburban literature.

Canada's anti-suburban David Suzuki Foundation says, "density defines the city."[61] Karen Danielson, Robert Lang, and William Fulton express a similar view: "The most basic smart growth housing strategy is the creation of higher density."[62] Finally, in promoting alternatives to urban sprawl, the Sierra Club considered density to be the central issue, as was indicated in an e-mail announcing the first edition of the Sprawl Calculator: "Density does it! Neighborhoods come in patterns, where all these vary in the same direction, in lockstep. Density is the best single descriptor of these patterns."[63]

Parenthetically, however, it is not just any density. The anti-suburban movement favors sprawl that is based upon walking and urban sprawl that has been created by mass transit. What it opposes is sprawl based upon the automobile. Therefore, to call the anti-suburban movement an anti-sprawl movement is not technically correct; it is much more accurately described as an anti-automobile movement.

Changing Urban and Suburban Definitions

Throughout history, most urban growth has been on the periphery, or suburbs, of urban areas. However, through time, perceptions of the suburbs and the core have been changing. Many of the suburbs of 100 or more years ago are now considered part of the core. London, Paris, and New York can illustrate this changing definition of *suburban*.

> **London:** Urban development outside the one-square-mile City of London was considered suburban in medieval times. At the time of the great fire in 1666, the former newspaper row of Fleet Street, from which the City can easily be seen, was suburban. Today's Oxford Street shopping district was beyond the suburbs. Yet, both Fleet Street and Oxford Street are now considered within the urban core. London's suburbs are miles away and its exurbs—even more distant than the suburbs—lie beyond the greenbelt, sprawling over an area of more than 5,000 square miles.

> **Paris:** In the early 17th century, the walls of Paris enclosed less than two square miles. Suburbs had developed outside the walls, such as Faubourg Saint-Germain, Faubourg Saint-Honoré, and Faubourg Saint-Martin. Today, these 17th-century suburbs are in the urban core and not at all suburban. Since that time, newer suburbs have continued to develop. The size of the core city grew to 5.2 square miles, then 13 square miles, and finally 40 square miles in the 1860s. Today all contiguous suburban development out-

side the 40 square miles is considered suburban, and comprises 1,000 square miles—25 times the size of the core city.

New York: In the early 19th century, much of Manhattan Island and virtually all of what is now the city of New York (Manhattan plus the boroughs of the Bronx, Brooklyn, Queens, and Staten Island) was either suburban or exurban. Today, the suburbs of New York are considered to be everything outside the city of New York (more than 3,000 square miles).

Transportation and the Evolution of Urban Areas

Transportation technologies have been a principal factor in shaping urbanization. This can be viewed as occurring in four waves.

The First Wave: The Walking Urban Area. Before the 19th century, some more affluent people had access to horse transport and even comfortable carriages. However, for most people, walking was the principal form of urban travel. This meant that residences had to be within walking distance of employment and stores. Because walking takes so much time, the urban areas tended to be comparatively compact and very dense. Ancient Rome had a population density of approximately 130,000 persons per square mile.[64] In the middle 17th century, Paris is had a population density of nearly 250,000 per square mile.[65] Paris was 100 times the current average U.S. urban density and 35 times the current Western European average.[66] London's urban area population density was 100,000 or more in the 17th and 18th centuries.[67] Generally, the urban footprint radiated nearly equally from the core, except where constrained by geographical features.

By one account, walking permitted the urban area to sprawl up to an area of approximately eight square miles (20 square kilometers).[68] There was considerable variation in population densities, so long as they remained small enough for walking to be practical. For example, the walking urban area of St. Louis had a population density of approximately 10,000 per square mile in the 1850s, one-tenth that of Paris or London.

The Second Wave: The Mass-Transit-Oriented Urban Area. Mass transit arrived in the early-to middle 19th century and made it possible for the urban area to sprawl more. Horse-drawn omnibus (large horse-drawn vehicles) service began in large urban areas, and was available at fares that were affordable to a large share of the population. More widely available mass transit made it possible for people to live farther away from their employment and stores. By the 1850s, omnibus service was placed on rails and became more rapid. Commuter railroads, interurban railroads, streetcars (trams or light rail), and metros (elevated railways, undergrounds, and subways) provided even more rapid service toward the end of the 19th century. Urban footprints began to exhibit spider legs of linear development, occurring far from the urban core along radial commuter rail lines. Mass transit provided greater mobility than had been available in the walking urban area.

The impact on urbanization was rapid. Urban areas expanded outward at a greater rate than their population increased. During the 19th century, London expanded its population more than four times and its developed land area at least 10 times. The most dense Paris arrondissements (districts) lost one-half of their population by the beginning of the 20th century. During the last half of the 19th century, New York's urban population density declined by one-third, despite enormous density increases in lower Manhattan from immigration.

Only a few walking urban areas had achieved a population of 1,000,000 by the early 1800s, such as London, Beijing, and Paris. However, mass transit made it possible for people to access much larger geographic areas, which allowed urban areas to grow in an unprecedented manner. By 1900, London and New York exceeded 4,000,000 residents, while Paris had more than 3,000,000. Population densities were substantially reduced, but still high. The urban densities of London and New York were between 40,000 and 50,000 per square mile, while Paris was above 55,000. The largest mass-transit urban areas covered less than 120 square miles.

The Third Wave: The Automobile-Oriented Urban Area. Like mass transit before it, the automobile transformed the urban area. The automobile brought personal autonomy to urban travel. As people obtained cars, they were able to go where they wanted, when they wanted in the urban area, no longer constrained by the mass transit route patterns or timetables. The automobile made it possible to travel from virtually any point in the urban area to any other, and without the inconvenience of transferring from one route to another. Sectors of the urban area that could not be conveniently reached on mass transit were now within easy reach by the automobile. Personal mobility—the ability to travel wherever and whenever one wanted—was no longer the province of the rich. The democratization of mobility had begun.

The automobile transformed land use. Housing filled in the spaces between the spider-like commuter rail lines. Businesses were able to locate throughout the urban area, not just where mass-transit service converged. The automobile-oriented urban area was geographically less centralized.

The high densities that had typified the pedestrian and mass-transit-oriented urban area fell. This is illustrated by the evolution of the New York urban area. Densities peaked at above 60,000 in the middle of the 19th century. By 1900, densities had dropped to 40,000 per square mile, as mass transit had made it possible for more people to live in the periphery and work in the core. By the end of the 20th century, New York's population density had fallen to 5,300. Even more spectacularly, the 250,000 densities of pre-mass-transit Paris dropped more than 95 percent to 9,200 by 1999 (see Figure 3.1).[69] The world's largest urban areas now covered more than 1,000 square miles and some, such as New York and Tokyo were above 2,500 square miles (see Figure 3.2).[70] Los Angeles, long thought of as the world's most sprawling urban area, covers less land area than Chicago, Boston, Philadelphia, or Atlanta.

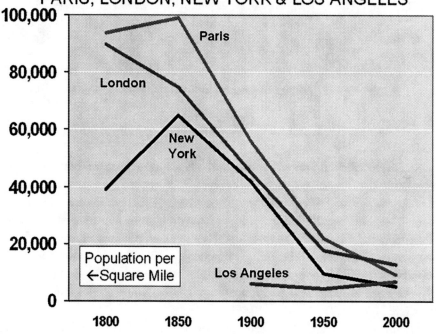

Historical Urban Densities
PARIS, LONDON, NEW YORK & LOS ANGELES

Figure 3.1

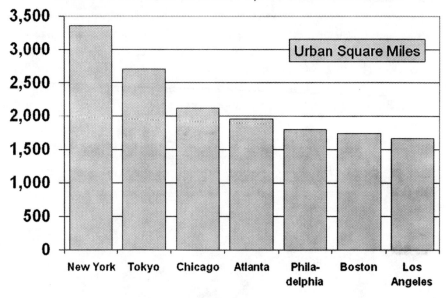

Figure 3.2

As automobile use has expanded and shaped development patterns, urban population densities have dropped substantially. Now, the average urban population density in the United States is approximately 3,000 per square mile, a more than 90 percent drop from the density of large pre-automobile mass-transit urban areas. Even the historically more dense urban areas of Western Europe are far less dense today than before the coming of the automobile. Western European urban population densities are approximately 7,000 per square mile, a decline of more than 80 percent from the densities of large pre-automobile mass-transit urban areas (see Figure 3.3).

The most sprawling urban areas are approximately 95 percent less dense than their pre-automobile predecessors. The least sprawling Western European urban areas are more than 60 percent below pre-automobile densities.

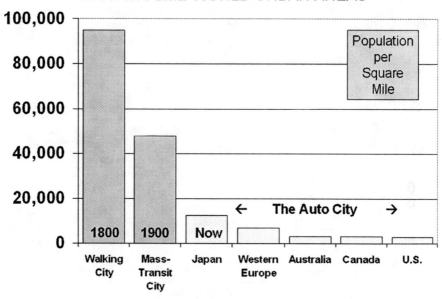

Urban Densities: Pre-Auto & Present
HIGH-INCOME WORLD URBAN AREAS

Figure 3.3

Today, urbanization is occurring principally in the suburbs in a narrow range of density that is far below the levels of pre-automobile urban areas. For example, at approximately 6,750 persons per square mile, the suburbs of Los Angeles are more dense than the suburbs of Western Europe and only 10 percent less dense than the suburbs of Japan. The suburbs of Portland, an urban area that has developed an international reputation for sprawl control, are less dense than the suburbs of Canada and less than one-half as dense as the suburbs of Los Angeles (see Figure 3.4).[71]

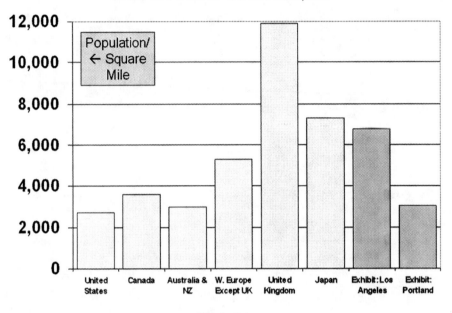

High-Income World Suburban Densities
URBAN AREAS OVER 750,000

Figure 3.4

The Fourth Wave: The Telecommunications Urban Area? Telecommunications, especially the Internet, could have an even more decentralizing impact on urbanization than the automobile. Telecommunications advances are making it possible for some people to live virtual urban lives far from urban areas. The extent of this influence is yet to be determined.

International Urbanization in Context

However, the ascent of the automobile-oriented urban area is not obvious to casual observers or even to many urban planners.

American (or Canadian or Australian) tourists travel to Western Europe to see sites that look very different from home. They buy their mass-transit day passes and travel from museums to art galleries on world-class metros. They sit beside artisans in cafés near the Louvre in Paris and observe the attractive urbanization that simply does not exist at home. They return home wondering why the urban areas of the United States, Canada, or Australia are so different from their perceptions of those in Europe. Like junketing American mass transit board members, they may even ask, "Why cannot we too have trains that take people every-where?" Of course, as in the New World,[72] the trains fall far short of taking peo-ple everywhere.

Urban planners ask similar questions. Like the tourists, they visit Paris, Lon-don, or Milan and marvel at the historical cores. They interact with their Euro-pean counterparts, who are only too eager to cite the purported superiority of the European urban form, while denigrating the more automobile-oriented forms of the New World.

There is a perception that automobile-oriented urban sprawl is limited to the United States. For example, the Lincoln Land Institute referred to urban sprawl as a "uniquely American phenomenon."[73] It is true that United States has more suburbanization than any other nation. However, to consider urban sprawl as a "uniquely American phenomenon" betrays a geographic myopia. Modern, auto-mobile-oriented suburbanization will be found around the world, wherever cars have become the principal mode of transport. This includes Western Europe, and Japan as well as the United States, Canada, Australia and New Zealand.

Most of the tourist sites of Paris are within a mile or two of Chatelet, the large Metro (subway or underground) station in the core of the city. The tourist sites themselves are concentrated in the pre-1860 city, which covers less than 15 square miles of the city's 40 square miles. The rest of the city itself contains little of interest to tourists. The tourist attractions can all be easily seen by mass transit or walking. However, the 1,000 square miles of suburbanization beyond the city makes Paris one of the world's most sprawling urban areas. The suburbs of Dal-las-Fort Worth and Houston each cover less area than the suburbs of Paris.[74] The suburbs of Paris are home to more than 80 percent of the metropolitan popula-tion and two-thirds of the jobs.[75]

The same is true in other Western European urban areas.

- The smallish, historic core of Brussels is surrounded by suburban development often not even visible from peripheral freeways because designers have so effec-tively camouflaged them with roadside vegetation.[76]

- Beyond the boundaries of the core city of Zurich are the nearby and distant suburban villages where all growth has occurred for decades. Since 1960, the city has lost nearly 75,000 residents, while the suburbs have gained more than 475,000 residents.[77]

- The city of Milan has lost more than 400,000 people in 30 years, with all growth captured by the leapfrogging suburbs that stretch more than 20 miles toward the Alps.[78]

- Barcelona is one of the most attractive central cities in Europe. However, tourists or planners never see much of the Barcelona urban area, because it is over a mountain range in a parallel valley, connected by freeways. Development extends further into the perpendicular valleys to the north. The city and inner suburbs have been losing population, while all population growth has been in suburbs that are more remote from the core. Since 1981, the city of Barcelona has lost 250,000 residents.[79]

Similar suburbanization will be found adjacent to all major historical cities in Europe, except where much of it has been forced to leapfrog over greenbelts even further away, as in the United Kingdom.

New World visitors to Western Europe understandably limit their tours to the historic cores. Few would be interested in spending their limited time visiting automobile-oriented suburbs that remind them of home.

However, urban planners have no excuse for limiting their vistas to the urban cores of Europe. The urban planning literature is filled with descriptions of how different European urban areas are from their American counterparts. But that perspective is, more often than not, the result of comparing historic, dense urban cores, as will be found in Paris or Stockholm, with the urban areas of the United States, including cores and suburbs.

The appropriate comparison is between European *suburbs* and American *suburbs*. The expansiveness of Western European urban areas cannot generally be observed from mass transit. Only cars provide the mobility necessary to examine the totality of the modern, automobile-oriented urban area, whether in Phoenix or Paris.[80] Perhaps what is most amazing is that some European planners have as myopic an impression of European urban areas as visiting American urban planners.

In fact, the same myopia even occurs in the United States, where regional planning organization reports sometimes give the impression that downtowns are the dominant work location and that little more of the urban area matters. Transportation planning and the pre-occupation with urban rail systems that principally serve the urban core illustrate this. But, in fact, the urban area includes all of the employment, not just the core employment, and all of the residences, not just the core residences. In addition, the urban area is now predominantly suburban in the United States, Western Europe, Japan, and Canada, with most residents living in the suburbs.[81]

Of course, there are differences between the suburbanization of the United States, Canada, Australia, Western Europe, and Japan. Densities are lower where there is a longer history of automobile ownership, as in the United States, Canada, and Australia (below). Building styles are different. Residential street widths are different. Some Western European countries have a larger share of suburban apartments, especially where personal income growth has been slower or more recent. Even so, single-family detached dwellings are built in ample supply where they are allowed, from Japan to Sweden, France, the United Kingdom, and the Iberian Peninsula.

Commercial Development

Suburbanization has occurred with respect to commercial functions as well as residences. One of the most obvious trends has been the declining importance of central business districts (CBDs, downtowns, centros, or hypercenters), which have also changed as transportation technologies have advanced. Robert Fogelson asserts[82] downtowns are a creation of mass transit. Mass transit, with its routes radiating from the core, concentrated commercial development in a way that had not occurred in the previous walking-oriented urban area. The mass-transit-oriented downtown area is most obvious in the pre—World War I urban areas of the United States, Canada, Australia, and New Zealand. These urban areas developed largely after mass transit had become available and did not have the large, less concentrated walking-oriented cores found in the world's older, larger urban areas. U.S. downtown commercial development tended to be concentrated in areas of one square mile or less, with the principal exception of New York, with a central business district substantially larger than any other.[83] Even today, employment densities in these areas can be very high—over 600,000 jobs per square mile in Midtown Manhattan, with more than 400,000 per square mile in Lower Manhattan and Hong Kong and more than 350,000 per square mile in Chicago's Loop. Many smaller downtown areas have employment densities of more than 100,000, such as Los Angeles, Adelaide, and Zurich.[84] These hyperdensities are far larger than the overall employment densities of under 1,500 per square mile in U.S. urban areas or 3,500 per square mile in Western European urban areas.

Mass transit made it possible to reach the concentrated business core of the urban area more quickly from longer distances than before. However, travel to areas outside the core was more difficult, because it would generally be necessary to travel to the core and transfer to another transit service to reach the destination. More often than not, this would require circuitous travel that took much longer than simply traveling to the core.

Thus, the core orientation and the difficulty of traveling to locations outside by mass transit provided a strong impetus for locating commercial activity in the concentrated downtowns of the high-income new world. The same considerations drove the radial design of mass transit toward the more geographically expansive cores of Western Europe or Japan

Pre-automobile American downtowns sometimes accounted for more than one-half of an urban area's employment. However, the car was to change this. With most people having access to automobiles, it was no longer necessary for so much commercial development to be in the core, where the mass-transit routes converged.

Suburban residential growth led to suburban commercial growth. Since 1960, nearly all new job creation in the United States, Western Europe, Canada, and Australia has been outside the core. Among the largest central business districts in the high-income world, only London is growing,[85] with losses in Tokyo, New York, Osaka, and Paris. Even among the urban areas with the largest downtowns, 80 to 90 percent of employment tends to be elsewhere. Manhattan, with its unparalleled concentration of skyscrapers, accounts for only one-fifth of the metropolitan area's employment. In high-income nations, core commercial areas tend to have, on average, only 10 percent of urban area employment. This may be surprising given the visual dominance of downtown office towers in many urban areas.

Further, concentrated downtown areas are no longer being built. Newer business centers, whether in cores or suburbs have been automobile oriented, not mass-transit oriented. Employment densities are far lower and buildings are often separated by large parking lots. For example, Phoenix experienced nearly all of its growth during the automobile era. Phoenix has nothing resembling a dense central business district. What is liberally called downtown Phoenix is a sparsely developed spine along Central Avenue, rarely extending a block in either direction.

Charlotte, North Carolina, which has emerged as one of the world's principal banking centers, built a few world-class skyscrapers, but resembles a dense downtown less than a suburban *edge city*, a term coined by Joel Garreau to denote the large commercial and office centers that have developed in suburban areas.[86]

After World War II, major retail stores began opening branches in the suburbs, and some closed their downtown stores. The more decentralized commercial and industrial development that has occurred relies principally on trucks for distribution. The flexibility of trucks, like that of cars, makes it possible for commercial facilities to be located throughout the urban area, rather than being concentrated in and near core areas, as was the situation in the mass transit and walking-oriented urban areas.

Survey of High-Income World Urban Areas

A review of the 29 high-income world urban areas[87] with more than 3,000,000 residents illustrates both the similarities and differences in suburbanization (see Table 3.1).[88] Most of the urban areas have fewer than 10,000 residents per square mile, an upper bound that is less than 1.5 times the density of Los Angeles. Hong Kong is by far the high-income world's most dense urban area. Hong Kong is more than 3.5 times the density of second ranking Singapore and eight times that of Paris Atlanta, the lowest-density large urban area has a population density below 2,000 per square mile. All of the urban areas except for Hong Kong have densities well below those of pre-automobile, mass-transit-oriented urban areas (see Figure 3.5)[89]

Table 3.1: High-Income World Urban Areas Over 3,000,000 Population

Rank	Urbanized Area	Population	Square Miles	Density	Compared to Pre-Auto Density
1	Hong Kong	6,475,000	85	76,200	1.59
2	Singapore	4,000,000	185	21,600	0.45
3	Osaka-Kobe-Kyoto	16,425,000	990	16,600	0.35
4	Athens	3,685,000	264	14,000	0.28
5	Madrid	4,900,000	365	13,400	0.28
6	London	8,278,000	627	13,200	0.28
7	Barcelona	3,900,000	310	12,600	0.26
8	Tokyo-Yokohama	33,200,000	2,710	12,300	0.26
9	Berlin	3,675,000	380	9,700	0.20
10	Paris	9,645,000	1,051	9,200	0.19
11	Nagoya	9,000,000	1,110	8,100	0.17
12	Essen-Dusseldorf	7,350,000	1,020	7,200	0.15
13	Milan	4,250,000	600	7,100	0.15
14	Los Angeles	11,789,000	1,668	7,100	0.15
15	Toronto	4,367,000	638	6,800	0.14
16	San Francisco	3,229,000	527	6,100	0.13
17	Sydney	3,502,000	651	5,400	0.12
18	New York	17,800,000	3,353	5,300	0.11
19	Montreal	3,216,000	671	4,800	0.10
20	Miami	4,919,000	1,116	4,400	0.09
21	Melbourne	3,162,000	803	3,900	0.08
22	Chicago	8,308,000	2,123	3,900	0.08
23	Washington	3,934,000	1,157	3,400	0.07
24	Detroit	3,903,000	1,261	3,100	0.06
25	Houston	3,823,000	1,295	3,000	0.06
26	Dallas-Fort Worth	4,146,000	1,407	2,900	0.06
27	Philadelphia	5,149,000	1,799	2,900	0.06
28	Boston	4,032,000	1,736	2,300	0.05
29	Atlanta	3,500,000	1,963	1,800	0.04

Pre-Auto Density: 48,000 (average of London, Paris, and New York in 1900).
Does not include urban areas in the more recently emerging high-income areas (South Korea and Taiwan)
Source: *Demographia World Urban Areas*

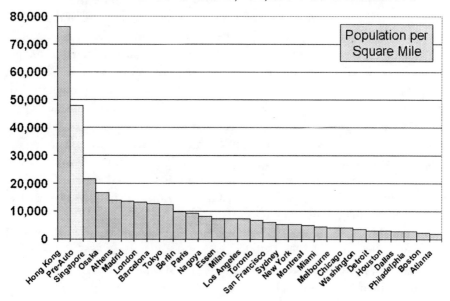

High-Income World Urban Densities
URBAN AREAS OVER 3,000,000 POPULATION

Figure 3.5

United States. The world's lowest urban population densities are in the United States. The 37 urban areas with more than 1,000,000 population had a density of 3,400 in 2000. The overall average urban density in the United States, including small urban areas,[90] was approximately 2,400 per square mile in 2000.[91]

For decades, Los Angeles has had the reputation of being the world's most sprawling urban area. However, nothing could be further from the truth. Los Angeles is now the *most* densely populated (least sprawling) urban area in the United States and it is more dense than any other urban area in the new world of the United States, Canada, Australia, and New Zealand. Los Angeles, at 7,100 per square mile, is 30 percent more dense than New York, with 5,300 persons per square mile. The high Los Angeles density results from suburban development that is considerably more dense than typical of most other U.S. urban areas.

Nonetheless, the inner core densities of New York are considerably higher than in Los Angeles. However, it would be a mistake to think that Los Angeles is without high densities. Los Angeles has more land area of above 15,000 per square mile densities than any U.S. urban area other than New York, and a greater expanse of over 10,000 per square mile densities than even New York.

The New York urban area covers 3,350 square miles, more than any other urban area in the world. A number of other urban areas cover more land than Los Angeles, including Chicago, Tokyo, Philadelphia, Boston, and Atlanta.

The world's least dense major urban area is Atlanta at approximately 1,800 per square mile. Smaller U.S. urban areas are even less dense, such as Charlotte, Nashville, or Raleigh. At the same time, Atlanta is the fastest growing major urban area in the high-income world. Dallas-Fort Worth and Houston, which also rank high in growth, are often considered highly sprawling, like Atlanta. In fact, the urban densities of Dallas-Fort Worth and Houston are nearly as high as anti-suburban model Portland, and higher than Philadelphia or Boston, which are often thought of as less sprawling. In fact, Boston, ranked as one of the least sprawling metropolitan areas by Smart Growth America, has suburbanized at densities little different than those of Atlanta.[92]

It is notable that San Jose,[93] which has largely developed since World War II and thus is virtually all an automobile-oriented suburb, is one of the most dense urban areas in the United States.[94] San Jose, at 5,900 persons per square mile, is more dense than New York and every other major urban area in the nation except Los Angeles and San Francisco.

With respect to core area densities, the core city of New York is in a class by itself. New York is the highest density major central city in the United States, at approximately 27,000 per square mile. The borough of Manhattan, which includes the central business district, has a population density of nearly 70,000 per square mile. San Francisco has the most dense large core city outside New York, at approximately 16,600 persons per square mile.

Suburban densities, however, are much lower.

- The suburbs of San Francisco are nearly as dense as those in Los Angeles, at 5,600 per square mile. (Los Angeles suburbs are 6,750 per square mile).

- New York's suburbs have only 3,100 persons per square mile.

- Boston's outer suburbs (largely developed since 1950) have a density of only 1,500 per square mile, less than the suburbs of Atlanta that developed over the same period of time.[95]

Western Europe. Urban densities are higher in Western Europe, averaging slightly more than those of Los Angeles. The average urban density is approximately 7,000 per square mile, more than double the large urban average of the United States. Population densities are higher in the United Kingdom (UK), which has had perhaps the free world's most stringent land-use regulation for more than 50 years. Urban population densities average 10,200 in the UK. The highest density urban areas in Western Europe are Athens and Madrid, at 14,000 and 13,400 per square mile respectively. Paris has a lower urban area density, at 9,200 per square mile. The high density of the city is masked by the much lower densities in the Paris suburbs that are only slightly more dense than the suburbs of Los Angeles.[96]

London is also comparatively dense, at 13,200 people per square mile. However, this is principally the result of intense UK land-use regulation. The urban area is enclosed by a greenbelt approximately 10 miles wide, in which no development is permitted. As a result, the urban area is artificially constrained and what would have been contiguous suburban development has been driven to exurban areas outside the greenbelt.

The highest density major core cities in Western Europe are Athens and Paris, at more than 50,000 per square mile, and Barcelona, at approximately 40,000 per square mile.

Suburban densities are, of course, much lower. For example, suburban densities in Antwerp, Brussels, Milan, Porto, Nantes, and Munich are 5,000 per square mile or less.

Japan. The largest urban areas of Japan are the most dense in the high-income world—outside the enclaves of Hong Kong and Singapore—with an average density of 12,500 per square mile. This is approximately 3.5 times U.S. large urban area densities and more than 1.8 times large Western European urban area densities. Japan contains the world's largest urban area, Tokyo-Yokohama, which is the fifth most dense in the high-income world, at 12,300 per square mile. Tokyo-Yokohama covers more land area than any of the world's urban areas except New York. Japan's other megacity, Osaka-Kobe-Kyoto is more dense, at 16,600 per square mile.

Among major core cities, Tokyo[97] has a population density of 33,000 per square mile, while Osaka has a population density of 31,000 per square mile. Suburban population densities in the three largest urban areas (Tokyo-Yokohama, Osaka-Kobe-Kyoto, and Nagoya) average 8,100 per square mile.

Canada. The urban areas of Canada with more than 1,000,000 population have an average density of 5,400 per square mile, approximately 60 percent above the U.S. large urban average. Nevertheless, overall, Canadian urban areas[98] have only slightly higher density than their American counterparts, at 2,500 per square mile.[99]

Toronto is the largest and most dense urban area in Canada, at 6,800 per square mile. This is below Los Angeles, but higher than all other major U.S. urban areas. Montreal has the second highest population density, at 4,800 per square mile. The core of Toronto[100] is the most dense in Canada at approximately 18,000 per square mile.

Australia. Australian urban areas are somewhat more densely populated than U.S. urban areas. The average population density of urban areas over 1,000,000 is 3,600, compared to 3,400 in the United States. The largest urban area, Sydney, has a population density of 5,500, one-fifth less than that of Los Angeles. The cores of Australian urban areas tend to have densities similar to the newer, more automobile-oriented central cities of North America. The highest density municipality in the Sydney area, Waverly, has fewer than 20,000 persons per square mile.[101]

The Enclaves: Hong Kong and Singapore. The highest urban densities in the high-income world are in the political enclaves of Hong Kong and Singapore.

Hong Kong. By far the highest densities are in Hong Kong, with approximately 75,000 persons per square mile. Hong Kong is an assortment of very high densities and comparatively low densities, with little in between. Nearly 3,000,000 people—nearly one-half of the urban area's population—live at densities above 200,000 per square mile. This is by far the highest concentration of such hyper-densities in the high-income world. New York, with the second highest such concentration, has fewer than 40,000 people living at such a high density.

Hong Kong's exceedingly high population density, however, is the result of politics even to a greater extent than in London. Between 1950 and 2000, Hong Kong's population expanded three times, as people left China in response to the unique political and economic factors. The factors that produced Hong Kong's hyper-densities are unique and not likely to be replicated. Hong Kong is the only high-income world urban area with a population density higher than the large pre-automobile urban areas of Paris, London, and New York in 1900.

Singapore. Singapore is the second most dense urban area in the high-income world, with a population density of 21,600 per square mile, with the exception of urban areas in the more recently emerging economies of South Korea and Taiwan. This is considerably less than the nearly 50,000 per square mile densities of pre-automobile Paris, London, and New York in 1900. Like Hong Kong, Singapore is a political enclave. It covers approximately the same land area as the city of Chicago. Singapore has experienced a large flow of immigration, which is typical for a high-income area surrounded by middle-and low-income nations. Even so, Singapore's high density is partially the result of a larger than average household size. If Singapore households were the same size as in the United States, Western Europe, or Japan, its population density would be similar to that of Madrid or London.

More Recently Emerging, High-Income Urban Areas. In recent years, South Korea and Taiwan have achieved high-income status. Their urban areas retain substantially higher densities, as would be expected because car ownership developed later. For example, Seoul-Incheon has an urban population density of 43,200 per square mile, while Taipei's urban density is 39,300 per square mile. In each case, however, virtually all population growth is occurring in the suburbs or exurbs.

Differing Rates of Motorization. While all of the high-income world's largest urban areas now have automobile-oriented densities well below that of the pre-automobile city, the lowest densities are in U.S. urban areas. It seems likely that the principal factors for the lower U.S. densities are earlier affluence, the resulting earlier motorization, and the substantial urban growth that has occurred as the nation was becoming more automobile oriented.

The United States was the first major nation to achieve broad automobile ownership. The automobile-oriented urban area thus came to the United States well before it developed elsewhere. The limited data available suggest that as late as 1920, urban mass-transit market shares remained at approximately 50 percent, near the current rate of Tokyo-Yokohama and five times the present Western European rate. However, during the 1920s, the automobile became the dominant form of transportation, and mass transit's market share dropped to 20 percent in 1930. By this time, there were 0.75 automobiles for every household in the United States. Automobile gains continued during the economic upheavals of the 1930s. Mass transit's urban travel share rebounded during World War II, as gasoline and rubber were rationed, but then fell to 20 percent in 1950 and 2.4 percent today (including school buses and private shuttles).[102]

The 1930 U.S. automobile ownership rate of 0.75 per household was not achieved until much later in other nations. Canada, which has been the second leading economy (in per capita measures) through much of the last 75 years, achieved the 1930 U.S. automobile ownership rate only in the mid-1950s. The 0.75 cars per household rate was achieved in Australia in the mid-1960s. The delayed economic advance of war-torn Europe and Japan led to later motorization. France and Germany achieved the 1930 U.S. automobile penetration rate in the 1970s, while it took until the 1980s in the United Kingdom. Japan achieved the 0.75 automobiles per household rate in the late 1980s. A principal reason that U.S. urban areas are less dense and more automobile oriented is that the automobile became the dominant means of transportation from two to six decades earlier than in the rest of the high-income world.

However, there is more than the mere passage of time. During its longer period of wide automobile ownership, the United States has experienced far more urban growth than other high-income nations. Since 1930, the U.S. urban population has increased more than 220 percent. This population alone would have required a near tripling of urban development, plus land for residential and commercial building replacement. Canada's urban areas have grown nearly 140 percent since achieving the 1930 U.S. automobile ownership rate, while Australia's urban areas have grown more than 80 percent.

On the other hand, much of the post-war growth in Western Europe and Japan happened before the automobile achieved dominance. Urban areas in France grew only 18 percent since achieving the 1930 U.S. automobile availability rate. Urban areas in Japan have grown only 13 percent since achieving 0.75 automobiles per household. Thus, the greater extent of suburbanization in the United States and its low-density nature are the result of many more years of automobile availability and the higher growth that has occurred during that period (see Figure 3.6).[103]

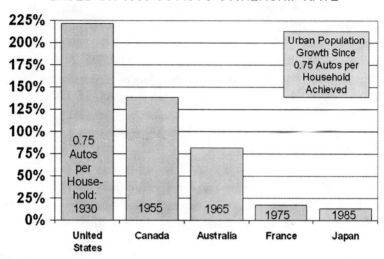

Figure 3.6

Causes of Suburbanization

Suburbanization is the result of various related factors, the most important of which are population growth, falling household size, the entry of women into the workforce, and the attractiveness of suburban living.

The Great Migration: Rural to Urban. For decades, people have been moving out of rural areas, especially to larger urban areas where larger, more efficient labor markets have produced greater economic opportunities. This has been the principal source of suburban growth, rather than the reduction in core populations so often cited by analysts. This "great migration" has been particularly strong in high-income nations and is now occurring in middle-and low-income nations, some of which remain considerably more rural than urban (such as China and India).

Urban areas are magnets of opportunity. In recent decades, urban areas have accounted for most overall economic growth, which has made them even more attractive to residents of small urban and rural areas. At the same time, technological advances in agriculture have substantially reduced labor requirements, which hastened migration to urban areas. No nation has achieved modern high-income status without a major movement of its population from small towns and rural areas to larger urban areas.

Nearly all population growth in the United States has been in urban areas since World War II. Since 1950, nearly 130,000,000 people have been added to urban areas, compared to only 2,000,000 in rural areas.[104] A major factor was the exodus of African Americans from the rural South to metropolitan areas principally in the Northeast, Midwest, and California.

A similar phenomenon occurred in Japan. From 1950 to 2000, metropolitan areas of more than 1,000,000 residents experienced a population increase of 41,000,000.[105] This compares to a much smaller increase of 2,000,000 in rural areas and smaller urban areas. Tokyo-Yokohama itself, the largest metropolitan area in the world, added more than 20,000,000 residents, more than reside in any other urban area in the world.

Canadian metropolitan areas accounted for more than 70 percent of growth from 1951 to 2001. Metropolitan areas with more than 1,000,000 population have nearly doubled their population since 1965 in Australia. The enclaves of Hong Kong and Singapore have more than doubled their populations since 1965. Growth has been less in Western Europe, but is still substantial. Since 1965, metropolitan areas of more than 1,000,000 have grown nearly 25 percent.[106]

Falling Household Size. Besides population growth and distribution, average household size has declined substantially since World War II. As a result, more housing units have been built than if household size had remained at its previous level. This has required more land for urban development.

By 2000, the average household size in the United States was 2.7, down nearly one-quarter from the 3.5 of 1950. Household sizes have declined similarly throughout the high-income world. In many urban areas that have had core city population declines, there have actually been increases in the number of occupied housing units. For example, the core city of Chicago lost 20 percent of its population between 1950 and 2000, yet added four percent to its stock of occupied housing units. From 1950 to 2000, 85 percent of the expansion in U.S. urban land area can be attributed to the increase in housing units, which is the result of smaller household size. In fact, U.S. housing densities have declined less than 20 percent since 1950 and have risen slightly since 1980.[107] This indicates that suburbanization is occurring at a rate virtually equal to the rate of household formation.

Entry of Women into the Workforce. Employment has expanded substantially since World War II. In the United States, employment rose at a rate more than 1.5 times that of the population from 1950 to 2000. A principal factor was the entry of millions of women into the work force (see Figure 3.7).[108]

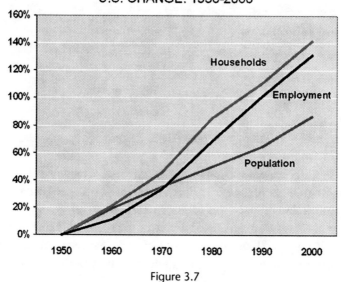

US Population, Households & Employment
U.S. CHANGE: 1950-2000

Figure 3.7

Larger Commercial Space Requirements. Moreover, the nature of the new commercial development was much different. Large commercial buildings and factories became more horizontal, often spread out (sprawling) in single-story configurations. This generally made commercial operations more efficient, lowering product prices for consumers. The more horizontal structures required more land, which was available at much lower prices than in the core or even in the inner suburbs.

Data are available for the Paris area, where the automobile-oriented outer-ring suburbs that have developed since 1950 have commercial development that occupies more than twice the land area per employee as in the inner-ring suburbs, mass-transit-oriented suburbs that developed with a more mass-transit orientation between 1900 and 1950 (see Table 3.2).[109]

Table 3.2: Commercial Area and Employment, Paris: 1999

Sector of Metropolitan Area (Ile de France)	General Period of Development	Acres per 1,000 Jobs	Compared to inner ville de Paris
Ville de Paris: Inner (Arrondissements I–XII)	Walking Era: (Before 1850)	2.4	1.0
Ville de Paris: Outer (Arrondissements XIII-XX)	Walking Era (1850–1900)	3.9	1.6
Suburbs: Inner (Petite Couronne)	Mass Transit Era (1900-1950)	17.9	7.5
Suburbs: Outer (Grand Couronne)	Automobile Era (1950-)	41.0	17.1

Source: http://www.demographia.com/db-paris-comml.htm

Quality of Life. Household economic factors may have been as important as population and household growth in fueling suburban growth. Incomes rose substantially. From 1960 to 2004, per capita gross domestic product increased more than 150 percent (inflation adjusted)[110] in the United States, Canada, the United Kingdom, and Sweden. Italy, Austria, and Norway experienced per capita economic growth exceeding 200 percent. In Japan, the per capita gross domestic product grew more than 400 percent.

As would be expected, higher incomes led households to seek a better quality of life. The higher quality housing was available at the best prices on the urban fringe. Automobiles became affordable and their higher speeds relative to mass transit made it possible for households to locate even further from employment. Commercial development followed residential development, so that work trip distances and travel times were less than they would have been if the decentralization of employment had not occurred.

French Automobile Association executive and "father" of the RER suburban rail system in Paris, Christian Gerondeau details the quality of life advantages of European suburbs and concludes, "It is a lifestyle…that has gradually become the most common in Europe. "Suburbia" gives its inhabitants a quality of life with which the majority is satisfied…"[111]

Unsustainably High Core Densities. Some suburban growth occurred because of central city losses. As transportation improvements have occurred, the formerly hyper-dense cores of central cities have lost population. Perhaps the most important factor was that their population densities were unsustainably high for the emerging, more affluent era of the automobile and smaller households. At the end of World War II, there were housing shortages, and central cities were generally overcrowded. Government programs were enacted in various nations to reduce population densities and improve sanitary conditions.

However, the process of urban population decline started much earlier. In Paris, core arrondissements began losing population in the 1830s, as did core New York wards. Kenneth Jackson found that core wards of Philadelphia began to lose population even earlier, between 1800 and 1820.[112] The formerly most dense areas of Paris, London, New York, and Tokyo now have population densities 60 percent or less than their historical peaks.[113] Core population losses have occurred in virtually all of the urban areas that were built around walking or mass transit, as people have taken advantage of the opportunity to enjoy more space.

The losses extend to the municipal level. It is generally well-known that central cities of the United States have lost population. St. Louis has lost the most population, dropping nearly 60 percent from 1950 to 2000. Pittsburgh, Detroit, and Buffalo have lost more than 50 percent of their population, while Washington, Minneapolis, and Chicago have lost more than 20 percent. In all of the U.S. cases except Pittsburgh, the population of the corresponding metropolitan areas, including suburbs, has increased.

What is less well-known is that historic core cities have lost population in Western Europe, Japan, Canada, and elsewhere. Manchester, Liverpool, and Glasgow have lost more than 45 percent of their population. European central cities perceived as vibrant and attractive have also lost population. Copenhagen's population dropped approximately 40 percent from its peak; Paris has lost more than 25 percent of its population, while Zurich and Vienna have lost 20 percent or more. The core cities of Tokyo, Osaka, Toronto,[114] and Montreal have also lost population. Again, generally, metropolitan area populations, including suburbs, have generally increased.

Core city losses have been pervasive throughout the high-income world. Among the high-income world central cities (municipalities) that have achieved 400,000 population at some point and neither annexed nor consolidated, only one, Vancouver, is at its peak population.[115]

However, the core losses accounted for comparatively little of the suburban growth. In the United States, less than 30 percent of suburban growth from 1950 to 2000 was attributable to central city losses in the metropolitan areas where such losses were the greatest.[116] Only 22 large historic core cities in the United States retain approximately the same boundaries as in 1950. Every one has lost population. However, the surrounding suburban growth has *not* been principally fueled by core city losses. More than twice as many people moved to the suburbs from outside the area than from the cities. Even in St. Louis, with the largest percentage population loss in modern history among major cities, less than one half of the suburban growth was attributable to central city losses.

Less than 15 percent of the population growth in the major metropolitan areas of Western Europe is attributable to central city losses since 1965. For example, the ville de Paris reached its population peak in 1921. Since that time, the city has lost more than 775,000 residents. However, this loss is less than 10 percent of the approximately 8,000,000 gain in the suburbs of Paris.[117]

The core city losses in Japan have been only a minor contributor to that nation's explosive suburban growth. The core of Tokyo reached its population peak in 1965. Since that time, the population has declined nearly 800,000, while the suburbs have added 11,600,000 residents. Thus, more than 90 percent of Tokyo's suburban growth has been from small town and rural areas, rather than from the core area. Over the same period, the core city of Osaka has lost approximately 550,000 residents, while the suburbs have added 4,800,000 residents. In Osaka-Kobe-Kyoto, approximately 90 percent of suburban growth has been from outside the metropolitan areas, rather than from the central city.[118]

In Canada, central city losses have represented only a small part of suburban growth. Since reaching its peak in 1971, the former city of Toronto has lost approximately 40,000 residents. The suburbs have added 2,000,000 residents, more than 50 times the central city loss. Over the same period, the core city of Montreal lost 175,000 residents, while the suburbs added nearly 900,000 residents.

The same core area decline can be observed in a number of developing world urban areas as well. The central delegations (wards) of Mexico City lost 45 percent of their population from 1960 to 2000. This more than 700,000 loss was more than offset by a 12 million increase in metropolitan area population. Small losses have been sustained in the urban area of Shanghai, while the metropolitan area has experienced strong growth. Similarly, core population losses have occurred in Mumbai (formerly Bombay), which is one of the world's fastest growing urban areas. The core city of Buenos Aires has lost residents since 1947, while the suburbs have added approximately 8,000,000 residents. Population losses have occurred in a number of historic core cities outside the high-income world, such as Seoul, Manila, and Bucharest.

Lower Costs. A principal reason for the economic advancement of the high-income world has been lower costs. Commercial practices, including large retail stores, horizontal rather than multi-story buildings, better transportation, and the flexibility of truck transportation have all worked together to produce low prices. This improves the standard of living and facilitates greater choice by producing more disposable income.

"Push" Factors. Further, many central cities have experienced serious difficulties in retaining residents who have the means to move to the suburbs because
they are perceived as insufficiently accommodating places to live. Educational
performance may be inferior, which leads families with children to move to the
suburbs. The cost of living is often higher in central cities. Central city crime
rates also tend to be higher. Often taxes are higher. In addition, it is not unusual
for central city public services to be inferior to those in the suburbs. Additional
push factors were operating in American urban areas, which are described in
Chapter 4.

Suburban World

The modern patterns of suburbanization are irreversible. To restore the pre-automobile patterns of the mass-transit-oriented urban area would require abandoning between 60 and 95 percent of urban land area and forcing suburban residents
to move into a far more dense urban core, except in Hong Kong. Not even ardent
critics of urban sprawl propose this. The smaller increases in population density
that anti-sprawl programs would bring to urban areas like Portland and Toronto
fall far short of the thresholds that would be required to materially change the
urban form, much less transfer a material amount of demand from cars to mass
transit.

For decades, nearly all growth in high-income world urban areas has been suburban. Among metropolitan areas of more than 1,000,000 population in the
high-income world, approximately 95 percent of urban growth has been in the
suburbs. In the United States, Canada, Japan, and Oceania (Australia and New
Zealand), more than 90 percent of growth has been in the suburbs since 1965. In
Western Europe the share of growth in the suburbs has been even greater, at 114
percent, reflecting the continuing central city population losses (see Figure
3.8).[119] Stated in terms of the urban sprawl definition, nearly all urban population growth has resulted in *the spreading of urban development on undeveloped land*
near urban areas for decades, whether in the United States, Western Europe,
Japan, Canada, Australia, or elsewhere in the high-income world.

International Suburb Growth Share
METROPOLITAN AREAS OVER 1,000,000

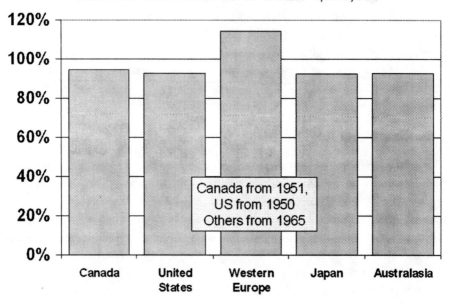

Figure 3.8

Generally, suburbanization occurred because people preferred it, whether in Los Angeles, Atlanta, Paris, or Nagoya. The housing was newer, bigger, better, and less expensive than could be obtained in the central city for the same price. People moving to the suburban neighborhoods normally perceived them as better. The wide availability and flexibility of the automobile brought the entire urban area within reach of nearly everyone, for the first time. All in all, households throughout the high-income world moved into what David Brooks has characterized as the "future tense," and it has become a suburban world.[120]

4

Planning and the Post-War American City

The Unique Decline of U.S. Core Cities

The decline of the central city has been more pronounced in the United States than elsewhere. There is a widely accepted belief that this decline is principally due to "white flight," the exodus of a prejudiced white population, fleeing increasingly African American cities. This is a simplistic and puritanical view.

Core city population losses have generally been greater in the United States than in other high-income nations. Among the 14 largest U.S. core cities that did not expand their boundaries and had virtually no room for fringe development,[121] 12 experienced population losses greater than can be explained by falling household sizes. The losses have been very large in some cases; St. Louis lost nearly 60 percent of its population, a larger loss than that of any major city in the world. Pittsburgh, Buffalo, Detroit, and Cleveland lost approximately one-half of their population. These four cities are the core of the American "rust belt," which suffered serious industrial losses as international competition increased, beginning with the European and Japanese recoveries from World War II. The two cities in which the loss can be explained by falling household sizes are San Francisco, which lost five percent of its population from 1950 to 2005, and Chicago, which lost more than 20 percent of its population.

At the same time, other core cities, such as Portland, Atlanta, Houston, Denver, and Seattle expanded their boundaries (annexed) and experienced growth. Analysts often make the mistake of assuming that because these cities grew, they somehow escaped the difficulties experienced in the cities that did not annex substantial new territory. In fact, in nearly all cases, core population losses have occurred, which have been masked by increases in population due to annexation, consolidation, or "greenfield" development (development on previously rural land) that looks no different from the suburban development surrounding cities that did not annex. The same movement of people from the core has occurred in cities that have annexed large expanses of territory. The development in these

55

areas, while technically in the central city, is no different than the development in suburbs that have not been annexed. For example, most of the land area of the central cities of Toronto, Phoenix, Portland, Indianapolis, Columbus, Los Angeles and others is covered by post-World War II suburban development little different than that of suburbs that have not been annexed to the central city.

Misunderstanding Core Cities

There is a wide range of differences between core cities. Some are very small compared to their metropolitan areas. For example, the cities of Atlanta and Boston have 10 percent or less of their respective metropolitan populations. At the other end of the scale, San Antonio has nearly two-thirds of its metropolitan area's population. In U.S. urban areas, poverty and lower-income households tend to be concentrated in the geographical cores, irrespective of the share of the population in the core cities. Thus, all things being equal, smaller core cities will have higher rates of poverty and more low-income households. Expanding the boundaries of such cities would do nothing more than mask the same poverty with a larger surrounding population.

Urban areas are not constrained by political or administrative boundaries. Municipal boundaries can be drawn virtually anywhere. Core cities represent substantially varying percentages of urban area populations and are thus very different. Comparisons between core cities are, as a result, often misleading.[122]

This is illustrated by the work of David Rusk.[123] Rusk, a former mayor of Albuquerque, has proposed a "city elasticity" theory. Among his observations is that more elastic cities—those that can or have annexed suburban areas, have less poverty and higher incomes than cities that have not been able to annex. As noted above, this is to be expected, since poverty and lower incomes are concentrated in urban cores, regardless of the size of the central city. Rusk also claims that metropolitan areas with elastic core cities have less racial segregation.

However, this city elasticity theory simply measures the characteristics within what are arbitrary municipal boundaries. At the urban area level, the characteristics Rusk identifies are not evident. In fact, poverty is lower in the urban areas that are *less* elastic, while average incomes are *higher*.[124] With respect to racial segregation, it appears that the driving force is growth. In a Brookings Institution report, Edward L. Glaeser and Jacob L. Vigdor show that segregation has declined most where population growth has been the greatest.[125]

This same difficulty is evident in other research. A Brookings Institution report on the 2000 Census outlines income trends in major U.S. cities and classifies cities from "balanced" in terms of their array of income groups to "stressed," where there is a higher concentration of low-income households.[126] The city of Louisville, Kentucky, is rated in the least healthy category, as distressed. The state capital, Lexington, is in the healthiest category, as balanced. Not surprisingly, the poverty rate in the city of Lexington is less than in the city of Louisville. However, matters are different when the entire urban area is considered. The Louisville poverty rate is less than that in Lexington. The difference is that Lexington had combined with its suburbs in a city-county merger, while Louisville had not. The higher poverty rates in the city of Louisville are a simple matter of where municipal boundaries have been drawn.

The Simplistic Answer: "White Flight"

The old adage that history is written by the victors, or at least the survivors, is true of U.S. city history. The general story line is that U.S. core cities, with their massive population losses, were decimated by "white flight," as a uniquely prejudiced American white population refused to live with African Americans, and moved to the suburbs instead. The reality is not so simple.

This is not to suggest that racial prejudice was not a factor in the decline of U.S. core cities. However, analysts have been far too hasty to suggest that racial attitudes in the United States are worse than they might have been in other countries with similar challenges. Around the world, tensions generally increase where there is an influx of what Statistics Canada calls "visible minorities[127]," and segregation often occurs.

For example, some of Stockholm's new towns are highly segregated. For example, a visit to Tensta will reveal few native Swedes. Instead, there is a preponderance of immigrant residents from nations like Turkey and Iran. The British Broadcasting Company has referred to internal migration trends in France as white flight.[128]

The Great Migration

The economic boom that accompanied and followed World War II attracted virtually millions of African Americans off the farms of the South to large urban areas in other parts of the country, especially in the Northeast and Great Lakes area. On the eve of World War II, the 1940 census found that less than one-quarter of African Americans lived outside the South. This was to change radically, as African Americans, like rural residents throughout the high-income world, sought the opportunities that were only available in the large urban areas. From 1940 to 1970, nearly 80 percent of African American growth occurred outside the South. This "great migration" added at 5.4 million more people to the population outside the South compared to what would have been expected if the African American population distribution had remained the same as in 1940. Most of the gain was in the large urban areas. Even in the South, African Americans were moving in large numbers away from the rural areas to the larger urban areas, to take advantage of economic opportunities.

However, this was a time of great natural growth in the United States. During the 1950s, the nation's population increased more than in any other post-war decade, at approximately 20 percent. Virtually all of the growth was in urban areas, as people—African Americans and others—left rural areas. Under any set of circumstances, accommodating the new residents would have been difficult. It would be particularly difficult with respect to a largely poor, visible minority.

The new residents were to find pervasive racial prejudice outside the South, though much less of it was imbedded in law. African Americans could, for example, generally send their children to the same schools as whites, because segregated school systems had not been established. However, they faced serious legal barriers with respect to housing and were barred, often by deed restrictions, from living in many neighborhoods.

There is no doubt that white flight was a factor in the decline of U.S. core cities. However, it is an oversimplification to indict Americans as inherently more prejudiced than others, as the white flight of Sweden and France shows. However, there is much more to the story. America's core cities faced additional serious challenges, some of them the direct result of public policy.

How Urban Planning Hastened Core-City Decline

Rapid population growth, low-income migration, and African American migration might have been more gracefully accommodated had it not been for the destructive role of urban planning. The policy instruments were urban renewal and urban freeway construction.

Urban renewal and urban freeway construction were not confined to U.S. urban areas. Nor was the devastation of urban planning limited to the United States. For example, Romanian dictator Nicolai Ceaucescu tore down thousands of homes and churches to build his "Palace of the People"[129] and the monumental boulevard leading to it. However, generally, U.S. urban areas experienced more planning-based devastation than in other nations.

It is often implied that these programs were imposed from the outside on the cities by the federal government. In fact, urban renewal was a part of a deliberate effort by city leaders, downtown business interests, and urban planners to remove what they deemed to be blight. The freeways were not imposed on the cities.

Large-city mayors had objected when early drafts of Interstate highway legislation did not include urban freeways. They successfully lobbied Congress to add the urban freeway miles that revisionist historians have been blaming on the federal government for decades.[130]

These post-war urban planning strategies were a principal cause of the uniquely intense destruction that occurred in U.S. core cities. In the 1950s and 1960s, cities bulldozed large swaths of inner cities for urban renewal and construction of freeways. Generally, low-income housing areas adjacent to downtowns were removed for new development. Little thought was given to replacement housing for the dispossessed. Those fortunate enough to own their homes were compensated, but they were by no means the majority. Indeed, the urban renewal sites were often empty for years following the demolition. For example, some lots cleared in the 1960s in the Los Angeles Bunker Hill redevelopment project were still undeveloped 40 years later.

Moreover, planners appear to have chosen the routes of least political resistance for their urban freeways, which meant that low-income areas were leveled to a greater extent than other neighborhoods. As a result, the urban freeway projects became virtual extensions of the urban planning "slum-clearing" initiatives.[131] According to housing advocate Catherine Bauer: "The planners saw redevelopment as the means for more rational and efficient organization of central cities, by removing wasteful and inappropriate land uses and facilitating new development in conformance with some kind of plan for the area."[132]

Moreover, these programs provided the impetus for an unprecedented growth in the number of urban planners[133] and may be considered the foundation of the profession's present influence.[134]

How Urban Planning Destroyed Neighborhoods. The areas that urban planners deemed to be slums or derelict development, however, were home to the residents who lived there, and the small businesses that served them. The strength of many such communities was either not perceived by the planners or not of interest to them. African Americans, recently arrived from the rural South, occupied the soon-to-be-leveled communities. Noting that "blight, like beauty is in the eye of the beholder,"[135] Mindy Thompson Fullilove describes the African American core-city neighborhoods that were to be destroyed by urban renewal: "Although they were areas of filth, crime, and poverty, those funky neighborhoods provided the doorway to the American dream."[136]

At the same time, the white households who perceived themselves to be forced out of their neighborhoods by the new African American entrants created just as much demand for housing elsewhere. The neighborhoods that the whites left were communities, like the bulldozed neighborhoods of African Americans. The selling households sought new housing elsewhere in the urban area, which fueled artificially high demand for new houses, mostly in the suburbs.

A late 1960s federal commission headed by Illinois Senator Paul Douglas estimated that urban renewal programs from 1949 to 1967 had demolished more than 400,000 houses. Fullilove indicates that 1,600 neighborhoods were destroyed. The commission report estimated that 330,000 additional houses had been demolished due to urban freeway construction, and projected a further 250,000 demolitions in the next five years. These two federal programs alone would destroy nearly 1,000,000 housing units and many thousands of businesses. However, there was more demolition going on. The commission cites a National Association of Home Builders report, which estimated total government demolitions in urban areas, including those not related to federal programs at 2.4 million.[137] The 1.0 to 2.4 million demolished through government programs could have housed between 3,000,000 and 7,000,000 or more people.[138] This is at the same time that millions of people, whites and African Americans were moving to the urban areas, and at a time of strong natural population growth.

There was little, if any provision made for the displaced. Fullilove notes that less than 11,000 new homes were built under urban renewal programs, 97 percent less than would have been needed to replace the demolished 400,000 homes.[139] Nor was relocation assistance provided, though homeowners were compensated for the taking of their property. However, it seems likely that most African American and low-income victims did not own their own homes. The urban freeway program had virtually no relocation assistance element through most of its implementation, whether for owners or renters. The underlying, "let them eat cake" philosophy on relocation had been expressed by the President's Commission on Home Building and Home Ownership decades before, in 1932:

> We do not concur in the argument that a slum must be allowed to exist because there are persons dwelling in them who could not afford to dwell in better surroundings. It is our view that the slums must, nevertheless, be removed for the benefit of the community. We are confident that a large portion of the group displaced by slum clearance will be able to find suitable accommodations elsewhere.[140]

The federal Housing Act of 1949 had anticipated building millions of units of public housing, but this was not in anticipation of urban renewal, it was rather a strategy for addressing the housing shortages that followed World War II.

Where new residential units were constructed, they were usually well beyond the means of the displaced residents. For example, Portland, Oregon, is proud of its south side urban renewal project that removed low-income households and businesses to provide leafy boulevards and high-rise residential buildings far too costly for the long-since-displaced residents. Los Angeles drove low-income residents out to build skyscrapers for bank headquarters, a museum, and a performing arts center, albeit decades later. The bank headquarters have long since moved away.

Thus, urban renewal and urban freeway construction took homes away from millions of households, many of whom had low incomes. One of the most important "externalities" of mid-20th-century urban planning was the financial setback imposed upon low-income, often minority households. It seems likely that these programs drove some households into poverty and lengthened the time in poverty for others.

Destroying Neighborhood Business. The impact on small businesses may have been as great. For example, the African American and other communities that were dismantled by urban planning were served by local businesses, owned by people who lived in the neighborhoods. There were professional offices, such as medical doctors and dentists. As is typical of small businesses, many of these operated on low profit margins, and their proprietors could not afford to move. Those who owned their properties were, of course, compensated, but most did not.

In addition, like the residents forced out, the uprooted businesses received almost no assistance from the governments that displaced them, which, in effect, forced them to close. Even if these businesses could have moved, their customers would have been dispersed and a new customer base would have had to be developed. To planners who often fail to understand the mechanisms of entrepreneurship and wealth creation, the impact of their policies on small businesses may seem slight. It was, however, no slight matter to owners who were driven out of business by the urban planners.

Prison-Like Public Housing

Some of the displaced moved into new public housing. However, the long public housing waiting lists made this difficult. Some households managed to find accommodations in the high-rise-tower apartment blocks built consistent with the urban planning doctrines of the time. This was a further disaster.

The now-demolished Robert Taylor Homes in Chicago are a good example. This line of 16 story apartment blocks stretched along the east side of the 12-lane

Dan Ryan Expressway. The land cleared for this public housing project and the freeway may have dispossessed more low-income African Americans than any other "urban improvement" project in the United States. Yet, the urban planners of the day saw this as a singular triumph of urban planning.

However, what looked so ideal to the urban planners was a virtual hell to its residents. The Robert Taylor Homes and the many smaller but similar complexes around the nation often resembled prisons both in their design and environment.

My university colleague, Officer Walter Schwalm (retired) of the Cook County, Illinois, Sheriff's Department describes the squalid conditions in the Robert Taylor Homes and other city of Chicago public housing projects.

> Conditions at the CHA housing projects for the most part could only be described as grim and inhumane. The worst conditions were at the high-rise projects where large numbers of poor people were packed into high-density multi-floor buildings. Elevators in these buildings were frequently out of order, requiring tenants to walk up many floors to their apartments. The stairs in the buildings were unheated and open to the elements. Often the stairs and hallways smelled of urine and were littered with trash and garbage. And frequently the lights on the landing of the stairs were out, requiring tenants to walk up the stairs in total darkness.

> Many of the CHA high-rise buildings had boarded-up and abandoned apartments. I remember sometimes whole floors of a building were boarded up due to a fire or some other reason. Thus, tenants in a building might be living in an apartment where all of the apartments above or below them were boarded up and unrented. Abandoned apartments were often broken into and used by street gangs for various criminal activities such as drug sales, hideouts for gang members, etc.

> Many of the high-rise buildings were designed so that each apartment was accessible only from an outdoor hallway, which was open to the air and fenced in from floor to ceiling by a metal screen. This gave the CHA tenants the feeling that they were living in a huge cage, almost like animals at a zoo.

> I remember an elderly woman who lived on one of the upper floors of one of the projects telling me that crime was so bad at the projects that once the sun went down at night she never left her apartment for any reason until the next morning. The combination of unreliable elevators, dark and unlit hallways and stairs, street gang activity in the stairwells, and abandoned apartments all created an unsafe environment for housing residents and visitors.[141]

However, climbing the stairs was just the beginning. Chicago is a very cold place in the winter. Its temperatures are routinely far below those reached in most other major U.S. urban areas. Few, if any, Western European urban areas have such bitterly cold weather. In addition, the summers are humid. The staircases at the Robert Taylor Homes were unheated and exposed to the weather. Apartments opened to hallways that were themselves exposed to the weather. Chainlink fences were on one side of the hall, and apartment doors on the other.

Many of the conditions described by Officer Schwalm would not have been allowed to exist in much of the city's regulated private apartment rental stock. City authorities would have closed privately owned apartment buildings that were in such a poor state of repair. However, government has routinely been ineffective in regulating itself, despite its frequent failures. Perhaps it should take a page from basketball and other sports, which do not allow members of the opposing teams to serve as referees.

Blockbusting: Urban Planning's Harvest

Other displaced households with somewhat greater resources sought housing in the private market. The combination of the African American migration from the South and core-city displacement of African American households generated by urban planning led to a virtually unprecedented demand for housing. There was a great need for new housing and for more rapid turnover of existing housing in the resale market.

The real estate industry responded to the planning market distortion by a distortion of its own, called *blockbusting*—a process that systematically used racial fears to "scare" people into selling their houses at steeply discounted prices.[142] For the blockbusting real estate agent (white or black), it was like printing money; there was a substantial opportunity to receive commissions from a much larger volume of sales than would have occurred in normal circumstances. White residents feared that allowing African Americans into their neighborhoods would lower property values. There was also a perception that crime rates would rise.

This destroyed some households financially and certainly left most victim households considerably less affluent than they had been before. Obviously, this only made the achievement of racial harmony more difficult. White victims tended to blame the new African-American residents for their losses, rather than the urban planners or even the blockbusters, whose profits were so unwittingly facilitated by the planners.

As planners and their principally downtown business allies implemented their dreams of more tidy cities, they intensified and even created opportunities for blockbusters. It is perhaps the ultimate irony that in their pursuit of a better city, urban planners helped to destroy communities by both bulldozing and propelling a market reaction that extended the destruction to stable, working-class, inner-city neighborhoods that had escaped physical demolition.

1960s Urban Disorders

All of this dislocation was not without its consequences. U.S. central cities experienced destructive civil disorders in the middle and late 1960s, in which there were many deaths and massive destruction, by fire, of principally African American neighborhoods. A number of these actions were precipitated by law enforcement incidents and a number immediately followed the assassination of Dr. Martin Luther King, Jr. The Kerner Commission, empanelled to report on the disorders, linked urban renewal, along with other factors, to the discontent that fueled the disorders.[143]

Increasing the Demand for Suburban Housing

Even without the destructive urban planning policies, there would have been some white flight, because the lowest-cost available housing tended to be in working-class, white neighborhoods near the urban core. The new African American households gravitated to these core areas, because house prices were lower.

Of course, when an African American household purchases a house from a white household and moves in, the white household moves. This is not white flight; it is rather the nature of a housing sale. With the large influx of African American households into the core cities, it is to be expected that a similar number of existing households, mostly white, would move away. In this environment, core cities could not have retained their white households. There just was not enough room.

Learning from History

By the early 1970s, it was becoming clear that serious mistakes had been made. Jane Jacobs[144] had questioned the entire direction of urban planning in her 1961 book, *the Death and Life of Great American Cities*.[145]

The huge Pruitt-Igoe public housing complex in St. Louis was demolished less than 20 years after it was opened. Many were to follow, including the infamous Robert Taylor Homes. The Chicago Housing Authority Robert Taylor Homes Internet site indicates that the "Robert Taylor property became a national symbol for the errant philosophy of post-war public housing." This assessment would have shocked the Chicago and federal planners of the time, whose commitment to what they believed was good for the community involved building these prisons.[146]

Of course, it is not possible to turn back the clock to undo the mistakes of urban planning that had so much to do with the decline of the American central city. What is important is to learn the lessons. The urban planners of the post—World War II era believed very much that they were doing right. They did not intend to destroy the city. Yet, their good intentions were insufficient to annul the negative consequences that they could not at the time either foresee or understand. The post-war urban planners believed that they were doing good. However, in fact, they were doing wrong, and it was very wrong.

There is an important lesson for today and the future. Urban planning doctrines have consequences. The doctrines of the 1950s destroyed communities, families, and lives. The doctrines of the early 20th century are already destroying the hope of home ownership, and its attendant advantages, for many households, which could lead to economic losses that could spread throughout the urban economy, not just the core cities.

"Push" Factors

Other factors contributed to the decline of U.S. city cores. These are referred to as push factors, because they tended to push core-city residents to the suburbs. For example:

- **Inferior Municipal Performance.** U.S. core cities have historically been characterized by high taxes, poor services, and high comparative expenditures per capita. Suburban areas generally had lower taxes and better municipal services. Moreover, core-city governments are more susceptible to special interests, which virtually always seek higher expenditure levels. This includes, for example, business interests seeking subsidies, and municipal employee labor unions, which also use their political power to bar cost-saving service delivery options.

- **Political Corruption.** U.S. core cities have, through their history, been objects of political corruption. Corruption can occur in smaller municipalities, but it is likely to be far less pervasive, both because the potential rewards for the wrongly inclined are less and because governments tend to be more responsive to voters, whose individual influence is much greater because it is not diluted in a much larger electorate.

- **High Crime Rates.** Generally, crime rates have been higher in core cities. This has been a particular concern because of the perception that the judicial system had become far too tolerant of crime.

- **Poor Educational Performance.** Core-city educational systems perform poorly. As a result, households often leave the core cities by the time children enter school and households with school age children generally do not move to the core cities. Moreover, it is not simply a matter of insufficient financial resources, since many core-city school systems have higher-than-average spending levels.

- **Mandatory School Busing.** School busing was an important push factor, as anyone who had children in affected school districts at the time can attest. Legal interventions to eliminate de-facto racial segregation in city school systems often resulted in pupils having to be transported, by school bus, long distances to school, instead of being able to walk to school. This combined with a concern for the security of their children, led households to move to the suburbs, beyond the forced busing programs. Forced busing started in the 1970s. That decade was by far the period of greatest central city loss. More than one-half of the 1950 to 2000 core-city population loss occurred during the 1970s. It is ironic that current urban planning doctrines have now come full circle, embracing the neighborhood schools that the social engineers did so much to destroy in the core cities.

Moreover, the push factors drove more than white residents out of the city. For some years, *black flight* has been underway, as African Americans who can afford it have been moving to the suburbs. Suburban Prince George's County in Maryland has a majority African American population, with many residents having fled the high-tax, education, and public service disaster that is Washington, DC. Data from the 2000 census indicates that more than 40 percent of the 1,000,000 plus residents added to suburban Atlanta in the last 10 years were African American. With an influx of Hispanics and Asians into the suburbs, the non-Hispanic-whites accounted for less than one-third of the new residents. Of course, none of this should be surprising. There is a universal preference for a better quality of life, and households throughout the high-income world have been flocking to the suburbs for just that reason for decades. It is not a matter of white or black.

A Brighter Future: The Inner City Renaissance

It is perhaps surprising that, despite their victimization by urban planning policies, U.S. inner cities are now experiencing a renaissance. Even in St. Louis, which, it could be argued, has lost more of its population than any core city since the Romans sacked Carthage,[147] there is substantial new apartment and loft construction in the core area (though not without subsidy), after decades of decline.

There are reports that builders have run out of old commercial loft space for conversion and have begun building new loft buildings in the core of Chicago. The South Bronx, with destruction that looked like Dresden at the end of World War II when Presidents Carter and Reagan visited (separately) has been reborn as a vital, prospering community.[148] Something clearly has changed in the American core city.

- Generally, cities are no longer so involved in slum clearance, perhaps simply because there is no more money. This means that communities are allowed to thrive with less government intervention.

- Improving crime rates are a major factor. The cities are becoming far safer, at least in the areas where the new housing is being built or converted. Former Mayor Rudolf Guiliani's groundbreaking programs that reduced New York City's crime rates have been copied successfully around the nation.

- Demographic trends are also favorable. Millions of Baby Boom and younger households are now Empty Nesters. The children have gone, and they are now in their suburban homes with plenty of space. Some, though by no means most, Empty Nesters are moving to the new condominiums and lofts in places like downtown Seattle, Kansas City, Minneapolis, St. Louis, and Denver. However, these new residents do not leave their suburban, automobile-oriented lifestyles behind. The large, new condominium buildings on Chicago's north side have ample parking to accommodate the cars brought by the new urban residents from the suburbs. When the core area population losses were briefly reversed in the 1990s, mass transit's share of commuting in the core area declined.

The same is true elsewhere. In a number of areas, single-family detached housing is being developed that looks no different than the new housing in the suburbs.

However, poor educational performance of children in core-city schools remains a daunting issue. Mandatory school busing has been abandoned in many places. However, many households with children are still deterred by decrepit core-city educational performance. Nonetheless, the decline has been slowed or even stopped, at least in the cores of American central cities.

Overall, the American core city faces a more attractive future than in the past. Some of the current residential renaissance in the core is subsidy driven, either by direct payments or by tax incentives. Still, some of it has little to do with subsidies, and the prospect is that the market will look more kindly on core cities in the future. Finally, this renaissance is occurring both with and without anti-suburban policies. Some urban areas with a substantial core renaissance, such as Kansas City, Milwaukee and Atlanta have not adopted anti-suburban policies. Others, such as Seattle and Portland have adopted anti-suburban policies.

Core cities are not likely to ever be the dense urban centers that they were in the past. Nor will they be dominant in their respective urban areas. The trends occurring in U.S. core cities can be described as the *suburbanization* of the inner cities. A trip through nearly all large U.S. city cores will reveal a level of development and vibrancy that is without parallel over the past 75 years.

PART II
Demonizing the Suburbs

5

Hysteria over Land

One of the most frequently cited justifications for curbing suburbanization is the claim that it threatens agricultural production. This claim is simply wrong.

Urbanization: No Threat to Agriculture

Throughout the high-income world, the amount of land used for agriculture has been declining. Improved productivity is the reason, not expanding urbanization. There is, in fact, a surplus of production, which is why many high-income world governments provide price supports (subsidies) to agriculture.

United States. Even with the subsidies, there is less farmland in the United States than in 1950. Productivity has more than doubled, while the land used in agriculture has declined by 260 million acres. During that time, U.S. urban areas were adding a population of nearly 130,000,000—more than live in Japan today. Yet, the area consumed in new urban development was only one-sixth of the total farmland removed from production. Thomas J. Nechyba and Randall P. Walsh suggest that the anti-suburban "farmland loss threat" arguments are more rhetorical than real, characterizing it as "unlikely, for instance, that advocates of anti-sprawl measures worry primarily about the encroachment of city footprints on farmland, especially in the light of the fact that forests encroach significantly more on farmland than do cities."[149]

According to the 2000 U.S. Census, 2.6 percent of U.S. land was urban, leaving 97.4 percent of land in non-urban uses.[150]

Canada. The situation is similar in Canada, where the expansion of urbanization has been far less than the productivity-driven reduction in agricultural land. The total expanse of urbanization was approximately one-quarter the maximum agricultural land that has been withdrawn from production in the last 50 years.[151] The withdrawn agricultural land is nearly 1.5 times as great as the total land area of Nova Scotia. All of Canada's urbanization occupies approximately three percent of the total human footprint (urban plus agricultural land).[152]

Australia. Agricultural land withdrawals have greatly exceeded urban expansion in Australia as well. Since 1981, nearly 187,000 square miles of land has been withdrawn, an area approximately 25 times the land area of Australian urbanization (approximately 0.25 percent of land[153]). The agricultural land withdrawn from production is more than twice the size of the state of Victoria.

Rural Open Space

A related criticism of suburbanization is that it consumes open space or green space. This is most evident to urban dwellers that see land on the urban fringe being developed with houses, commercial facilities, and activity centers.

However, what is access to open space? If it is the ability to visit rural parks or sensitive rural areas, then suburbanization is not much of a barrier. Urbanization is routinely not permitted in rural parks, and the appropriate preservation of environmentally sensitive areas also prevents urbanization. Thus, suburbanization does not reduce access to open spaces that are generally available to the public.

Except for open space within urban areas, such as urban parks, it has virtually never been possible for residents of large urban areas to access open space except by mechanized transport, such as the car or public transport.

The geographical expansion of urban areas and high rates of automobile ownership have improved access to rural open space for urban residents. Urban residents had little access to rural open space before the automobile. Rural open space was too far away to access by walking. Mass transit served little rural territory, and often, to reach that open space required most residents to travel to downtown areas and transfer to services going to rural areas. The automobile changed all of this. Rural open space became far more accessible to the overwhelming portion of urban households with cars. Without the automobile, households find it difficult, if not impossible, to reach rural areas, little different from their predecessors in the pre-automobile age.

The speed of the automobile nullifies all but a small part of the additional time that might be required to access rural open space. For example, an urban area of 400 square miles might expand 20 percent to 480 square miles. This might appear to be a significant expansion. However, it would require little more than one additional mile around the perimeter of the urban area. The automobile or train traveler, eager to see agricultural areas or open space, would have to wait an extra minute or so at prevailing highway speeds before the rural greenery would appear.

Travelers on intercity highways may perceive that there is little open space left between cities. It may appear that there is commercial development at virtually every interchange. However, there is much more land than can be seen along the busy avenues of commerce that traverse modern nations. This largely undeveloped area can be seen along the many U.S. and state highway routes and other rural roads that are not freeways, and which constitute most of the intercity roadway mileage. Similarly, little development will be found along the secondary and local highways of rural Western Europe, Japan, Canada, Australia, or New Zealand.

Similarly, an airplane trip on a clear day gives a more accurate impression of urbanization's extent. Between Chicago and Los Angeles or Cleveland and Cincinnati, for example, little urbanization is evident in a sea of agricultural land and open space. In other areas of greater urban development, the impression is not much different. Between Chicago and New York, Toronto and Ottawa, Tokyo and Sapporo, Paris and Berlin, or Sydney and Canberra, urbanization is lost in a sea of agricultural land and open space.

The Shrinking Human Footprint

The anti-suburban movement could not have gotten the data more wrong than it has regarding agriculture and open space. Urbanization has not increased the human footprint over the past 50 years. Quite the contrary has occurred. The human footprint (urban development, rural development, and agricultural land use)[154] has decreased in the United States, Canada, and Australia, as significant amounts of agricultural land have been withdrawn and turned back into open space. In the United States, the human footprint has been reduced by 15 percent since 1950, an amount equal to the land area of Texas and Oklahoma combined. Improving productivity has allowed 5.3 acres of agricultural land to be retired for each new acre of urban land. In 1950, the human footprint accounted for 53 percent of the land area in the United States. By 2000, the human footprint had declined to 47 percent (see Figure 5.1).[155]

In Japan, the combination of urbanized and agricultural land fell slightly from 1965 to 2000. This is despite the fact that the nation was undergoing unprecedented urban growth, virtually all of which was in the suburbs.[156]

Similarly, in Canada and Australia the human footprint has also decreased, as the amount of land consumed by urban development has been miniscule compared to the land made unnecessary for agriculture by improved productivity.

There is no shortage of agricultural land, open space, or green space. In the high-income world, the human footprint is smaller today than it was 50 years ago. Moreover, it seems unlikely that the human footprint will expand, because population growth has slowed substantially, and projections call for even slower growth and, in some nations, a decline in population.

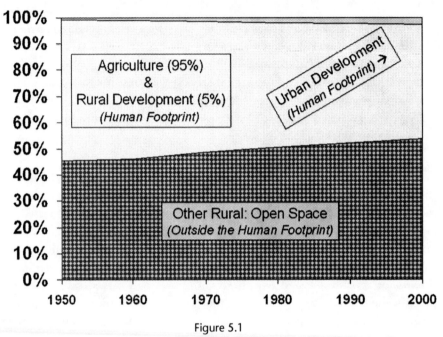

Figure 5.1

Urban Open Space

Further, modern suburbanized urban areas contain a great deal of open or green space. For example, the Chicago urban area includes more than 160,000 acres of forest preserve, equal to the land area of St. Petersburg, Russia, or Santiago, Chile. This represents more than 10 percent of the land in the area. If these areas had been developed, the Chicago urban area would be more compact (sprawl less). Similarly, counties throughout the Denver metropolitan area have undertaken aggressive programs to preserve open space. Large urban parks provide accessible space to residents of urban areas, such as the Bois de Vincennes in Paris, Griffith Park in Los Angeles, the Kings Domain in Sydney, Parc Mont-Royal in Montreal, and Ueno Park in Tokyo. Even road beltways in urban areas such as Atlanta or Brussels contain so much greenery that during most of the year, that little urbanization is evident.

Suburbanization has expanded private open space substantially. In many suburban areas of the United States, Canada, Western Europe, and Australia, owners of private houses maintain comparatively large yards. Atlanta's large lot development pattern provides residents with more than three times the private green space as in more dense Portland.[157]

Open space preservation, however, can induce greater suburbanization. In fact, where more land adjacent to an urban area is preserved, urban development becomes even more dispersed, as the exploding exurbanization of London (outside the greenbelt) and the San Francisco Bay area demonstrate (see Chapter 8).

"Leapfrog" Development

Leapfrog development is a term that sends shudders down the spines of anti-suburbanites. According to Burchell et al, leapfrog development is the very essence of urban sprawl.

> Sprawl refers to a particular type of suburban peripheral growth. It refers to development that expands in an *unlimited and noncontiguous (leapfrog) way outward* from the solidly built-up core of a metropolitan area.[158]

Leapfrog development occurs when new houses or commercial buildings are built outside the existing developed area. Usually this occurs fairly close to the present urbanization, but may be separated by a few hundred yards or even miles. This discontinuous development is criticized because it may not have urban services, such as water and sewer. Obviously, this problem is solved by providing the services, the cost of which should be borne by those in the leapfrog development. Moreover, virtually all of the on-site costs of roads, sewers, and water systems are paid by homebuyers, in their house prices.

Discontinuous development offends current urban planning tastes. An urban area with discontinuous development will not look as "tidy," for example, to many urban planners, to whom the appearance of the urban form is paramount.

However, leapfrog development plays an important role in moderating land prices on the fringe of urban areas, which makes it possible for land prices to be low enough to permit broad home ownership. If new development must be adjacent to older development, the few owners whose property is eligible for development are able to command a higher price, which is a principal reason for the escalating land costs that have occurred in urban areas implementing land rationing policies (see Chapter 8). The democratization of home ownership could not have occurred without leapfrog development.

Of course, there will be discontinuous development on and beyond the fringe of the urban area if people are allowed to live and work where they like. This is not a new phenomenon. Rather than being an ill, leapfrog development is a useful characteristic of the market. Discontinuous development lowers overall costs because it provides developers with a larger pool of sellers and makes it possible to obtain land for residential and commercial development less expensively. The alternative, fully embraced by the anti-suburban movement, is to require land to be developed serially—new land for development must be adjacent to already developed land. As will be shown in Chapter 8, this leads to higher land prices, higher housing prices, and lower rates of home ownership.

Leapfrog development is a transitional phenomenon. As the urban area grows, undeveloped areas are filled in by new urban development, resulting in the continuous form of urbanization that will be found generally in the United States, Japan, Canada, Australia, and New Zealand and in Western European nations such as France, Spain, Belgium, and Sweden.

Thus, besides being transitional, leapfrog development is not extensive. In the United States, more than 92 percent of residents in metropolitan areas of more than 1,000,000 residents lived within contiguous urban (urbanized) areas in 2000. The very nature of these urban areas is that they are contiguous—virtually devoid of leapfrog development. Outside the urban portion of these metropolitan areas, population densities are very low, and include preexisting rural, often agricultural population. This non-urban metropolitan density, at 51 persons per square mile, would include any leapfrog development, and is similar to the *rural* densities of Midwestern states such as Ohio, Indiana, and Michigan.

Similarly, there is little leapfrog development in Canada. Nearly 94 percent of residents in metropolitan areas of more than 100,000 residents lived within contiguous urban areas in 2000. Outside the urban areas, the population density was 43 per square mile, a density below that of many U.S. and Canadian rural areas.

Finally, the urban planning community seems to have little concern about leapfrog development when it is the result of their own planning. For example, much of the development that has occurred in the London exurbs over more than a half-century of stringent planning regulations is leapfrog development, spread as it is over thousands of square miles of land in southeast England. Urban planning regulations in Germany have forced major portions of urban growth to leapfrog outside contiguous urban areas.

In fact, cities are continually growing and changing. They are always a work in progress. If people are allowed to freely buy and sell, the fringe will always look somewhat untidy. The better quality of life that results for more people is well worth it.

Household Densities

In fact, urban land appears to have expanded little more than would be expected based upon the change in the number of households. The best available U.S. estimates indicate that total urban land area tripled from 1950 to 2000 in the United States. The number of households increased by nearly as much, leading to a net reduction in household density of less than five percent (see Table 5.1). Falling household sizes have been a principal driver of suburban development in other high-income nations.

Table 5.1: Change in U.S. Urban Population, Land Area, and Density: 1950–2000

Item	1950	2000	Change
Urban Land Area (square miles)	30,048	92,505	207.9%
Urban Population (millions)	96.5	222.4	130.5%
Population Density (per square mile)	3,210	2,404	-25.1%
Urban Households (millions)	28.5	83.5	192.9%
Household Density (per square mile)	949	903	-4.8%
Source: Calculated from U.S. Census data. 1950 urban land area estimated from U.S. Department of Agriculture Economic Research Service data.			

Smaller Urban Areas Sprawl the Most

The anti-suburbanites have directed most of their attention to the largest urban areas. In fact, however, the lowest densities are to be found in smaller urban areas.

In the United States, the top population quintile (one-fifth) of urban areas takes up only 10 percent of the urban land. The bottom population quintile occupies 30 percent of the nation's urban land; three times the area of the largest quintile. If all urban areas had as many people per square mile as those with more than 1,000,000 population, nearly one-third less land would be urbanized.

As in the United States, the larger urban areas of Canada cover proportionally less land than smaller urban areas. Toronto, which represents approximately 20 percent of the nation's urban population, accounts for only six percent of urban land. The urban areas with more than 1,000,000 population represent 40 percent of the population and only 19 percent of the urban land area. The smallest population quintile (20 percent) of Canadian urban areas covers 48 percent of the urban land.[159] If all urban areas in Canada were as dense as those with more than 1,000,000 population, urbanization would consume one-half less land.

The greatest suburbanization is not to be found in Los Angeles, Toronto, Atlanta, or Edmonton. It is rather in less familiar places such as Eugene, Prince Albert, Meridian, Waterloo, Harrisonburg, and Kelowna.

The Appropriate Urban Density?

Without a threat to open space or agriculture, it cannot be plausibly argued that land is being wasted in urbanization. Urban settlements have had a wide range of densities.

Neighborhood densities of up to 5,000,000 per square mile are reported to have existed in Hong Kong's Kowloon Walled City before it was demolished in the early 1990s.[160] At this density, the entire population of the world could be housed within the Paris or Houston urban area. Even after dismantling the Kowloon Walled City, neighborhood densities of 1,000,000 per square mile exist in Hong Kong, density that would allow all humanity to be housed in an area approximately the size of the Tokyo and New York urban areas together.

However, densities could be far higher than the Kowloon Walled City, which had building heights of up to 14 floors. Building heights can be more than 100 floors, which would indicate that urban densities, with today's technologies, could be perhaps 10 times as great, which would allow all of the world's population to be accommodated in a seven mile radius.

At the other end of the scale are the very low urban densities of Avignon, France (1,300), Sudbury, Ontario (1,000), and Barnstable, Massachusetts (850).

Thus, it is theoretically possible for the footprint of urban development to be shrunk to well beyond the point suggested by the Sierra Club in its withdrawn Sprawl Calculator, or perhaps even to the extent that James Howard Kunstler or Dolores Hayden might require. However, there is a more important question: is it necessary?

The answer is a resounding no. There is no threat to agriculture. There is more open space than before, and it is more accessible to more people. The human footprint—the amount of land used for urbanization and agriculture—is getting smaller. The anti-suburbanites have identified no imperative that justifies interfering with the right of people to live and work where and how they like by forcing them into higher density environments.

6

Missing the Transportation Connections

At least as much attention is directed to urban transportation in the anti-suburbanization debate as to land use.

Suburbanization and Traffic Congestion

One of the most frequently recurring themes of the critics is that automobile-oriented suburbanization increases traffic congestion. Like so many of the anti-suburban claims, the claim that sprawl makes traffic congestion worse could not be more wrong.

In fact, automobile-oriented suburbanization is associated with *less* intense traffic congestion. This can be illustrated by examining the international evidence. There are still a few large international urban areas with densities approximating the pre-automobile era (the mass transit era).[161] In these urban areas, daily vehicle hours (total hours that cars and trucks are in operation) per urban square mile was more than three times as high as in the urban areas with automobile-era densities.

However, this is just the beginning. Among the urban areas with automobile-era population densities, traffic congestion was greater where population densities were higher. Urban areas with more than 10,000 hours driven per square mile densities had more than four times as many vehicle miles per square mile than urban areas with less than 3,000 per square mile densities (see Figure 6.1).[162] The reason is simply that higher population densities produce more intense traffic congestion.

The fact that higher density results in greater traffic can also be illustrated by comparing driving in the high-income world's most dense urban area, Hong Kong, to levels in other areas. Hong Kong hours driven per square mile is more than three times the rate of Los Angeles, which has the worst traffic congestion in the United States. Hong Kong hours driven per square mile is 10 times that of low-density Brisbane.[163]

As would be expected, work trips show the same relationship—higher densities mean longer travel times. In the more dense urban areas of Western Europe
and Asia, with their higher quality mass-transit systems, work trip travel times are
considerably longer than in the United States. On average, Western Europeans
spend one third more time commuting to work in urban areas with more than
5,000,000 residents, and commuters in large Japanese urban areas spend 50 percent more time.[164] Work trip travel times are longer in Western Europe and
Japan because traffic congestion is worse and a larger share of workers use transit,
which is generally slower than cars. With the world's highest densities, Hong
Kong's work trip travel time is nearly double that of the United States, despite its
high level of mass-transit service. In 1990, the average Hong Kong one-way work
trip was 44 minutes, which compares to 26 minutes in Houston, one of the high-
income world's most sprawling urban areas. As a result, Houston commuters
spend three hours less per week traveling to work than do Hong Kong commuters. This is despite the fact that the average work trip is at least 2.5 times as long
in Houston.[165]

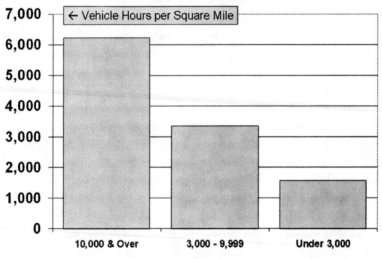

Figure 6.1

The same relationship is indicated throughout the United States. An analysis
prepared for the United States Department of Transportation indicated that traf-

fic volumes in small sectors (census tracts) rise with population density (see Figure 6.2).[166]

There is further evidence that U.S. traffic congestion is worse where densities are higher, as indicated by Federal Highway Administration and Texas Transportation Institute data (see Table 6.1). In 2002 :

- Traffic intensity (vehicle miles per urban square mile) was the greatest in the most dense urban areas at more than double the intensity of the least dense areas. Urban areas with densities above 4,000 per square mile averaged 96,500 vehicle miles per square mile, while urban areas with less than 2,000 per square mile averaged 46,700 vehicle miles per square mile.

- Because congestion slows down traffic, the difference in vehicle hours is even greater. Vehicle hours per square mile in the above 4,000 density category were 2.6 times the rate in the below 2,000 density category.[167]

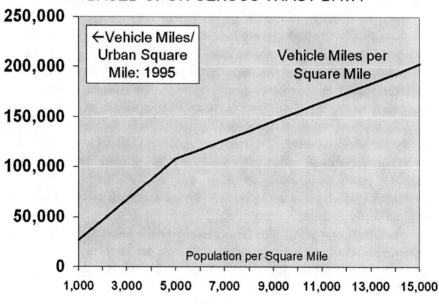

Figure 6.2

Table 6.1: Traffic in Large U.S. Urban Areas: 2002

Urban Area Population Density	Vehicle Miles (per square mile)	Vehicle Hours per (square mile)
4,000 & Over	96,545	1,675
3,000–3,999	72,103	1,237
2,000–2,999	54,524	911
Under 2,000	46,724	609

Vehicle hours are for freeways and principal arterials only. Source: Calculated from Federal Highway Administration and Texas Transportation Institute data.

Portland versus Kansas City. A comparison of more dense Portland with less dense Kansas City illustrates how a less dense urban area tends to have less traffic congestion. According to Texas Transportation Institute 2002 data Kansas City had approximately one-third more total vehicle miles than Portland, which has a similar population. Yet, because of Kansas City's lower density (larger land area), traffic congestion was considerably less. In Kansas City, peak-hour travel averaged 10 percent longer than travel in non-congested conditions.[168] In Portland, peak-hour trips averaged 38 percent more than during non-congested periods, nearly four times the figure in Kansas City. This illustrates an important distinction that is often missed—that a higher volume of traffic does not translate into more traffic congestion if there is sufficient roadway capacity. More dense urban areas generally do not provide sufficient roadway capacity and, as a result, traffic congestion tends to be worse. The average Kansas City driver spends less time in traffic congestion than the average Portland driver, despite the fact that the overall traffic volumes are higher in the urban area. At the same time, despite the lower overall level of traffic in the Portland area, the average driver spends more time in traffic congestion.

It is true that lower population densities are generally associated with less driving per capita. However, the reduction in driving per capita is not enough to negate the overall increase in driving that occurs because there are more people and cars in the area. This should not be surprising. Where there is less of a concentration of anything, things are less crowded. Where population densities are lower, people will generally be able to make their trips more quickly, and less travel will be in stressful conditions of intense traffic congestion. Peter Gordon and Harry Richardson of the University of Southern California have noted, "sub-urbanization has turned out to be the traffic safety valve."[169]

Freeways and Suburbanization

Anti-suburbanites often claim that suburbanization would not have occurred without freeways. However, as noted above, automobile-oriented suburbanization has been the dominant form of urban development for decades.

Automobile-oriented suburbanization has occurred regardless of the intensity of freeway networks. For example, Sydney has the least comprehensive freeway system of any major high-income world urban area. Yet, even before most of its freeway network was built, Sydney had managed to sprawl at automobile-oriented densities. Even today, there are virtually no genuine freeways in Adelaide,[170] yet the urban area is dominated by low-density automobile development, like areas with dense freeway networks. Surprisingly, Hong Kong, the high-income world's most dense urban area, has the highest concentration of freeways in the high-income world.[171]

Atlanta is also a surprising example. To the casual observer, Atlanta appears to be well served by freeways. Interstate 75, in suburban Cobb County, may have been the widest freeway in the world in the late 1990s, with 17 lanes. However, what traveling on Atlanta's mega-freeways does not reveal is the vast expanse of low-density suburbs that have little freeway access. Atlanta has the greatest extent of suburbanization in the world that is not served by "cross-town" (non-radial) freeways. This lack of freeway coverage has proven no barrier to suburbanization in its most advanced form. The combination of a weak freeway system and a poor, arterial-grid street system have made Atlanta one of the few very-low-density urban areas with substantial traffic congestion.

Anti-suburbanites also claim that belt routes or ring roads are major drivers of suburbanization. However, David Hartgen and Daniel Curley, at the University of North Carolina, found that beltways make little difference in the extent of suburbanization.[172] This is illustrated by development in urban areas like Dallas-Fort Worth, Atlanta, and San Antonio, where urban development spills many miles beyond northern beltways and is comparatively sparse along the southern alignments of the same roadways.

The Purported Superiority of Mass Transit

Anti-suburbanites claim that mass transit is superior to the automobile in a number of ways. There are dimensions in which mass transit is superior to the automobile, but an examination of the claims shows that these are very limited.

Energy

A principal claim is that mass transit is more fuel-efficient than the automobile. In fact, at least in the United States, there is little difference between mass transit and cars in relative energy consumption. In 2002, cars were slightly less fuel-efficient than all mass-transit services and more fuel-efficient than buses. Small trucks (including sport utility vehicles) were less fuel efficient than mass transit, but slightly more fuel-efficient than buses (see Table 6.2).[173] Thus, the wholesale substitution of mass-transit use for automobile use, even if possible, would make little difference at all in energy consumption. In fact, however, material substitution of mass transit for automobile and personal truck use is impossible, because the overwhelming majority of urban trips cannot be made in a competitive time by mass transit, whether in the United States or Western Europe (see Chapter 9).

Table 6.2: Energy Consumption by Passenger Transport Mode: 2002

	Passenger Miles	BTUs	BTU/Passenger Mile
Personal Vehicle			
Automobile	2.604	9,326	3,581
Personal Truck	1.201	4,873	4,057
Total	3.805	14,199	3,731
Mass Transit			
Bus	0.022	90.9	4,126
Urban Rail	0.015	49.3	3,266
Commuter Rail	0.010	25.8	2,715
Total	0.047	166.0	3,560
Mass Transit Relative to Automobiles			99.4%

In Trillions of Passenger Miles and British Thermal Units
Calculated from Table 2.13 USDOE Transportation Energy Book #24

Air Pollution

The automobile is often characterized as a horrendous environmental polluter. Indeed, the automobile has been the source of much air pollution in its time. However, air pollution preceded the automobile by centuries, as a seemingly inevitable consequence of economic progress. In his book *The Skeptical Environmentalist,* Bjorn Lormborg shows that air pollution in London in 1600 was more intense than today,[174] despite the fact that London today has 40 times as many people and millions of automobiles.

There is sometimes a tendency to forget that urban areas of 100 years ago were much less healthy than today. For example, the use of coal for heating tended to make air pollution intense. Coal is no longer used in large quantities, but the legacy survives. Old buildings can still be seen in some core areas that have been blackened by coal. The wide use of horse-based transport produced its own pollution.

However, automobile air pollution has been reduced substantially over the past three decades. The Environmental Protection Agency reports that highway volumes increased 155 percent from 1970 to 2002. Yet, aggregate[175] air pollution *declined* 48 percent (see Figure 6.3).[176] Similar improvements have been made in Europe. It is probably not an overstatement to suggest that large urban areas have better air quality today than at any time in their histories.

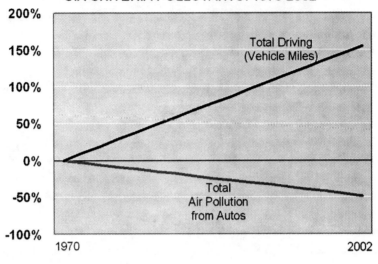

Figure 6.3

Anti-suburbanites claim that higher-density urban areas have lower *overall* levels of motor-vehicle-produced air pollution. This depends on a number of factors, such as the average speed of traffic and the extent to which "stop and start" conditions prevail. Air pollution emissions are generally more intense in slower urban traffic. They are the most intense in "stop and go" traffic. For example, according to the U.S. Environmental Protection Agency,[177] cars tend to produce more than 2.5 times the carbon monoxide and volatile organic compounds at 15 miles per hour as at 55 miles per hour. Thus, a principal strategy in the control of air pollution should be to improve the flow of traffic.

Of course, the densification strategies of the anti-suburbanites would do just the opposite. Higher densities are associated with higher local travel volumes, slower speeds, and less consistent traffic flows. This means greater air pollution emissions.

Randall O'Toole has shown that more severe air pollution classifications are associated with higher densities.[178] This mirrors the international evidence, with air pollution production per square mile lower where population densities are lower.[179] Thus, air pollution emissions are lower in the lower-density urbanization of the United States and Australia than in higher-density Western Europe or

Asia.[180] The impact of higher traffic densities on air pollution is readily apparent to any walking in the dense cores of urban areas such as London, Paris, or Tokyo.

Moreover, air pollution conditions will continue to improve. According to Joel Schwartz, air pollution from motor vehicles will fall even further, with a decline of 80 percent over the next 20 years, *after* taking into account the projected additional driving.[181] Given that air pollution is closely related to energy consumption, little would be gained by transferring demand from cars to mass transit, even if it were possible.

Finally, it is misleading to cite air pollution statistics for entire urban areas as justification for densification. The negative health effects of air pollution do not occur at the urban area level, they occur in the neighborhood and they are related to the intensity of the breathed pollution. People breathe the air pollution where they live, not all of the air pollution produced over hundreds or thousands of square miles. Thus, the higher neighborhood air pollution levels associated with densification can be expected to impair health much more than the lower emission levels that would occur in less dense conditions. More intense air pollution in a local area is a more significant health risk than the gross amount of pollution in an entire urban area.

Greenhouse Gas Emissions

A more recent argument against suburbanization is the role of land-use planning in greenhouse gas reductions. The assumption is that if suburban development is limited, people will use mass transit more and their cars less, resulting in lower greenhouse emissions.

For example, in some nations, such as Canada, the mere mention of greenhouse gas emissions can often trump arguments. Rarely is any further analysis provided. Newspaper columnists routinely condemn any highway improvement because of an assumption that the result will mean greater greenhouse gas emissions. In fact, however, cars play a comparatively small role in greenhouse gas emissions and local transportation and land-use policies can have, at best, miniscule impacts.

In 2003, cars and light trucks emitted only 12 percent of Canada's greenhouse gases.[182] If Canada were to stop using cars and light trucks, the savings in greenhouse gas emissions would be barely enough to cover *one-half* of the nation's committed reduction under the Kyoto Accords.[183]

Short of imposing taxes and restrictions that induce severe economic losses (something no nation seems inclined to do), there is little potential of materially reducing greenhouse gas emissions through land-use or transport policies. A report by researchers at the U.S. Oakridge National Laboratory estimates that doubling urban population densities would reduce greenhouse gas emissions from personal vehicles by approximately five percent.[184] It is inconceivable for an urban area to double its density because that would mean the abandonment of up to one-half of the urban form, with the suburban evacuees forced into an already crowded urban core. On the other hand, the Oakridge report concluded that fuel economy measures was an effective strategy for reducing automobile and light truck greenhouse gas emissions.

Mass Transit's Unparalleled Cost Effectiveness Decline

Anti-suburbanites also claim that automobiles and highways are more expensive than mass transit. They cite the labor efficiency of trains, which can carry hundreds of people with just a few staff on board, as opposed to cars, which often carry only the driver. They cite the long lives of rail cars, which can sometimes exceed 30 years, compared to the comparatively short life spans of cars. However, costs are evaluated based upon monetary expenditures, not the number of employees or how long a rail car lasts. Moreover, by monetary measures, mass transit is far more expensive than the highway system.

In 2004, all of the costs of the automobile-based system were approximately $0.22 per person mile.[185] This includes all of the private costs to purchase, maintain, and operate cars and the government costs of roadway construction, maintenance, patrol, and research (including the tax subsidies to local roads, which is less than $0.01 per person mile).[186] By contrast, mass-transit expenditures were $0.95 per person mile, 4.5 times the full cost of the auto and highway system. Moreover, mass transit carries little, if any, freight. As recently as 1960, mass-transit expenditures per person mile were nearly the same as automobile expenditures.[187]

In fact, mass transit expenditures in the United States have virtually exploded. From 1970 to 2004, mass transit spending increased 275 percent, after adjustment for inflation.[188] At the same time, mass-transit passenger usage has increased only 14 percent. The gross expenditures in excess of inflation (real expenditure increase) are more than $475 billion, more than the approximately $425 billion required to build the US interstate highway system. Since 1970, mass transit's increase per passenger mile has exceeded even increase in health care costs as measured by the Consumer Price Index.[189]

This means that mass transit has produced a return of $0.05 for each new dollar of expenditure.[190] At the same time, automobile expenditures per person mile have stayed virtually the same (inflation adjusted), meaning that approximately $1.00 in value has been obtained for each additional $1.00 in expenditure.

Gaining new mass transit ridership is difficult and expensive. From 1970 to 2004, the cost per new mass-transit passenger mile in the United States was nearly $6.00—more than 30 times both the total rate for automobiles and sport utility vehicles (approximately $0.22). If as much had been spent on all automobile and sport utility travel in the U.S. over the same period, $23 trillion would have been required, approximately double the national income.

Moreover, U.S. mass-transit authorities have shown strong resistance to cost-effective reforms. Urban areas in Europe and Australia have implemented competitive contracting (competitive tendering) programs that use private operators and subject public authorities to competition, resulting in lower unit costs and more service. U.S. mass-transit agencies still rely principally on costly government monopolies. In the few urban areas where significant programs have been implemented, such as in Denver[191] and San Diego, there have been substantial cost savings and services have been expanded (as has also occurred in places like London, Stockholm, and Perth).[192]

Another contributing factor is that urban-rail systems have been so expensive that each new daily rider could be given a new car, in perpetuity, for less.[193] Urban-rail projects have been subject to gross cost escalation, especially between the time they are adopted by governments and completed. Bent Flyvbjerg, of the University of Aarlburg (Denmark), who studied an 80-year span of infrastructure projects in North America and Western Europe, attributes the underestimated costs to "strategic misrepresentation, namely lying, with a view to getting projects started."[194]

He also singles out urban-rail projects for particular criticism.[195] Indeed, future historians could well surmise that mass transit in the U.S. had been controlled in the last third of the 20th century by those seeking its demise.

Car and Highway Subsidies

However, the anti-suburbanite view of highways and mass transit becomes even more distorted when subsidies are considered. They characterize the highway system as highly subsidized and claim that mass-transit subsidies are much less than subsidies to highways and local streets. This view can be described as Orwellian, in the sense that the language conveys the virtual opposite of reality.

The problem begins with confusing user fees and subsidies. Subsidy occurs when taxpayers pay for a good or service without regard to their individual use. Subsidies dominate mass transit. Three-quarters of mass-transit revenues are from subsidies—paid by people through general taxes or user fees paid by drivers. Users or commercial sources pay only one-quarter.

By contrast, in 2003, highway users paid amounts equal to more than 70 percent of the gross expenditures on highways and local streets through highway user fees. These user fees usually take the form of special taxes on highway fuels. These are taxes that are not charged on other commodities or services. Only those who drive pay highway user fees. Those who do not drive do not pay.

Highway user fees are similar to the bills paid to municipally owned electric utilities. No one would classify a payment made for electric service as a subsidy, whether a private or government utility supplies the electricity. Similarly, payment of a user fee that builds highways is not a subsidy. In fact, rate per gallon levy is comparatively efficient. It tends to raise the cost of driving for less fuel-efficient vehicles and makes it less costly for more fuel-efficient vehicles. Highway user fees are prices, not subsidies. Characterization of user fees as subsidies demonstrates profound misunderstanding, or worse, intellectual dishonesty.

However, the special levies on highway users pay for other things as well. Since 1982, billions of dollars have been made available for mass transit from highway user fees. The philosophical justification for this is a presumption that mass transit reduces highway demand. Yet, since the diversion of highway user fees to mass transit began, urban roadway volumes have increased more than 100 times that of transit volumes. Mass transit's urban market share has dropped more than one-third. There are also substantial diversions at the state level. For example, one quarter of the Texas gasoline tax is used for education.

In fact, nonuser subsidies to mass transit are nearly 80 times those paid to support local streets, highways, and automobiles on a person mile basis.[196]

Externalities or Social Costs

It is often suggested that the highway-based transportation system carries with it substantial social costs that are not reflected in the actual economics. This would include such factors as the health impacts of air pollution and travel delays. In fact, the entire subject of social costs, or externalities, is contentious, and there are no broadly accepted standards for measuring such costs. Indeed, the Nobel Laureate Frederik Hayek noted that costs could not be known outside the market—that is, genuine market costs cannot be reliably established through administrative or political processes.[197]

Nonetheless, even an avid advocate of social costing found that the automobile was comparatively efficient. Mark DeLucci, of the University of California, is an author of seminal work on the social costs of the automobile. His research indicates that, on average, subsidies to mass transit in the United States are between 3.4 and more than 10 times the total external costs of the automobile.[198]

Believing in Yesterday

There is an abiding belief that the urban areas of Western Europe depend principally on mass transit, to the contrary of urban areas in the United States. This is illustrated by an experience I had when addressing a conference at the James E. Clyburn University Transportation Center at South Carolina State University in Orangeburg. The conference theme was mass transit, and, as a result, it was not surprising that my comments would be particularly provocative to some in the audience. One questioner seemed taken aback by my assertion that, consistent with virtually all urban planning forecasts in the high-income world, the automobile would continue to be dominant and that failure to supply sufficient new road capacity would result in substantial increases in traffic congestion. His said that, when he visits Europe and Japan, with their trains and superior mass-transit systems, he feels like he is seeing the future. My answer was that, to the contrary, what he had seen is the past.

Of course, cars are used more in the United States than in Western Europe, but it is simply a matter of degree. The overwhelming share of urban travel is by car in both Western Europe and the United States. In U.S. urban areas, more than 97 percent percent of motorized travel is by cars and SUVs. In Western Europe, the urban automobile market share is 80 percent in the larger urban areas and is estimated at approximately 90 percent for all urban areas.[199] The automobile market share in Japan is lower, with huge mass-transit shares still evident in Tokyo-Yokohama and Osaka-Kobe-Kyoto. However, outside these two areas, the automobile market share appears to be 80 percent.[200] U.S. automobile market shares were at Western European levels as late as 1955.

Mass transit's U.S. market share has steadily fallen since that time, to little more than 1.5 percent (see Figure 6.4).[201] Moreover, substantial losses have occurred in the market in which mass transit has the greatest potential to reduce traffic congestion—work travel during peak periods. There has been a steady erosion of mass-transit's commuter market. In 1960, 12 percent of commute trips were by mass transit. Today, the number is below five percent. From 1960 to 2000, the nation added nearly 64 million jobs, and 1.7 million fewer people use mass transit to get to work.[202] A principal contributing factor to this loss has been the market share loss of downtown areas, as employment has spread throughout other parts of urban areas.

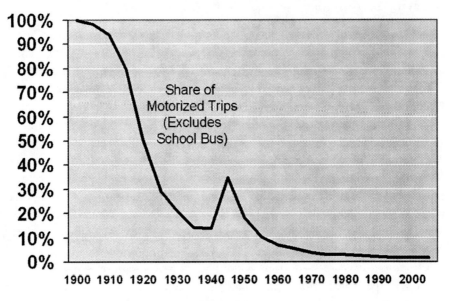

US Mass Transit Market Share History
ESTIMATED: 1900-2005

Share of
Motorized Trips
(Excludes
School Bus)

Figure 6.4

However, the impressions of travelers can be much different. Urban and transportation planners, like tourists, travel to Western Europe and see the historical cores. This is where mass transit is the strongest—in the large core sections of cities that were developed before the automobile. Mass transit provides effective mobility within and to these small cores, just as it does in the old, pre-automobile cores of New York, Boston, Toronto, or Montreal. However, like these North American urban areas, most jobs and residents in Western Europe are outside the cores, in the expansive suburbs and exurbs that have developed since World War II. In these areas, the great majority of travel is by car.

Moreover, it is not unusual for anti-suburbanites to misread travel trends in the urban areas of Western Europe or Japan. It is often implied that urban areas in the United States should aspire to Western European or Japanese mass-transit usage levels. However, neither Europe nor Japan has *aspired* to its present mass-transit usage rate; both are experiencing mass-transit losses as automobile use increases. This is an inevitable process as the dispersion of urban areas continues, as described in Chapter 3. As households gain more discretionary income, they choose to live in larger dwellings in the suburbs and seek to take advantage of the automobile to access locations throughout the urban area with a convenience and comprehensiveness that is simply not possible with mass transit.

Mass-transit market share has generally declined in Western European urban areas since 1980. Overall, the annual compounded loss rate has been 1.6 percent annually. Declines have occurred in nine of 11 urban areas for which data are available, with only two urban areas (Brussels and Zurich) experiencing small increases.[203] Mass-transit market share dropped 17 percent from 1980 to 1995 in both Munich and Amsterdam. In Hamburg, mass transit's share dropped 35 percent. Paris, with perhaps the most comprehensive system in the western world, world, has seen its mass-transit market share drop from over one-third since 1960.[204]

Western Europe's Love Affair with the Automobile. An often-repeated mantra is that "Americans have a love affair with the automobile." But, a more compelling case could be made for a Western European "love affair." Western Europeans use automobiles for nearly as much of their travel as Americans.

Western Europeans drive despite serious disincentives. Fuel has been up to five times as expensive in Western Europe as in the United States because of exorbitant tax rates. Highway tolls are also greater, on average. Urban traffic is much more intense. Parking is far more scarce, and more expensive. Finally, with better mass-transit systems, somewhat more trips can be made on automobile-competitive services.

However, of course, Western Europeans do not drive their cars out of affection, any more than do Americans. It could be as plausibly argued that Americans and Western Europeans have a "love affair" with refrigerators or flush toilets. In fact, people, be they Americans or Europeans, tend to use technologies that enrich their quality of life. The car enriches people's opportunities and their lives, like a host of other modern conveniences.

The continuing market share losses and rising costs led Remy Prud'homme, of the University of Paris, and a team of researchers to question whether mass transit is sustainable in Western Europe.[205]

Asia. While the later affluence and automobile availability kept mass-transit market shares higher in Asia, the same downward trends are evident. Since 1990, *all* new travel demand in Tokyo-Yokohama, Osaka-Kobe-Kyoto, and Nagoya has been by automobile, as mass transit's share has continued to fall.[206] Even Hong Kong, with the high-income world's largest mass-transit market share, experienced an approximately 10 percent loss from 1980 to 1995. Singapore, where a renowned road pricing system has been in operation, experienced a loss of 23 percent over the same period.[207] However, there is an important difference about mass transit in affluent Asia. In the larger urban areas it is largely supported by commercial revenues, principally fares. Even the subways of Tokyo receive comparatively little in subsidies. This means that, unlike their counterparts elsewhere in the high-income world, mass transit is financially sustainable in affluent Asia.

Canada. It is an easy and often-taken trek for mass-transit managers and board members to go north to see what may be the best mass-transit systems in North America. In the Toronto and Montreal urban areas, mass transit has a higher market share than in any U.S. urban area, at between 10 percent and 15 percent. Like Western Europe and Asia, mass-transit shares are dropping in Canada. From 1980 to 1995, Toronto's mass-transit market share was down 41 percent, while Montreal's was down 24 percent. The story is the same in Australia and New Zealand, where mass-transit market shares have declined in most large urban areas.

Moreover, the declining mass-transit market shares around the world have occurred during a period of unprecedented urban-rail construction, which promoters typically claim will reduce traffic congestion. Urban areas, especially in Western Europe and Canada, have built and expanded metro, light-rail, and commuter-rail systems, while their share of travel generally declines or is at best stagnant. Moreover, because mass-transit systems principally feed the core commercial districts (downtowns or central business districts), these systems are routinely built to areas of generally declining actual population and declining employment market shares (see above).

The Automobile: Expanding Mobility

Finally, it is often suggested that the automobile has taken travel away from mass transit. This is true only to a limited degree. As late as 1950, when automobiles were broadly available in the United States, annual travel per person by mass transit was equal to that of pre-automobile 1900. In fact, the automobile expanded travel opportunities. Today, urban travel per capita is nearly 20 times that of 1900. Thus, the principal role of the automobile has been to expand mobility, well beyond levels that were possible with mass transit (see Figure 16).[208]

This is why, as soon as people can afford them, cars have emerged as the dominant form of urban transportation from Phoenix to Portland, Paris, and Nagoya.

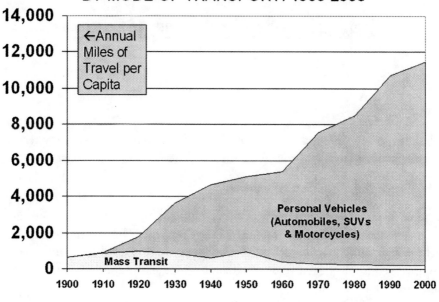

Figure 6.5

7

Costs, Community, Obesity, Fear, Ad Nauseam

There are other, unfounded indictments of suburbanization, principally relating to costs and community. From there, they degenerate toward silliness.

The Trumped Up Costs of Sprawl

One of the most enduring myths about suburbanization is that it is more costly to government budgets than more dense development. This claim is particularly believable because, on the surface, the broader spaces required by suburbs would appear to consume greater resources than development in the core city. The data show the opposite.

The logic then proceeds to an assumption that more densely developed areas subsidize less dense suburban areas. As noted above, Peter Blake wrote of "bankrupting most suburbs"[209] forty years ago. A late 1990s study financed by the U.S. federal government, *The Costs of Sprawl Revisited*, concluded that the future costs of suburbanization are "unaffordable."[210]

In Australia, these "costs" of suburbanization are being used as a principal justification for some of the world's most radical land rationing policies. Urban planner and former Australian National University professor Patrick Troy reviewed the "suburbs versus core" literature on which much of Australian densification policy is based and found it to be wanting. He notes that the studies included private costs, such as the user charges residents pay for water and sewer service, which are not costs of government at all. Troy also notes that some studies included the theoretical costs of additional travel time, which even if accurate, cannot be considered a government cost by any stretch of the imagination. Not surprisingly, Troy found the studies highly sensitive to cost and planning assumptions, which he found to be often questionable.[211]

Considerable research has been conducted on sprawl and municipal costs in the United States. The U.S. government financed what was perhaps the most influential study. *The Costs of Sprawl—2000*, concluded that costs in the United

States would be more than $227 billion higher over the next 25 years. This was a follow-up to the previous *Costs of Sprawl-Revisited* report that had characterized future suburbanization as "unaffordable." The researchers attempted to estimate the costs of greater suburbanization down to the regional level.[212]

It is useful to consider their "impressive" number in context. The $227 billion projection from *Costs of Sprawl—2000* may appear to be large on the surface. However, big or small numbers are not, in and of themselves, significant. For example, it might have taken you 5,000,000,000 nanoseconds to read this sentence. This is an impressive number, which expresses an insignificant amount of time—five seconds. To understand numbers, it is necessary to consider them in context, something that *The Costs of Sprawl—2000* does not do.

In fact, $227 billion, in context, is not such a large number. The context is that $227 billion amounts to an average increase of $30 per capita each year. This amount pales by comparison to the approximately $40,000 per capita income in the United States. This is less than the cost of a dinner for two at an inexpensive restaurant. It is an exaggeration of gargantuan proportions to suggest that $30 per capita annually is "unaffordable."

Less comprehensive studies have come to similar conclusions in New Jersey, South Carolina, Oregon, Colorado, and other areas. However, each of these reports suffered from a fatal flaw. The reports simply added up theoretical comparative costs, without checking the results against the actual experience. Of course, projecting future costs is difficult. However, believable projections can only be developed if the results based upon "ivory tower" theoretical assumptions are reconciled with the actual experience.

Public and Private Costs. However, even the small amount of $30 per capita per year does not represent costs to the public. Much of the $30 is made up of private costs—the costs of residential street, sewer, and water construction, which are routinely paid by developers and then passed on to homebuyers in house prices.

No one forces a household to buy a new house in the suburbs. The costs of a new house, including the included infrastructure costs, are a matter of private choice. Generally, private financial choices are not a legitimate concern of government.

There are system utility costs that are not paid in house prices, such as sewer and water trunk lines to the new development and additional roadway capacity for the additional traffic. These costs have been historically funded by community wide user fees and taxes in the United States and some other nations. The same is true of services provided by the private sector, such as telephone lines.

The cost of the system improvements is borne by the entire rate base. Because telephones are a private sector enterprise, governments have not been required to concern themselves about system infrastructure costs. The same potential is available for sewer and water services, which in many locations are also provided by the private sector. Much of the French water and sewer system is private. System expansion is not viewed as a threat by the private sector, but rather an opportunity.

When Do the Bankruptcies Start? If, truly, the costs of sprawl were unaffordable, it would be readily apparent by now. Central cities would be surrounded by suburbs that had "gone broke," as Peter Blake predicted decades ago. Doubtless, many suburbs would have sought mergers with the more healthy central cities. Yet, the opposite is true. Few suburban jurisdictions have gone broke, and most are in demonstrably better fiscal shape than the older, more dense central cities. Some jurisdictions have, indeed, gone broke. However, financial collapse has predominantly occurred among the central cities, not the suburbs. Examples include New York, Philadelphia, Cleveland, Pittsburgh, and others.

The suburbanization that has occurred in the United States is unprecedented in the world, perhaps principally because its automobile era urban population growth has been greater than anywhere else. The slower projected growth rates mean than suburbanization is likely to slow in the future. The "inevitable" suburban bankruptcies that Blake imagined have not occurred in the last 60 years. Nor are they likely to occur in the future.

The Reality: Suburbs Cost Less. The theoretical projections are not only insignificant, they are also wrong. Joshua Utt and I reviewed actual expenditure data from more than 700 U.S. municipalities reporting to the Bureau of the Census in 2000.[213] In the functions most impacted by new development—sewer and water services—the data reveal exactly the opposite of the theoretical predictions.[214] The lowest per capita sewer and water fees are in the newest suburbs, those that are generally farthest from the core. The highest sewer and water fees are in the core cities (see Figure 7.1).[215] The research also found that suburban areas generally have lower total municipal expenditures per capita than core cities.

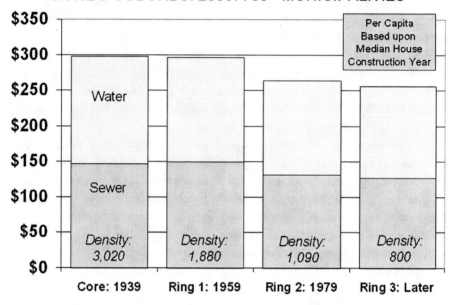

US Water & Sewer Fees: City & Suburb
CORE & SUBURBS: 2000: 700+ MUNICIPALITIES

Figure 7.1

A similar conclusion is obtained in a more detailed analysis of locally financed municipal spending (federal and state funds excluded) in Pennsylvania. In 2001, average local (municipal and county) spending per capita was approximately twice as high in Philadelphia than in the suburbs. Spending in the city of Pittsburgh was 150 percent more per capita than in the suburbs. Moreover, quite to the contrary of the "suburbs going broke" predictions, suburban jurisdictions had much lower debt levels. Annual interest on debt per capita in Philadelphia was 40 percent above the level in the suburbs. Pittsburgh's debt per capita was seven times suburban levels.[216] In 2004, Pittsburgh entered the state equivalent of receivership, a condition Philadelphia had narrowly averted in the early 1990s.

Moreover, the suburbs subsidize the cities, contrary to the anti-suburban view. In the United States, the less dense suburbs tended to receive less than one-half as much assistance from the federal and state governments compared to the more dense core areas. Thus, the suburbs are not only less costly, but they subsidize the more dense areas through higher federal and state taxes.[217] Patrick Troy makes a similar observation with respect to suburbs in Australia.[218]

Moreover, anti-suburbanites often suggest that infill—new development in the dense cores—would save money because the infrastructure is already in place. But often, existing infrastructure is nearly obsolete and requires substantial improvement to accommodate additional capacity. Alternatively, it may not meet current environmental standards.

Why Central Cities Cost More. Theoretical studies, such as *Costs of Sprawl—2000* may suffer from a "length of pipe fallacy"—the assumption that market labor and materials rates determine comparative local government costs. In fact, older, inner city government labor rates are often higher than suburban rates, and regulation requirements may be higher.

The difference between the theory and the reality may be explained by politics. While the competitive market determines the costs of goods and services in the private sector, no such market operates in the public sector because there is no competition. Costs in the public sector are determined politically. The generally higher spending levels of the older municipalities may be due to a process of political entrenchment that occurs as time goes by.

"Entrenchment" may have first been noted by Adam Smith in *The Wealth of Nations,* when he pointed out that the historical control of guilds in the older cities had produced a situation where prices were lower in the suburbs, beyond the reach of the guilds, which kept prices above market levels.[219] Economist Mancur Olson similarly postulated that, as time goes on, political and special interests become more entrenched in older national governments.[220] Stronger bureaucracies, more powerful employee organizations, strong local business interests, political interests, and more rigid operating procedures may have developed over a longer time period that force costs in older municipalities higher than they would be in newer municipalities.

Reflecting such entrenchment, older municipalities have often been notably resistant to cost-effective management innovations such as privatization, competitive contracting, more flexible labor arrangements, and innovative management techniques. For example, the oldest quartile of municipalities had a general government expenditure level 23 percent higher than in the youngest quartile.[221]

An entrenchment theory of municipal finance would be consistent with the findings of economist Charles Tiebout, who argued that people tend to "vote with their feet," to move to newer communities that better meet their desires and needs. The lower suburban tax levels are an important component of this thesis, which characterizes the new communities as competing with one another for new residents.[222]

Lower Consumer Costs in the Suburbs

It is also claimed that suburbanization raises the private costs of consumers. The anti-suburbanites miss this point. For example, the Surface Transportation Policy Project has issued reports purporting to demonstrate that consumers pay higher transportation costs in areas of greater suburbanization. However, expenditures are not a reliable indicator of the cost of living. The data used in these reports are from the U.S. Department of Labor Consumer Expenditure Survey, which, for example, counts all expenditures to purchase automobiles, including $50,000 luxury cars and subcompacts that might cost $10,000. There is virtually no difference in the mobility provided by the luxury car and the subcompact car. The extra $40,000 spent on the luxury car is not a necessity, and cannot be considered a cost of living. It is, rather, the cost of a preference.

For the most part, detailed cost of living data are not available for sectors within urban areas. An exception, however, is Pennsylvania, where the state's Center for Rural Pennsylvania commissioned research on the cost of living by county.[223] The cost of living tends to be lower in suburban areas than in core cities.[224] In the Philadelphia metropolitan area, the city of Philadelphia (which is also a county) is the most dense and rated by Smart Growth America as the least sprawling county in the area. The cost of living in Philadelphia was 20 percent or more above the Philadelphia suburban county average. A similar relationship was found in the Pittsburgh area, where Allegheny County, which includes both the central city of Pittsburgh and inner suburban jurisdictions. The lower density, less sprawling suburban counties had an average cost of living five percent below that of Allegheny County.

The same general situation appears to exist at the metropolitan level—urban areas that have greater suburbanization have a lower cost of living. In the United States, the principal difference in the cost of living between geographical areas is housing. This is illustrated by an analysis cost-of-living data from ACCRA, the principal source of such information in the United States. Among the 31 metropolitan areas with more than 1,000,000 residents for which 2002 data was available, 67 percent of the variation in the cost of living was attributable to housing. Moreover, housing is most expensive where there is less suburbanization.[225]

According to 2000 U.S. census data, urbanized areas with the *greatest* suburbanization had the most affordable housing markets. Among urban areas with densities of under 3,500 persons per square mile, the median house value was 2.8 times the median household income. Higher-density urban areas, with densities of from 3,500 to 5,000, had median house value multiples averaging 3.2. The highest-density urban areas (least suburbanized), those with a population density exceeding 5,000 per square mile, had the least affordable housing markets.[226]

The Housing Subsidy Canard

Anti-suburbanites also claim that government subsidies and home ownership programs in the United States have been a principal cause of suburbanization. After World War II, the United States undertook special efforts to increase home ownership and to make it easier for veterans to buy homes. There was the "GI Bill of Rights" as well as other programs to make housing finance more readily available. Interest on mortgages was made deductible in calculating income subject to taxation. However, this claim does not stand up to scrutiny. A report by the U.S. Government Accounting Office found the subject too complex to isolate any specific material relationships between suburbanization and federal programs.[227]

If housing programs were responsible for suburbanization in the United States, then it would be logical to presume that suburbanization did not occur in nations without such programs. In fact, as has already been shown, automobile-oriented suburbanization is virtually universal among high-income urban areas, demonstrating that housing programs in the United States were not a material cause. Again, reflecting their geographic myopia, the anti-suburbanites seem unaware of the suburban developments that have, for decades, accommodated nearly all new urban growth around the world (see Chapter 3).

Longing for Central Ownership or Central Planning

Indicating the otherworldliness that emerges so often in the anti-suburban literature, *The Costs of Sprawl—Revisited* bemoans the lack of "central ownership or central planning" as a driver of suburbanization.[228] Perhaps what is most remarkable is that *The Costs of Sprawl—Revisited* statement was published a number of years after most communist and socialist economies with central ownership and central planning had collapsed, as had been forecast decades before by economists such as Ludvig von Mises. The United States, of course, had been a leader in resisting the spread of the central-planning-and central-ownership-based ideologies. Yet, the very same United States government financed a study implying that central planning and central ownership would be preferable.

The prescriptions of the planners would radically change things. Instead of the current, generally decentralized approach to planning, the anti-suburbanites would install comprehensive regional planning or even regional government consolidation. The result under either approach would be to move planning decisions from local control to regional government agencies, which are more remote from citizens.

Indeed, some planners would exert far stronger influence over private property. The American Planning Association, in its federally funded *Growing Smart Legislative Guidebook*, proposed "amortization of nonconforming uses." A better term would be confiscation of property. For example, a home owner whose property subsequently was rezoned for apartments would have a certain number of years to convert the property to the new zoning use—that is replace the house with apartment units. An early attempt to use "amortization of nonconforming uses" in Aurora, Colorado, met with such opposition that it was quickly dropped.

The most fundamental problem with central planning[229] is that it is fundamentally undemocratic. A basic principle of democracy is that decisions ought to be made at the competent level of government closest to the people,[230] a concept the European Union calls "subsidiarity." For example, the national government will be the lowest competent level at which national defense or national taxation can be administered. Intermediate governments, such as state, provincial, and county or regional special districts will be the lowest competent level with respect to other functions, such as highways, mass transportation, and air pollution control. Local governments can competently administer other functions. However, unless there is a compelling need, local democracy should take precedence over the more "out-of-touch" political processes that necessarily exist in larger governments.

Regional Planning. In fact, the record of comprehensive urban planning has been less than stellar, at least in the United States. Substantial authority for urban transportation planning was given to regional planning organizations in the United States in the early 1990s. Since that time, a generally ideologically based approach has lavished spending on mass transit, while roadway capacity has been allowed to fall far behind demand. The result, of course, is that roadways have become more crowded. Mass transit has continued to lose market share because it is ill suited to most urban travel (see Chapter 9).

But, as planning moves farther from the people, planners tend to substitute a distortion of democracy, which might be labeled "manipulocracy;" more decisions are made through hearings and public participation forums, such as "charettes." In charettes, meeting attendees are shown illustrations of alternative future visions and asked to choose. The planners and consultants who lead these meetings often come well armed with their own ideology. It is not surprising that illustrations appear to be carefully chosen to evoke desired responses.

The planners can then take their plans to elected officials for ratification, claiming community support manipulated from the unrepresentative attendance lists at their meetings. The more remote planning process empowers the planners to project their preferences on the few and unrepresentative attendees and dilutes the legitimate role of the electorate. It is an illegitimate process for policy development. Informal democracy tends to be dominated by those who have a passion for political activity. Informal democracy gives such participants far more policy influence than would result from their disproportionately high voting rates. This is not a representative sample of the people or the electorate as they vote in elections.

The result is a distortion of policy that favors urban views and is biased against the views of suburban citizens. This is because the very nature of dense living is much different than living in more sparsely settled suburban areas. When people live closer together, as in dense urban areas, there is a greater need for government regulation. The simple matter of noise can illustrate this. In my Paris apartment, for example, it was not unusual to be disturbed by excessive noise from the neighbor's stereo. However, in my suburban St. Louis home, the same noise volume from the neighbor's stereo will not be a disturbance. Where there is ample distance between residences, the same noise level that would disturb a neighbor in an apartment will not be audible to a neighbor.

Higher densities create an incentive for greater political involvement, because proximity creates greater potential for interests to be in conflict. Because people tend to get in one another's way less frequently in the suburbs, there is likely to be less political organization. As a result, in more dense areas, people may have a tendency to participate in daily political activities, such as political committees and hearings, more than in less dense areas. Regional planning or government amalgamation is likely, therefore, to favor core urban interests at the expense of suburban interests.

Local Government Amalgamation: Economies of Scale for Lobbyists

Local government amalgamation is sometimes suggested by anti-suburbanites. Amalgamation can achieve the same purpose of centralizing planning authority in larger governments, which, of course, dilutes local democracy. Often it is suggested that governments should be amalgamated because larger governments are less costly than smaller governments. It is routinely argued that economies of scale exist that make larger governments less costly than smaller ones. Virtually all of the local government amalgamations that have occurred in North America have been justified on this basis.

However, in fact, the cost savings of larger local governments are only theoretical. The 2000 census data indicate that medium-sized U.S. municipal governments have the lowest expenditures per capita. More importantly, the data indicate that the largest municipalities have the highest costs per capita (see Figure 7.2).[231]

The Pennsylvania data support the same conclusion. Locally financed municipal spending per capita is the lowest in municipalities with a population below 5,000 and highest in the municipalities with the largest population.[232]

My own experience is similar. When I was a member of the Los Angeles County Transportation Commission, there were discussions of merging that agency with the largest mass-transit operator we regulated, the Southern California Rapid Transit District. The theory was that this would reduce the number of bureaucrats and save money. Some years after I left the commission, the merger took place, despite my advice against it to former colleagues. What followed was an escalation in costs that eventually led to a cost crisis so severe that the U.S. Federal Transit Administration suspended funding for an already-under-construction subway, a virtually unprecedented action.

Pietro Nivola of the Brookings Institution has rightly pointed out that "fragmentation" is not a barrier to effective urban planning. He notes that decentralized planning is the rule, rather than the exception, in Europe. The Paris metropolitan area, for example, has nearly 1,300 units of general local government[233] and spreads across seven departments. Somewhat smaller Chicago, often criticized for its "fragmented" local government, has fewer than 650 general government jurisdictions.[234] In fact, Paris seems to function as a successful urban area as well as any with 10,000,000 residents.

Andrew Sanction, at the University of Western Ontario, comes to similar conclusions from his review of U.S. and Canadian city consolidations—that larger municipalities tend to be more costly.[235] Perhaps one of the most naïve propositions is that municipalities should consolidate to reduce the number of elected officials, thereby reducing costs. Such false economies weaken the ability of the elected representatives of the people to exercise proper stewardship over the local government.

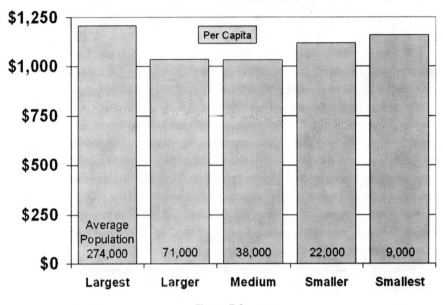

US Spending by Municipality Population
2000: 700+ MUNICIPALITIES

Figure 7.2

Perhaps the greatest problem with local government amalgamations is that they dilute democracy in favor of central city interests and bureaucrats. The former core cities tend to exert considerable political control in the new, larger jurisdictions. Local government becomes more remote and political participation is likely to be less in a larger jurisdiction because the power of an individual citizen or group is less in a larger jurisdiction. There may be more of a tendency to believe that "you can't fight city hall," in a larger jurisdiction. On the other hand, fighting city hall is much simpler in a smaller jurisdiction, where there is a possibility that the individual citizen will be a personal acquaintance of one or more of the elected decision makers. Indeed, if larger municipal governments are superior, and less costly, why not consolidate all of them into a single local government for each state? Or, indeed, why are states needed at all?

Mancur Olson's theory of entrenchment (above) appears to be at work in making larger jurisdictions less efficient and effective. For example:

- Much of Pittsburgh's higher spending is the result of city employee compensation is more than three times the per capita rate of suburban jurisdictions.[236]

- The core city of Chicago pays higher wages to its employees than the adjacent suburbs, all of which are considerably smaller. Moreover, Chicago has more employees per capita. City employee expense is 2.6 times that of the suburbs.[237]

- Mass transit costs in the United States are generally much higher in the larger agencies.[238] Moreover, the larger agencies, exhibiting their entrenchment, tend to be more resistant to cost-saving measures, such as competitive contracting.[239]

However, there are few, if any, economies of scale for taxpayers in larger governments or remote planning processes. There are, in contrast, significant economies of scale for special interests, which are able to manipulate larger government units with fewer resources and more reliable results than smaller governments, whose elected officials are much closer to their constituents. This led me to insert the following statement into a number of speeches written for delivery to American Legislative Exchange Council meetings:

> Government of the people, by the people, and for the people is government that is closer to the people.

Concocting Economic Losses from Suburbanization

One of the newer criticisms is that suburbanization and smaller governments retard economic growth. This contention appears in a Brookings Institution report diagnosing the competitive situation of Pennsylvania and strategies for improvement.[240] Brookings provides virtually no evidence to demonstrate a connection between suburbanization and a more stagnant economy. There was simply a claim that "a radical pattern of sprawl" had occurred in Pennsylvania and that in some way not described, the state's anemic growth had resulted from it. In fact, the pattern of suburbanization in Pennsylvania has been little different from elsewhere in the United States, and Pennsylvania's slower than average economic growth has been comparatively typical for a Northeast or Midwest ("Frost Belt") state.[241]

In fact, however, there is evidence that suburbanization cannot be a material inhibitor of economic growth. Three of the four fastest growing urban areas in the high-income world are among its most suburbanized.

- Atlanta is the high-income world's least dense (by some accounts, most sprawling) urbanized area over 3,000,000 population. Atlanta is also the fastest growing such metropolitan area.

- Houston and Dallas-Fort Worth are the fourth and fifth least dense among the 29 high-income world urbanized areas over 3,000,000 population. They are also the fourth and third fastest growing areas respectively.[242]

Community: Misunderstanding the Dynamics

The old adage that things look better from afar is probably no better illustrated than in the anti-suburban description of "lost community." Suburbanization is criticized as having destroyed community. In *Bowling Alone*, Robert Putnam[243] outlines a number of measures by which he believes community has been eroded in the United States. His characterization is similar to that of others, but the most detailed.

Putnam uses a number of indicators to illustrate how community has been lost. He finds that religious service attendance has fallen off dramatically since World War II, as people have moved to the suburbs. He notes that political participation is at lower levels than it used to be. He also finds that fewer people tend to volunteer for community activities because more of their time has been taken commuting due to suburbanization.

Even so, Putnam, with a perhaps unprecedented, quantitative informality, attributes only 10 percent of the cause of the perceived loss in community to suburbanization. Even Putnam's indicators of community miss much of the story.

Religious Participation. It could be argued that the principal cause of falling religious service attendance may have been the result of changes within religious organizations themselves. In the pre—Vatican II world of the 1950s, the Roman Catholic Church stressed the importance of church attendance. However, the 1962 Vatican II brought a more flexible attitude with respect to church attendance. It also removed, rightly or wrongly, long-standing traditions (such as the Latin liturgy). These were important factors in declining attendance.

Developments in the mainline Protestant denominations may have been even more disruptive. In much of mainline Protestantism (especially the historic churches descended from Europe, such as the Episcopal Church, the Methodist Church, and the Congregational Church, now a part of the United Church of Christ), theology has been substantially revised, some would say de-mystified. The membership losses in such mainline Protestant denominations have been substantial, while newer churches, offering theology that has not been revised, have made strong gains (such as the Church of Latter Day Saints (the Mormons) and Pentecostal denominations such as the Church of God in Christ and Assemblies of God, independent churches, and local "mega-churches"). The trends in the United States have been mirrored in Canada, Australia, and New Zealand.

Western Europe is different, having experienced an even greater religious service attendance drop, but generally without the rise of new churches.

From the perspectives of many Roman Catholics and Protestants, it is not the people who have lost the faith, but rather the religious organizations themselves. The interplay between community and religion is far more complex than can be explained by suburbanization.

Political Participation. Political faith has been lost as well. For most of American history, an idealized civics was taught in the nation's schools. Politics was portrayed as a noble profession, to which were drawn high-minded people driven by an interest in improving the lives of their fellow citizens. Much of the nation and many of its teachers fervently believed it to be the case. There were, of course, the corrupt central cities, where such an interpretation of history was less believable. However, for most students, who lived in rural and suburban areas, urban corruption was distant. To them, the nation was far more rural and suburban and the story of American democracy was, for the most part, something to be admired.

This widely held perception was swept away by Watergate and other very public scandals. It is now generally recognized that Washington, Sacramento, Albany, and Augusta are places where political decisions tend to be driven by special interests of the right, center, and left. This is not to suggest that American politics serves the populace less well than in the past (it may or may not). Nor is it to suggest that many who seek public office do not approach it with the same idealism as in the past. What has changed, at a minimum, is the perception. Improved telecommunications have made people more aware of government and public processes than in the past. Moreover, the very nature of the media is to report what goes wrong, rather than what goes right. It is not surprising that voter turnout has fallen. Lower voter turnout may have virtually nothing to do with suburbanization.

Volunteerism. There is also the matter of questionable analysis. Putnam notes that voluntarism has declined and suggests that it is because people are spending longer times commuting to work because of urban sprawl. However, the claim of longer commute times does not hold up. At the time of Putnam's writing, the Nationwide Personal Transportation Survey showed a small average decline in commute times from 1969. Given the fact that so many commuters switched from slower mass transit to faster cars, it seems likely that today's average work trip travel times are less than in the immediate post-war period. If there is less voluntarism, it is not because people spend materially more time commuting due to suburbanization—because they do not.

Changing Technology. Technology has also been a factor in changing community. The mobile (cellular) telephone, Internet, and other technological advances have radically and irrevocably redefined community. One may not know the neighbors, but may be in nearly constant contact with people who live thousands of miles away over the Internet.

The mobile telephone has played an important role in redefining community. This is illustrated by my experience in the Paris pedestrian quarter of Montorgueil, where I lived briefly. The streets are filled with pedestrians much of the day. Surely, according to the current urban planning dogma, this should be a cohesive community at the street level, with high density, people milling together and no cars. However, I also noticed many people talking on their mobile telephones. As a result, I conducted a survey for a few days. I counted the people who had stopped to talk to someone and those who were talking on their mobile telephones. The results were rather surprising. Out of more than 3,000 observations, approximately 80 percent of the people chose talking on mobile telephones, while only 20 percent had stopped to talk to someone on the street. Given the opportunity, common interest seems a more important determinant of community than geographic proximity.

At the close of the 19th century, community was local, because it could not be otherwise. Without personal transportation and with high telephone long-distance rates, people spent more time with those who were in close proximity. Social activities and conversations were generally held with these neighbors. People did not have most of their contact with physical neighbors because they had the most in common with them. People spent time with the neighbors because there was no alternative.

However, all of that has been changed by modern transportation and communications. The neighbors with whom people have the most significant contacts no longer need to be within walking distance. Community is no longer where one can walk or what one can see from the window. Community can be local or it can be remote and even international. Community limited by geography is obsolete. There is more to community than proximity.

To the urban planner who knows little of Portland beyond the West Hills or Atlanta beyond what can be reached by the MARTA subway, community does indeed appear to be absent in the suburbs. People are not walking in crowds on sidewalks between the yuppie boutiques. They do not spend their afternoons commiserating with their neighbors at trendy coffee shops.

More to the point, suburban areas are strong communities. Just ask the Portland planners, whose densification efforts stirred up so much trouble in low-density neighborhoods that their land-use dictates had to be severely constricted by a public vote. There are the "soccer moms," friends who get together in shopping mall coffee shops, fast food outlets or even sidewalk cafes ringed by parking lots in suburban strip malls. Volunteer fire departments are more likely to be found in the suburbs than in central cities. Urban planners who perceive suburbs as not having community may as confidently dismiss Mecca as nonreligious because there are no crosses. Patrick Troy characterizes the same kind of thinking as "romantic" and "inconsistent with the realities of urban living."[244]

New Urbanism: Salvation by Architecture

However, the anti-suburbanites have an answer: "new urbanism." New Urbanism seeks to bring back the romanticized 1900 American small town. Its proponents exhibit a belief in "salvation by architecture, through which such designs would restore the purportedly lost community. A number of New Urbanist communities have been constructed in the United States and Canada. I personally find some of these communities attractive.

Ticky-Tack Thinking: New Urbanist communities provide an alternative to the suburban housing that anti-suburbanites have, in elitist terms, labeled as "ticky-tack." Anti-suburbanites do not seem to appreciate that the modest houses of Levittown or Lakewood were the best their parents and grandparents could afford at the time. The purchasers were not manipulated by home builder advertising into buying what anti-suburbanites have labeled as ticky-tacky, 1,100-square-foot houses, rather than the tasteful two and three story colonials in today's leafy Boston or Atlanta suburbs.

The choice was rather between the ticky-tack house in Levittown and a crowded rental apartment in the city. If the Levittowns, Plaisirs, Honjos, Markhams, Kellyvilles and Manukaus had not been built, there would be less home ownership today. Households would be less prosperous, because more of their housing budget would have been used for rents on properties others own, rather than mortgages on property they themselves owned. It seems likely that some who demean ticky-tack houses have themselves benefited, with educations and estates that would simply not have been there if their parents and grandparents had paid rent instead.

The same is true of the other high-income world nations where suburbanization made it possible for people to enter the economic mainstream through home ownership. Middle-income households have never had it so good.

The Limits of New Urbanism. But, perhaps the ultimate irony is how reality has conformed New Urbanism to suburban values. Most New Urbanist communities are built in the suburbs, far beyond the urban core locations that would be necessary for them to achieve their purported "transit-oriented development." This is noted by strident anti-suburbanist Jane Holz Kay, who characterizes New Urban communities as "developer driven," and "suburban" as a result, relying on the automobile.[245]

Consistent with this view, New Urbanism is best understood as a suburban design movement. New Urbanist commercial designs are now showing up on wide suburban streets. Usually, not more than a block of such development is produced, but the neighborhood is not transformed. One block will have a strip mall, the next a New Urbanist architect's interpretation of an early 1900-era, small town downtown and the next block a large self-service gasoline station.

The evolving community has a look similar to that of the traditional county courthouse, built in the 19th century, to which a glass-curtained, international-style annex was attached in the 1960s. New Urbanism, like much of anti-suburbanism, is about micro strategies that simply do not add up to a macro vision.

There is nothing wrong with allowing New Urbanist designs. However, many New Urban proponents go further, seeking to make their preferences mandatory. It is no more appropriate to mandate New Urban designs than it was for Josef Stalin to mandate the architecture of socialist realism. It is always a mistake to legislate preferences. At the core, this is why the United States Constitution forbids the establishment of religion. Government establishment of architectural style is also inappropriate.

Separating Romance from Reality. The anti-suburbanites take their case too far when they propose that their designs are better for community. Community tends to be a philosophical, or perhaps even a theological, concept, but it is not an architectural concept. The changes that have occurred to community are much more complicated than can be explained by suburbanization.

The world has changed considerably in the last six decades. Neighborhoods and communities are different today than they were when Harry Truman was president. The old ethnic neighborhoods so characteristic of Northeastern and Midwestern urban areas have dispersed into suburban neighborhoods, or moved to the South or the West.

While old central cities had their Polish neighborhood events before World War II, the sons and daughters may have married Norwegians or Germans and the bond of the "old country" no longer exists as the cement of community. The migration of people from small towns and rural areas to the metropolitan areas has also served to change community, whether in the United States, Japan, or Canada.

Enunciating a New Urbanist vision of what some think the early 20th century small town was like is simple enough. However, the romance is more intense from the perspective of 100 years. Poverty was substantially greater. The average household lived on real incomes below today's poverty levels. Urban areas were far more polluted, with waste from the horses that moved commercial goods and the smoke from coal heating. Men sought to avoid horse refuse as they crossed the streets. Women, with their long dresses, encountered even greater difficulties. The extent of the air pollution is evident in soot darkened, not yet sandblasted, older buildings in core areas. For example, the Houses of Parliament in London were transformed from black to their original much lighter colors, as the effects of coal pollution were removed. Urban picture books show late 19th and early 20th century cities covered by industrial smoke, a condition that lasted in some places to after World War II.

Thomas Sieverts, of the University of Darmstadt (Germany), cautions about romanticizing the dense European cores so beloved by anti-suburbanites.

> ...the presumption that the density of the in the 19th century functioned so well is misleading. It could only be built so densely because the provision of communal services and facilities, especially open space, was irresponsibly poor, but above all because there were no cars. Anyone who has had to bring up small children in such an otherwise attractive and urban quarter from the 19th century knows that, because the streets are much too dangerous, children have to play in special fenced-off playgrounds, which they can only safely reach when helped by adults.[246]

Toward Silliness: The Obesity and Diet Disconnect

In recent years, the anti-suburban interests have seemingly become desperate for new arguments to advance their cause. This has led to a number of studies that could be called frivolous or even silly, especially in the field of public health. Obesity has taken center stage, a campaign that seems intent on making sure that how much we eat is kept out of the discussion.

The anti-suburbanites have been trying to demonstrate that obesity has increased in the United States because people who live in suburbs get less physical exercise. The most quoted is a Smart Growth America and Surface Transportation Policy Project report, which used an econometric model to predict a statistically significant relationship between obesity and suburbanization, using a Centers for Disease Control (CDC) dataset.[247]

However, the report was rife with difficulty. The apparently statistically significant results were insignificant. The statistical method used is highly sensitive to
skewing based upon "outliers"—cases far out of the normal range, principally
four counties within New York City[248] that are so much more dense than the
other observations as to render them unrepresentative. In the face of a general
view that obesity is associated with lower incomes, household income data were
excluded from the analysis, despite being available to the researchers in the CDC
dataset.

Even so, the results from the questionably designed research were less than
compelling. The predicted average weight difference between San Francisco, the
nation's least sprawling county outside New York and the most sprawling suburban county was less than 2.5 pounds. The predicted difference between highly
urban Cook County (which includes the central city of Chicago) and the most
sprawling county in the metropolitan area was less than 1.5 pounds. It is hard to
imagine a weight-loss firm purchasing time on late night cable television to tout
the potential of its products to trim 2.5 pounds over the course of a lifetime.

Somewhat untypical for what purported to be dispassionate research, members of Congress were briefed and an entire issue of a medical journal (*American
Journal of Health Promotion*) was taken over with a summary of the research,
along with related articles. Promoters were less than careful as they pointed out
that U.S. Centers for Disease Control (CDC) data were used, so that some media
outlets referred to the study as a CDC report.[249]

A further installment was provided by Professor Lawrence Frank of the University of British Columbia (UBC), who led researchers on a study of neighborhood obesity in the Atlanta metropolitan area. The results indicated that people
who drive more (and live in less urban settings) tend to be more obese. However,
the sample included a disproportionate number of people who were in cars more
than five hours per day, and can thus be considered representative of nothing.[250]
Again, there was a marketing campaign untypical of dispassionate academic
research. There were press conferences and an impressive spread in a special *Time*
magazine issue on obesity. Again, the study had design flaws. While the researchers managed to collect data on body weight and household income, the survey
sought no information on eating habits or diet. Meanwhile, one of the study's
coauthors has gone out of his way to disclaim the principal thesis of the marketing campaign, that suburban lifestyles cause obesity.

A principal difficulty with the "suburbanization makes you fat" studies is the
order of events. The large increase in obesity came after 1980.[251] Yet, there has
been little change in urban land-use patterns since 1980. The greatest suburban-

ization—the major reductions in density—occurred before 1980 (see Chapter 5). A recent study by the Transportation Research Board (TRB), a unit of the National Science Foundation, dismissed the "suburbs make you fat" contentions, stating that "research has not yet identified" sufficient causal relationships to demonstrate that "changes to the built environment would lead to more physical activity."[252]

However, more fundamentally, studies that exclude plausible causes from their analysis cannot be taken seriously. The econometric researcher has an obligation to include information on every potential contributor to a problem. What might be the most important driver of obesity—food consumption—has routinely been excluded from analyses.

Yet, changing eating habits are a more plausible cause of rising obesity. There are indications that caloric consumption has increased markedly since 1980. One report indicates that there was a more than 15 percent increase in consumption during the first one-half of the 1990s.[253] This idea was rhetorically stated in the title of an article by Dr. Ronald D. Utt of the Heritage Foundation, "Obesity and Life Styles: Is it the Hamburger or Your House?"[254]

More Silliness

The extent to which the anti-suburban claims have degenerated is illustrated by an Ontario College of Family Physicians[255] report, which examined the literature relating to suburbanization and health. The college found, for example, that driving in traffic congestion worsens stress, as it naively accepted the fallacious argument that suburbanization increases traffic congestion (see Chapter 6). They cite research purporting to associate suburbanization with "fear." Other studies associate "roadside blight" or "visual clutter" with suburbanization and make the predictable mental health connections. The array of public health justifications for densification is great indeed, but much more could follow. Perhaps future studies will show causal relationships between suburbanization and bad breath or hemorrhoids—everything "but the kitchen sink."

No Imperative for Anti-Suburbanism Demonstrated

For all of their efforts, the anti-suburban movement has failed to identify any imperative that justifies interfering with the right of people to live and work where and how they like. Coupled with reasonable environmental regulation, there is no reason that the present and virtually universal pattern of suburbanization should not continue, so long as people choose it.

Part III
War on the Dream

8

Rationing Land, Home Ownership, and Opportunity

Home Building Productivity and Land-Use Policy

Anti-suburban policies have consequences. The most important is inordinately higher housing prices, which represent a substantial threat to the quality of life and the economy.

As was discussion in Chapter 2, home building is comparatively productive in the United States compared to most other high-income nations. The McKinsey Global Institute found that the U.S. home building industry was 25 percent more productive than in France, nearly 50 percent more productive than in Germany, and more than double as productive as in Japan.

The McKinsey research further suggests that a principal cause of U.S. home building efficiency is the general lack of excessive land regulation. This regulatory structure allows for larger-scale home building projects, greater standardization, and a highly competitive homebuilding market. The greater standardization that comes with larger home building projects can be substantial. McKinsey estimates that a 50 house development will tend to cost approximately 25 percent less per house than building a single house. Large, privately built housing developments are rare, if not absent, in Germany, France, and Japan.[256]

According to McKinsey, the Netherlands and Australia have similar competitive conditions. The Australian finding was attributed to the presence of small firms in the market, both homebuilders and subcontractors, which has increased competition. This competitive intensity improves productivity, which keeps house prices down, providing greater opportunity for homeownership.

The Regional Housing-Affordability Crisis

Some urban areas are experiencing serious housing-affordability problems. Housing affordability has been in crisis in Californian urban areas for two decades or more, principally San Jose, San Francisco, Los Angeles, and San Diego. In recent years, housing has become much less affordable in various locations, such as Boston, Portland (Oregon), Las Vegas, and the large urban areas of California. Housing has become less affordable in the United Kingdom, where the government has commissioned a major report to identify the causes and proposed solutions. Virtually all major markets in Australia and New Zealand have experienced extraordinary housing cost increases in recent years. Some Canadian markets have also experienced affordability problems, especially Vancouver.

However, the housing affordability losses are by no means universal. Many U.S. and Canadian metropolitan markets retain strong housing affordability. This has been confirmed in reports by the Harvard University Joint Center for Housing Studies and Wachovia Bank, which have noted that U.S. housing-affordability problems tend to be concentrated where land-use restrictions are the most severe.[257] Our *Demographia International Housing Affordability Survey* contains similar findings.[258]

In some markets in the United States, the rising cost of housing has made it more difficult for middle-and lower-income households to find housing they consider acceptable that is relatively close to their preferred employment. Government officials talk of a "workforce" housing problem, and frequently cite data to indicate that nearby residential areas are too expensive for households dependent on government employment, such as fire departments, police departments, and schools. Some have even gone so far as to suggest development of virtual dormitories for government employees to live in during the week so that they do not have to make the long commutes.

The supply of goods and services in a market economy generally meets customer demand. Grocery stores have little trouble supplying sufficient product for customer demand, nor do automobile manufacturers. Supply tends to be sufficient to meet demand in most commercial settings and nearly all the time. For example, soon after World War II, the home building industry was able to provide for substantially expanded demand. For the most part housing has been comparatively affordable since that time.

However, this has changed in some urban areas in recent years, where the supply of housing has not kept up with demand. The resulting scarcity of new housing drives prices up, as would be predicted by economic theory. Why is the home building industry failing to meet demand in these urban areas? There is no shortage of construction labor for homebuilders to employ, nor are the materials required to build homes in short supply. Construction costs have not escalated relative to inflation. What is in short supply is land that can be developed.

Land Rationing Policies

Land-use policies have changed significantly in recent years. Principally as a part of the anti-suburban agenda, certain land-rationing strategies have come into much wider use.

- Densification: These policies, which include urban growth boundaries, green-belts, urban consolidation (the Australian term), urban service areas, and other strategies remove significant amounts of land from potential development and attempt to force building instead into already-developed areas (infill).

- Excessive Development Impact Fees (Excessive Infrastructure Fees): Some communities have imposed fees on the construction of new houses and apartments to recover purported costs to the community for schools, roads, sewers, water, and other community services. Often these fees are considerably higher than justified.

- Mandated Amenities (and New Urbanism): Zoning regulations may require expensive and unnecessary amenities as a part of new house construction. These may range from sodded lawns to new urbanist (early 20th century) design requirements.

- NIMBY: "Not in my backyard" (NIMBY) attitudes represent an interest in keeping neighborhoods and communities as they are, generally closing them to new development. NIMBY-ism is not generally considered a strategy of the anti-suburban movement. However, anti-suburban groups have embraced NIMBY strategies where they are perceived to advance their overall objectives. Such support has principally occurred with respect to "down zoning" (also called "exclusionary zoning"), also called "large lot zoning."

Densification

The anti-suburban densification policies remove large amounts of land from potential urban development by placing restrictions on urban fringe or "green-field" development. At the same time, policies are intended to transfer housing demand to "brownfield" or infill development sites closer to urban cores. Proponents of densification suggest that their regulations can be developed so that they do not force housing prices higher. Christchurch, New Zealand, developer Hugh Pavletich is not so optimistic, pointing to the "strangled" housing markets" densification policies in Australia and New Zealand have created.[259]

Urban Growth Boundaries and Urban Consolidation. Urban growth boundaries (UGB) prohibit urban development outside specified areas. Because urban growth boundaries are typically associated with policies that would force development into infill or brownfield areas, they are generally synonymous with "urban consolidation," the title by which such policies go in Australia.

Perhaps the world's best known urban growth boundary is in Portland, Oregon. In the 1970s, the state of Oregon enacted a requirement that urban areas designate urban growth boundaries outside of which development would not be permitted. More than 95 percent of the state of Oregon is outside urban growth boundaries and barred for urban development. UGBs have also been adopted in a number of San Francisco Bay area communities. The Denver area has imposed an urban growth boundary through its regional planning organization, with voluntary adoption by cities and counties in the region. Similar development boundaries have also been adopted in Vancouver, British Columbia, and a number of urban areas in Australia and New Zealand.

Urban service areas are also similar to urban growth boundaries. Urban service boundaries encompass the area in which urban services, such as sewer or water, will be provided. For example, Minneapolis—St. Paul and the city of Austin, Texas, have urban service boundaries.

Greenbelts. Greenbelts designate a ring of non-developable land around an urban area. Perhaps the world's first and most-significant greenbelt was in London, where development is prohibited in a ring approximately 10 miles wide outside the urban development as it existed before World War II. The London greenbelt is so extensive that it makes off-limits to development more than three times as much land as urbanization it encircles.

Greenbelts have subsequently been adopted on the outskirts of urban areas such as Seoul and Canada's Golden Horseshoe (Toronto-Hamilton-Niagara Falls). Generally, development is forced outside greenbelts, which leads to a pattern of leapfrog development, as new urbanization takes place farther away from the urban core. Development outside the greenbelt may still be subject to severe restriction, as is the case in the United Kingdom.

Impact on the Housing Market. Depending on the stringency of the regulation, the housing-affordability loss may be delayed. This occurred in Portland, for example, which included substantial land for development within its original urban growth boundary. The land shortages developed only later, as development filled up more of the land inside the urban growth boundary.

Not all land development prohibitions have the same price-increasing effect. For example, large expanses of forest area have been preserved in the Paris area.

However, these areas have tended to radiate outward in the outer suburbs. Between the forest areas, there has been abundant land for the strong residential and commercial growth that has occurred since World War II. The forest preserves have channeled development rather than restricted it.

The critical issue is whether the regulation interferes with the market to create an imbalance of demand over supply, or scarcity. If the regulations create scarcity, then housing affordability can be expected to decline. Steeply falling housing affordability has generally been the experience where strong land-use policies are adopted.

There are a number of ways that land development prohibitions and restriction ration the supply of houses relative to demand and increase prices.

Sellers' Market: Higher Land Prices. Urban growth boundaries create seller's markets. Land that can be developed increases in value. At the same time, land that cannot be developed loses value. It is typical for densification policy to provide sufficient land for 20 years of additional development.

The problem can be illustrated by examining the impacts in a medium-sized urban area similar to Columbus, Ohio, which had a population of approximately 1,100,000 in 2000. Based upon current growth rates, an urban growth boundary approximately one mile beyond existing development would be sufficient to accommodate 20 years growth. Over the 20 years, it can be expected that virtually every property within the urban growth boundary will be developed. Property owners will be aware of this and will be able to negotiate higher land-sale prices because they do not have to compete with potential sellers of property for development outside the urban growth boundary.

On the other hand, if there were no urban growth boundary (as is the case in Columbus), developers could open up land further from the core for home building and commercial structures. If, for example, households generally want to live within 15 miles of downtown—an area encompassing three miles beyond the urban growth boundary, then only one-quarter of the land would be developed over 20 years. There would be healthy competition among potential sellers of land, and land prices would be lower.

Once an urban growth boundary, or greenbelt, is defined, much less property is potentially developable, which can quickly raise the price of the developable property. Property inside the urban growth boundary will be worth much more than an adjacent piece of property outside the urban growth boundary. The differences can be stark. For example, Dr. Tim Leunig of the London School of Economics has reported that agricultural land reclassified for residential development in the London area can increase in value 500 times.[260] The higher values on the land designated for development translate into higher prices for potential homebuyers.

Where more land is available for development, the resulting urban form will not be as compact. However, development will tend to be closer to, rather than farther away from, the urban core. Moreover, as time goes on, the interplay between land buyers and sellers continues. The areas leapfrogged over become developed (see Chapter 5). Moreover, they are developed at lower prices than if they had been developed in a regulatory environment that prohibited discontinuous development.

Hoarding (Land Banking). Policies that restrict land development induce developers and builders to engage in speculative hoarding activities for their own profits and survival. A homebuilder requires a supply of land on which to build in the future. In a generally free, or unstrangled, market, the homebuilder can assume that there will be sufficient land available for sale to be developed in the future. But, if planning regulations severely limit the amount of land that can be developed, a home builder's survival will require obtaining developable land sufficient upon which to build for a number of years and rationing development to maximize the financial return.

As the Barker Report, prepared for the Deputy Prime Minister of the United Kingdom, indicates many house builders "trickle-out" houses especially from large individual developments—controlling rates of production to protect themselves against price volatility, and to ensure that they do not adversely influence prices in the local housing market."[261]

This kind of market manipulation would not be possible without the scarcity arising from densification policies.

Testimony before the Australian Productivity Commission's inquiry into affordability of housing for first-time buyers indicated that as much as 15 years worth of residential land supply is currently "banked" in the Melbourne area, which already has some of the most restrictive land-use policies.[262]

Higher Construction Costs. The scarcity of land can be expected to drive smaller homebuilders out the market, because they cannot find land on which to build. This leaves a more concentrated market of larger builders. The reduced competition is likely to lead to higher prices for construction itself. The fewer home builders in the more concentrated, less competitive market will now be able to charge not only higher prices for the land on which they build, but also for the houses as well. Higher profit margins can be charged on material and labor than if the market were more competitive. All of this further increases the price of housing, independent of the land price increase, the hoarding impacts.

Builders Go "Upmarket." Land rationing tends to impose an overall limit on the number of new houses that will be built, whether by planners' design or by the impact of land banking (hoarding). There is a natural tendency to maximize revenues in any particular transaction, and houses are no different. Thus, when homebuilders are able to choose to build a smaller number of houses without a threat of substantial competition, there will be incentives to build more expensive units—to go "up-market." This behavior mirrors what occurred in the automobile market. When the United States imposed import quotas on Japanese cars, the Japanese manufacturers began to ship a more expensive array of cars to the United States than had been the case before.

Infill. Densification policies may be accompanied by infill or brownfield development targets. For example, Australia's largest urban area, Sydney, has a target of providing more than 60 percent of its new housing in already-developed areas, and less than 40 percent in greenfield areas on the urban fringe. Further, it is typical for such authorities to require new greenfield development to be at higher densities than occurred in the past.

The planners seem to believe that if there is sufficient land for densification within developed areas, their policies can readily force infill development. Indeed, there appears to be a belief among planning authorities that increasing densities can reduce housing prices. This is based upon the assumption that smaller building lots will be less expensive. However, the price of smaller lots is driven up when there is a scarcity of land for development. The smaller building sites in Portland are more costly than the larger sites previously allowed. Moreover, Portland's small building lots are considerably more expensive than the larger lots in faster growing metropolitan areas such as Atlanta, Dallas-Fort Worth, and Houston.

Moreover, substituting infill development for urban fringe development raises construction costs. It is generally more expensive to construct a dwelling in an already-developed area. Further, the economies of scale, which the McKinsey Global Institute cite as cost advantages for home builders in the United States, cannot be achieved because the required, larger number of adjacent units required simply cannot be built in a developed area.

In fact, the costs of building infill housing are often above the price the market is willing to pay in many U.S. jurisdictions. As a result, infill housing often involves substantial government subsidies, such as in Portland's Pearl District.

Speculation. Anti-suburban policies also encourage costly speculation in housing. As densification policies have led to an explosion in housing prices, housing has become a more attractive element of investment portfolios. The business press is filled with articles on the long-term investment value of housing, treating the rising costs as if it is some inherent good, like rising stock market prices. There are frequent articles about a coming "bursting of the bubble." This treatment is not unlike what might be expected of commodity markets in scarce metals, such as gold, or highly speculative markets, such as venture capital and emerging technologies.

However, the business writers concerned about a property boom and fearful of a "bust" should view the matter in a broader context. What if, for example, a government imposed restrictions that created scarcity in food? This would surely be an outrage. Policies that artificially raise housing prices and retard the quality of life are indeed an outrage in modern societies. The democratized prosperity that has been developing, in part due to policies that allow low-priced housing on urban fringes, is threatened by densification policies. Anti-suburban policies threaten to consign future generations to a lower standard of living, and for no reason.

Excessive Development Impact or Infrastructure Fees

Development impact fees (or infrastructure fees) represent a comparatively new method for financing public services. Previously, these services were financed by the general tax base, rather than by "entry" fees to residents. Some public officials believe that development impact fees are justified based upon the growth challenges that municipalities have faced in the last decade. In fact, the financial challenges faced by municipal governments were much greater, and the growth was much greater, in the 1950s and 1960s.

Development impact fees are not permitted in some states. However, some jurisdictions have used "proffers," which are "contributions" from extracted (if not extorted) developers for infrastructure in exchange for project approvals.[263] Proffers have the same general economic impact as development impact fees—they raise the price of housing and reduce affordability. Proffers are used extensively, for example, in the northern Virginia jurisdictions of suburban Washington, DC.

According to a California state report, impact fees on new houses add an average of 10 percent to the cost of new residences, and 20 percent to the cost of new apartments in California. Impact fees can exceed $60,000 for a detached house and $40,000 per apartment.[264]

In the United States, development impact fees tend to be a fixed amount that is applied to a new house or a new rental unit, rather than being related to the value of the property under construction. Thus, a $200,000 house will incur the same development impact fee as a $500,000 house. As a result, development impact fees tend to be a greater barrier for low-and middle-income households than for those that are more affluent.

The impact on the supplier market is significant. Impact fees raise the initial cash requirements of developers. In Los Angeles County, this amounted to an increase of 16 percent, while in Contra Costa County, the cash requirement was increased 53 percent according to the state of California study.[265] Such a requirement creates a significant financial burden on multi-unit developers and can be expected to reduce the number of firms that can or will compete in the market and the number of housing units produced.

University of Chicago researchers[266] found that development impact fees in the Chicago metropolitan area increased not only the cost of new housing, but also existing housing.[267] They also found that development impact fees induced homebuilders to build higher-cost housing units to recover higher profit margins.

Making New Urbanism and Other Amenities Compulsory

Requiring housing to have unnecessary amenities or unnecessarily expensive designs also raises prices. For example, a community might require brick facings on houses, which would add to the cost of houses. There are campaigns to redraft building zones and zoning regulations to include New Urbanist (early 20th century housing design) amenities. There is nothing wrong with voluntary New Urbanism, but everything wrong with making New Urbanism the state architecture. Peter Gordon found that New Urban housing tends to be approximately 25 percent more costly than contemporary housing designs.[268] On a more fundamental level, attempts to require particular housing styles, such as New Urbanism, are nothing more than attempts to regulate taste, which is not a legitimate role for government.

Among advocates of New Urbanism, this cost differential is often characterized as a benefit. For example, Song and Knapp found "consumers willing to pay a premium price for a home in a New Urbanist neighborhood."[269] There is nothing wrong with upscale builders supplying housing for upscale buyers. However, there is a significant injustice if these more expensive designs are mandated by building codes and regulations that raise the price of entry-level housing, thereby restricting home ownership. Such New Urbanist sentiments betray an elitism oblivious to the fact that many potential home buyers are not in a position to "pay a premium" and would thus be precluded from home ownership altogether.

"Not in My Backyard," Down Zoning, and Exclusionary Zoning

NIMBY-ism is an acronym meaning "not in my back yard." It denotes strategies by which residents of an area attempt to bar or control new development in their neighborhoods. This is understandable, especially in a new suburban area to which households might have been attracted by the rural surroundings. As population growth continues, development expands, and the formerly rural surroundings become urban.

"NIMBY-ism" will not be found in lists of anti-suburban policies. However, in fact, NIMBY-ism is a form of growth management and anti-suburbanites have supported such strategies to advance their own objectives.

More often than not NIMBY-ism will be found in the sparsely populated suburbs and exurbs, where middle-and upper-middle-income homeowners seek to maintain the bucolic nature of their surroundings. The same interests will also be concerned about maintaining their comparatively high property values and will generally oppose the building of smaller houses, houses on smaller lots, or multiple-unit housing (apartments).

For example, in Loudon County, Virginia (suburban Washington, DC), much of the county had been down zoned for development at four houses per acre. To control growth, the county board rezoned many areas for a single house per acre. This, of course, increased the price of land for development, which had the effect of excluding many potential new homebuyers. This process is also known as "exclusionary zoning," because of its apparent association with efforts to keep central city households and lower-income households out of suburban areas. The Heritage Foundation's Ronald D. Utt has characterized NIMBY-ism as a process whereby suburbanites seek to "upgrade their demographics."[270] The ultimate impact is injury to lower-income households, who are denied housing opportunity by the artificially higher prices NIMBY-ism generates, or who must move even further away from their jobs to find housing that meets their needs. The urban planning strategies of NIMBY-ism exacerbate the jobs-housing balance by artificially moving housing opportunities further away from employment. In addition, because a disproportionate share of lower income households is of minority populations, the urban-planning policies of NIMBY-ism have the long-term effect of being anti-minority. Whether intended or not, this is the inevitable result.

Exclusionary zoning was identified by the Kemp Commission as one of the most important regulatory barriers to affordable housing. Exclusionary zoning is the use of local zoning powers to exclude types of housing development that are considered undesirable. Exclusionary zoning has been directed at keeping low-income households out of communities and neighborhoods, by restricting or even banning the more affordable types of housing, such as rental units, manufactured housing, or modular housing. The Kemp Commission also found evidence that exclusionary zoning has been used to keep particular types of households out of neighborhoods or communities, especially minorities.[271]

The anti-suburban literature expresses a strong rhetorical commitment to equal opportunity housing. Yet, anti-suburban interests have allied themselves with suburban efforts to implement exclusionary zoning measures where it has suited anti-suburban purposes. This has included support of measures to implement larger-lot zoning in northern Virginia and development bans in Ventura County, California.

NIMBY-ism itself can lead to an even more restrictive situation, now so widespread that it also has earned a descriptive acronym. BANANA refers to "build absolutely nothing anywhere near anything." The net effect of extending property rights beyond owned properties, whether by NIMBY-ism or BANANA-ism is to create a matrix of interests that make development nearly impossible.

Had NIMBY-ism banned development to the north of our new house near St. Louis, those of us fortunate enough to have purchased our property at the right time would have a nicer environment and better views of the rolling countryside. However, the households whose new housing would not have been permitted would have had their choices severely limited. Perhaps they could have moved into generally smaller housing within already-developed areas. More likely, they would have moved to the inevitable housing developments that anti-suburban policies have generated in the London and San Francisco areas. But in a metropolitan area with millions of people, the price of our exercising control over property we do not own would be to deny housing opportunity to those choosing to buy later. Had our neighborhood been interested, public policies might have granted us the right to deny opportunity to these neighbors. It might have been legal, but it would not have been fair.

The victims of NIMBY-ism and down zoning are the people who are denied the housing that would permit them to live in an area. They are typically younger, lower-income, and disproportionately minority. This is a fundamental flaw that, in the longer run, is likely to lead to a more divided society and a greater distribution of economic resources based upon privilege, as opposed to the market. NIMBY-ism is significant step backward for the American economy, because it threatens to undo the trend toward democratization of prosperity.

The basic problem with NIMBY-ism was characterized by historian Richard Pipes, as he described the expansion of unwarranted rights noting, "there is no limit to such rights since they are purchased at someone else's expense."[272]

Unintended Land Rationing

Scarcity is also created by policies not principally intended to regulate, such as government land sales that lag well behind the underlying demand for new housing development, such as in the Las Vegas and Phoenix areas.[273] Administering agencies gloat about their rising revenues, apparently oblivious to the longer-term economic and social damage their homeownership-reducing policies are creating.

The Incumbents Club

All of the anti-suburban policies favor "haves" over "have-nots." The price of new housing is driven up for new entrants to the market. Robert Bruegmann of the University of Illinois refers to the effect as creating an "incumbents club."[274] However, it is a step backward to favor the interests of the "haves" over the "have nots," or of favoring incumbents over new entrants to the community. In societies that purport to provide equality of opportunity, it is inappropriate to grant a right to some to deny the opportunities of others. The boundaries of "my back yard" are specified in the deed.

Research: Land Regulation Raises Prices

Economist and *New York Times* columnist Paul Krugman may have best characterized the situation when he coined the term "zoned zone" to denote the regions of the United States in which land-use regulation has artificially driven prices up, while prices remain affordable elsewhere.[275]

Research is increasingly identifying insufficient supply as the main driver of excessive house-price escalation. Edward Glaeser and Joseph Gyourko,[276] in work published by Harvard University, reported that the principal cause of differences in housing affordability between U.S. metropolitan areas is zoning and land regulation. This is a particularly stark finding, since average house prices in U.S. markets range from over $600,000 in the San Francisco Bay area to under $150,000 in a number of Midwestern and Southern metropolitan areas.[277]

Based upon their findings, Glaeser and Gyourko concluded, in a Federal Reserve Bank article, that there was no national housing-affordability crisis.[278] Nonetheless, there are a number of urban areas in which housing costs have escalated substantially. Most of these areas also have land-rationing policies that have driven up housing prices by creating scarcity. A U.S. Department of Housing and Urban Development report refers to this as "misuse of smart growth:"[279]

Measuring Housing Affordability

However, in many areas, housing affordability has declined, as houses have become more expensive relative to incomes. This has occurred in areas where the supply of housing has not kept up with the demand, generally because of planning practices that have reduced the supply of housing. More recent data have only made the arguments against anti-suburban policies stronger. In recent years, housing affordability has plummeted in urban areas that have the strong anti-suburban policies that create housing scarcity. These trends are measured by the "median multiple," which divides the median house price by the median household income. Throughout the United States, Canada, Australia, and New Zealand, the median multiple has historically been approximately three (3.0). Today, many markets in the United States, the United Kingdom, Canada, Australia, New Zealand, and Ireland have median multiples far above the historic level. Moreover, there is a strong association between higher median multiples, or reduced housing affordability, and anti-suburban policies (see Figure 8.1 and Table 8.1).[280]

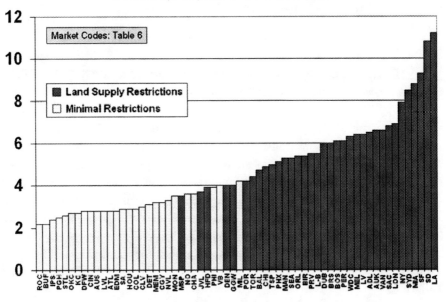

Figure 8.1

Table 8.1: Housing Affordability Market Codes Corresponding to Figure 8.1:
Median Multiples by Market

Code	Market	Code	Market	Code	Market	Code	Market
ADL	Adelaide	DET	Detroit	MEL	Melbourne	PRV	Providence
ATL	Atlanta	DFW	Dallas-Fort Worth	MEM	Memphis	ROC	Rochester
AUK	Auckland	DUB	Dublin	MIA	Miami	SA	San Antonio
AUS	Austin	EDM	Edmonton	MIL	Milwaukee	SAC	Sacramento
BAL	Baltimore	GGW	Glasgow	MON	Montreal	SD	San Diego
BIR	Birmingham	HFD	Hartford	MSP	Minneapolis-St. Paul	SEA	Seattle
BOS	Boston	HOU	Houston	NO	New Orleans	SF	San Francisco
BRS	Brisbane	IPS	Indianapolis	NVL	Nashville	STL	St. Louis
BUF	Buffalo	JVL	Jacksonville	NY	New York	SYD	Sydney
CGY	Calgary	KC	Kansas City	OKC	Oklahoma City	TOR	Toronto
CHA	Charlotte	L-B	Leeds-Bradford	ORL	Orlando	TSP	Tampa-St. Petersburg
CHI	Chicago, IL	LA	Los Angeles	PER	Perth	VAN	Vancouver
CIN	Cincinnati	LON	London	PGH	Pittsburgh	VB	Virginia Beach
CLV	Cleveland	LV	Las Vegas	PHI	Philadelphia	WDC	Washington
COL	Columbus	LVL	Louisville	PHX	Phoenix		
DEN	Denver	MAN	Manchester	POR	Portland		

United States. The first strong land-rationing policies were implemented in the United States in the 1970s. Thus, the last census in which incomes and housing values did not include the effects of densification policies was in 1970. Four of the five states with the largest loss in housing affordability had a strong densification policy influence (Oregon, California, Washington, and Colorado). The other state among the five with the largest affordability drop was Massachusetts, where NIMBY policies have been associated with land scarcity.[281]

The loss in housing affordability has been particularly stark over the past decade. This is illustrated by an examination of markets with more than 500,000 population (see Table 8.2).[282]

- In 1995, the highest median multiple in the nation was 4.3, in Honolulu. By 2005, the highest median multiple was 11.2, in Los Angeles. San Diego and Honolulu also had median multiples above 10.0.

- In 1995, no markets had median multiples higher than 5.0. By 2005, 18 markets were above 5.0.

- Among markets with strong anti-suburban policies, there was an average increase of 3.5 in the median multiple from 1995 to 2005. Among markets without such policies, the increase was 0.7, one-fifth the amount in the anti-suburban policy markets.

The higher-cost housing may already be taking a toll in growth. Many of the metropolitan areas with anti-suburban policies had been among the fastest growing in recent decades. Yet, among the metropolitan areas with more than 1,000,000, the ones with strong anti-suburban policies lost nearly 1.2 million domestic migrants[283] (1.6 percent of their 2000 population) from 2000 to 2005, while those without such policies gained more than 375,000 (0.5 percent of their 2000 population).[284]

A discussion of individual markets follows.

Table 8.2: U.S. Housing Markets, Median Multiples: 1995 and 2005

Median Multiple	1995	2005
3.0 & Below	56	20
3.1–4.0	7	17
4.1–5.0	1	9
5.1 & Over	0	18

Markets over 500,000 population.
Median Multiple: Median house price divided by median household income.
Source: *Second Annual Demographia International Housing Affordability Survey.*

California. The spread of anti-suburban policies began in the 1970s in California. The city of San Jose adopted what might have been the nation's first urban growth boundary. After the passage of Proposition 13, which limited property taxes, cities began to impose development impact fees. As might be expected from the extent of its anti-suburban policies, the most significant housing-affordability problem in the United States is concentrated in the largest urban areas of California.

As noted above, Los Angeles (including Orange County) and San Diego have seen unprecedented housing-affordability losses, with median multiples over 10.0. Other major California markets were also at unprecedented levels in 2005. The San Francisco area had a median multiple of 9.3. Riverside-San Bernardino and San Jose were over 7.0, while Sacramento and Fresno had median multiples above 6.0.[285]

The housing cost escalation has led to leapfrog growth over a mountain range. To find housing they can afford, many middle-income households are now traveling to the San Joaquin Valley, 60 or more miles away. From 2000 to 2005, population growth in the San Joaquin Valley metropolitan areas of Stockton, Modesto, and Merced was more than double that of the San Francisco Bay area, despite having a population base 80 percent smaller.[286]

There has been a strong outward domestic migration from California, with more than 650,000 persons leaving between 2000 and 2005.[287] Surprisingly, the San Diego metropolitan area, in recent decades one of the fastest growing in the nation, lost more than twice as many domestic migrants from 2000 to 2005 than Pittsburgh, which is alone among large metropolitan areas as having long been losing population. It seems likely that a principal factor in this trend is the high cost of housing.[288]

Oregon. The longer-term loss of housing affordability has been the greatest in Oregon, California's neighbor to the north. From 1970 to 2000, Oregon's median multiple rose more than 60 percent. This increase was more than four times the national average and was the largest affordability loss in the nation. In 1970, Oregon was the nation's 13th most affordable state. By 2000, Oregon had become 47th worst in housing affordability. Only three states and the District of Columbia were less affordable.

During the 1970s, Oregon adopted a comprehensive land-use law that required adoption of urban growth boundaries. Census data indicate that between 1989 and 1999, the housing-affordability loss in the three largest Oregon urban areas ranked first (Portland), second (Salem), and fourth (Eugene) out of the nation's more than 350 urban areas. Smaller Medford, the only other Oregon urban area in the list, experienced the 11th worst loss in housing affordability.[289] Congressman Blumenauer's claim that Oregon land-use policies expand housing choice is empty in the face of the housing-affordability losses that have produced fewer houses to choose from for virtually everyone. By definition, raising the price of housing *restricts* choice.

Finally, Portland's policies have led to less housing value, even after the housing cost increases. From 1995 to 2001, median new house size fell nearly 15 percent relative to the rest of the nation. The median lot size was reduced by nearly one-quarter. This, combined with Portland's inordinately escalating costs, contradicts the urban-planning expectation that smaller lot sizes should lead to lower prices.[290]

The Oregon law requires planning agencies to maintain a supply of developable land sufficient for 20 years of residential and commercial growth. In the early 1990s, it became clear that the existing plan would not accommodate 20 years of growth. Metro, the Portland land-use agency, began working on an updated plan. The agency determined that only a modest increase in developable land was necessary, based upon the assumption that there was the potential for significant densification. In the middle 1990s, Metro adopted a *2040 Plan* that provided for adding only 31 square miles—9 percent—inside the urban growth boundary by 2040.

The Portland Backlash. Metro proceeded to increase densities, consistent with the *2040 Plan*. Higher density, infill developments were built in existing neighborhoods, a development generally not welcomed by local residents. By 2002, a referendum had been qualified that would have severely restricted Metro's powers to force higher densities. In response, Metro placed its own, weaker-density limitation on the ballot. The Metro measure won by a two-thirds majority, and as a result, Metro will have significant limitations on densification until 2015.

As a result, the *2040 Plan* had to be revised. By 2004, Metro had expanded the urban growth boundary by 37 square miles—more than had previously been projected for 2040. However, the relaxation of the urban growth boundary may be just the beginning. A further potential limitation on the Oregon anti-suburban policies was enacted by voters in 2004, with the passage of Measure 37, which requires government compensation to land owners for zoning or land-use changes that reduce their property values. Portland's anti-suburban policies, along with those of the state, could be in the process of unraveling.

It remains to be seen whether the Portland urban growth boundary expansion will be significant enough to limit future price increases. However, even if housing prices do not continue their extraordinary increase, Portland remains considerably less affordable than it was before the scarcity associated with the urban growth boundary. It seems likely, however, that without a substantial rollback of anti-suburban policies, housing affordability will remain strained. It is an irony that Portland, which has been the source of so much anti-suburban thinking, and which is so revered by urban planners, has been forced to withdraw from its more aggressive strategies.

Portland Myths. But much of the Portland story was myth from the beginning. Portland's planners and promoters tended to claim success based simply upon the adoption of policies rather than their successful implementation. Even today, for all of the international publicity received by Portland, it is an urban area that sprawls rather liberally across the landscape. Among high-income urban areas outside the United States with more than 1,000,000 residents, only Perth and Brisbane have lower population densities. Portland's unearned reputation was noted by New Urbanist architect Andres Duany in a Portland *Oregonian* op-ed.

> I have visited Portland five times…in all cases I was "handled" by my hosts and shown the many wonderful paces that make it a great, livable city. On the fifth trip however, I "escaped" my hosts and went out to visit the famous urban boundary on my own. What did I find, to my surprise? That as soon as one left the prewar urbanism (to which all my prior visits had been confined) the sectors all the way to the urban boundary were chock full of the usual sprawl that one finds in any American city…[291]

In Portland, the changes in urban form have been modest, but the costs in lost housing affordability have been great. As in the San Francisco area, Portland's anti-suburban policies appear to have had a dampening impact on growth. U.S. census data indicate that from 2000 to 2005, more than 90 percent of domestic migration (both from within the area and outside) has been to counties in the metropolitan area *outside* the urban growth boundary. This is in contrast to the one-quarter of the 2000 population in counties outside the urban growth boundary. There is a strong trend of growth away from the urban core to the suburbs beyond the urban growth boundary.

Boston. The Boston metropolitan area has one of the most intense housing-affordability problems in the nation. A report commissioned by the governor[292] attributes much of the cause to exclusionary zoning strategies that include overly large lot size requirements, provisions that make development more difficult or slow, and absolute prohibitions on multiple-unit construction. In most communities, new housing must be developed at lower densities than the housing stock that already exists. The report cited the lack of affordable housing as the "greatest threat" to the economic vitality of the state and predicted that Massachusetts would "continue to lose population and fail to attract and retain highly skilled labor if our housing affordability crisis continues."[293]

A report by Edward Glaeser estimated that Boston area house prices had been inflated 60 percent by scarcity.[294] This "land-rationing premium" alone ($156,000) is enough to buy a median priced home in Dallas-Fort Worth, Houston, and 16 of the other 19 affordable markets in the United States.[295]

Anti-suburbanites have been sharp in their criticism of exclusionary zoning in the Boston area. However, Boston's policies are little different than those the anti-suburban interests have supported in Loudon County, Virginia; Ventura County, California; and elsewhere. Exclusionary zoning creates scarcity in land for residential construction. A report by the Massachusetts Institute for a New Community indicates that the state's comparatively low homeownership rate is the result of its high house prices.[296] As in San Francisco and London, this has led to substantial exurban development, bring hypersprawl to the Boston area. A Boston area "housing report card" noted that "home buyers are moving further from Boston to find affordable homes."[297]

Las Vegas. Las Vegas has been the fastest growing urban area with more than 1,000,000 population in the United States since 1990. Nonetheless, by 2000, housing affordability in Las Vegas was slightly better than average for the major urban areas. This changed radically in the new decade, as heavy affordability losses have occurred. The apparent cause is a shortage of land for home building, but it is not the result of densification policy. Nearly all of the land surrounding the Las Vegas urban area is either federally protected (such as national forest) or is owned by the United States Bureau of Land Management (BLM). BLM has a program to sell land for development. However, the pace of the BLM sales has lagged well behind demand, especially in recent years. According to National Association of Realtors data, housing prices increased more than 50 percent (approximately $100,000) in 2004 alone.[298] A major 2005 BLM land sale obtained more than $260,000 per acre. This is more than five times the price of residential land for development in the late 1990s.[299]

Australia. Few would think of Australia, with the lowest population density of any permanently inhabited continent, as an area with a shortage of land for urban development. There is an unbelievable, if not surreal, strain to Australian urban land-use policy. Reading the literature, it would be easy to get the impression that Australians live on a small island and that development is threatening to consume the last few parcels of land that exist between the urban area and the surrounding ocean. Yet, densification policies have been adopted in all of Australia's major metropolitan areas.

Overall, urbanization represents only 0.25 percent of Australia's land. At present rates, a single year's average reduction in agricultural land due to productivity would accommodate approximately 100 years of urban growth at present densities, without any need for urban consolidation policies. Those who find a shortage of land for development around Sydney, Brisbane, or other large Australian metropolitan areas might be expected to fret about the scarcity of sand in the Sahara Desert.

For the most part the densification policies have been adopted in a public policy environment driven more by ideology than reality. The government cost studies that are much of the foundation for densification are, as Professor Troy indicates, questionable. A national parliamentary leader indicated the extent to which policies are based in mistaken impressions, when he justified densification policies on the basis that "Sydney must not become the next Los Angeles."[300] In fact, Sydney "sprawls" at a density a quarter less than Los Angeles. Bernard Salt, writing in *The Australian,* challenged Australian planning authorities to stop trying to scare people by suggesting that Sydney, Adelaide, or any other place in Australia was headed toward becoming another Los Angeles—the Los Angeles area has almost as many people as all of Australia.[301]

A Brisbane planning report claims that its proposed urban consolidation policies are necessary because providing most housing on the urban fringe is "unsustainable in terms of land consumption and the cost of providing urban services." Given the fact that neither Australia nor Brisbane has a shortage of developable land, it is not surprising that the report provides little documentation of the land shortage claim.

The New South Wales state government's attempts to huddle Sydney residents into an artificially constrained area of urban consolidation is similarly irrational. The state of New South Wales has somewhat more land than the state of Texas. However, Texas, with its wide-open spaces, has three times the population of New South Wales. Moreover, despite local perceptions to the contrary, Sydney's growth is not spectacular. Dallas-Fort Worth and Houston are growing at annual rates 1.5 to nearly 2.0 times that of Sydney. At present growth rates, the pre-urban consolidation pattern would raise the share of New South Wales land occupied by Sydney from approximately two to three percent.

Today, approximately 30 times as much land in New South Wales is protected (such as in national parks and preserves) as is occupied by the urbanization of Sydney.[302] Indeed, there is enough land in New South Wales to house the entire population of the world, and still be less crowded than Singapore.

The results of urban consolidation policies have been devastating to housing affordability. The median multiple in Sydney was 8.5 in 2005, the highest outside the United States. In Melbourne, Brisbane, Perth, Adelaide, and Hobart, the median multiple was over 6.0. What may be Australia's world-record lack of housing affordability can be contrasted with a more affordable past. In each market, there has been an unprecedented increase in housing prices relative to incomes in response to "smart growth" (urban-consolidation) policies (see Figure 8.2).[303]

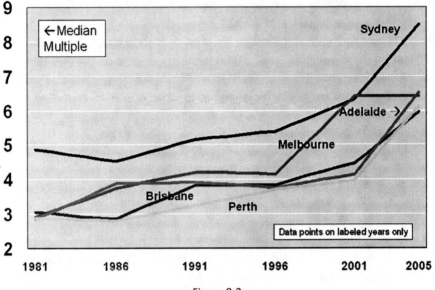

Australia: Median Multiple Trend
LARGEST MARKETS: 1981-2005

Figure 8.2

As would be expected from policies that ration land, much of the house price increase has been in land prices. In the mid-1970s, land represented 32 percent of the average new house cost in Sydney. By 2002, this figure had risen to 60 percent. Large increases in the land share of new house prices have also occurred in other major metropolitan areas, from a 50 percent increase in Melbourne to doubling in Brisbane, Adelaide, and Perth.[304]

However, there are indications that Australia's contrived land scarcity could be exposed. In Sydney and Melbourne, for example, organizations called Save Our Suburbs have begun to question the government's urban consolidation policies and are opposing neighborhood densification, similar to the public reaction that emasculated the planned Portland growth boundary.

United Kingdom. The United Kingdom's urban-planning policies have also reduced housing affordability. Since the 1940s, there has been strict planning control of urban development in the United Kingdom. Moreover, and not surprisingly, there is a well-publicized "housing shortage" in the United Kingdom. The Barker report indicates that land rationing is the "main" reason. From 1971 to 2001, average house prices increased 2.4 percent annually, more than double the 1.1 percent rate in Europe, where land-use regulation tends to be more restrictive than in the United States, but less restrictive than in the United Kingdom. The differential attributable to land-use regulation in the U.K. could exceed 30 percent from 1971.

By 2005, the median multiple in all major markets had risen to between 5.0 and 6.9. However, higher house prices do not necessarily translate into greater value. The average new house size in the United Kingdom is approximately 825 square feet, less than one-half the size of new houses in the United States, Australia, Canada, and New Zealand.[305]

Moreover, London's greenbelt has generated an explosion in leapfrog development. The population inside the greenbelt has declined, and all growth has been outside. If regulations had allowed development within the greenbelt, less than one-quarter would have been consumed. The radius of urban area would have expanded, on average four miles.[306] Households that today live from 25 to 45 miles from the urban core would instead be within 20 miles. As a result, work trip distances are greater and the people who have had no economic choice but to locate outside the greenbelt have considerably fewer employment opportunities. A report commissioned by the Corporation of London found that London's economic output per capita was less than that of Paris, at least partially because of its less comprehensive transport system,[307] which has to traverse so many miles of empty space to tie the region together (see Chapter 9). Those extra miles of commuting are the direct consequence of the anti-suburban policies, which have produced far more dispersed suburbanization than would have occurred otherwise.

Ireland. Severe housing-cost escalation has occurred relative to incomes in Dublin. The median multiple rose to 6.0 in 2005, as planning authorities have failed to make land for development available at rates required to meet the demand. As in the United Kingdom, these high housing prices are accompanied by small new house sizes, approximately one-half the size of houses being constructed in the United States, Australia, Canada, and New Zealand.[308]

Canada. There is similar evidence in Canada. Vancouver has been referred to as the "smart growth capital" of the Northwest. The unaffordability of the housing market confirms it. By 2005, Vancouver's median multiple had reached 6.6. The province of Ontario recently adopted draconian greenbelt policies that are likely to retard housing affordability substantially in the Toronto area,[309] where the anticipation of such policies has been a factor in raising the median multiple to 4.4. At the same time, the less regulated markets, such as Winnipeg, Edmonton, and Quebec[310] maintain median multiples below 3.0.

New Zealand. Urban consolidation policies appear to be having a similar effect in New Zealand. The median multiple in Auckland has reached 6.6, while in Christchurch the figure has risen to 5.9. Some homebuyers are being driven to the Hamilton area, more than 60 miles south of Auckland, to find more affordable housing.

Rationalizing the Loss in Housing Affordability

Until recently, the anti-suburban literature has largely ignored the housing-affordability consequences of their policies. However, as critics of anti-suburbanism began raising the issue, defensive reports started to appear. They might be called "sun rises in the West" studies, because of their interest in disproving the economic reality that rationing raises prices.

A study by the Brookings Institution, lead by Dr. Arthur C. Nelson,[311] has been frequently cited to prove that house prices are not increased by anti-suburban policies. A close reading of the study renders a different conclusion. The Brookings team commented, "The housing price effects of growth management policies depend heavily on how they are designed and implemented. If the policies tend to restrict land supplies, then housing price increases are expected."[312]

This is, of course, precisely the point. The problem is not demand, nor supply. It is rather the imbalance between the two—that supply has fallen short of demand. If policies lead to scarcity—a supply of new housing that does not keep up with the demand for new housing—then housing prices will rise. This can be expected to occur whether the cause is anti-suburban policies, overly restrictive traditional zoning, or other factors that reduce the supply of new housing. Significantly, the Brookings report expresses the view that housing-price increases can be mitigated by better design of anti-suburban policies. This hope, reminiscent of Gorbachev's view that communism could have succeeded if better designed, is probably beyond achievement.

Demand and Housing Affordability

Defenders of Portland's urban growth boundary contend that the area's high growth rate has created an excess of demand that has driven up housing prices. One report that attempts to minimize the impact of the urban growth boundary on housing prices concedes that, in the worst case, $10,000 might have been added to the average house price.[313] This is an exceedingly optimistic finding, because Portland's cost escalation has been extraordinary. If Portland prices had risen at the average rate of fast growing Dallas-Fort Worth, Houston, and Atlanta during the 1990s, houses would have been $35,000 less costly in 2000. Finally, adding $10,000 to housing prices may not place a barrier in the way of comfortable urban planners, but it can be the difference between home ownership and renting to many households.

Researchers writing in the Fannie Mae Foundation's *Housing Policy Debate* suggest that California's strong population growth rate was a principal cause of its inordinate housing cost escalation.[314] However, the view that housing-price increases are principally the result of growth or high market demand is not supported by the data.

Similarly, there is no justification for attributing California's huge housing-price increases to population growth. California has grown fast. Other states have grown faster, indicating stronger demand. Since 1970, California has ranked 12th among the states (and DC) in population growth. Yet, California has experienced the third largest increase in median house price in the nation, trailing only Oregon and Colorado, with their urban growth boundaries. Ten of the 11 states that grew faster than California experienced smaller increases in house values.

As noted above, Atlanta, Dallas-Fort Worth, and Houston are among the four fastest-growing, large metropolitan areas in the high-income world. Yet, housing affordability remains strong in these areas, which have remained free of anti-suburban policies. In 2005, the median multiple in Atlanta, Dallas-Fort Worth, and Houston was below 3.0, as it was in many other U.S. markets that have not embraced land rationing.

Interest Rates and Monetary Policy

Some in Australia and New Zealand have attributed the escalating housing prices to a "boom" in the property market, driven by low interest rates. However, the escalation in housing prices relative to incomes cannot be explained away by low interest rates. Interest rates have been low for a number of years. The low interest rates that have accompanied the housing-cost escalation in Los Angeles, Portland, Sydney, and Vancouver have also been present in markets where there has been little cost escalation, such as Atlanta, Dallas-Fort Worth, Houston, and Winnipeg. Further, the recent New Zealand experience demonstrates the immunity of housing-price increases to interest rate increases. The Reserve Bank of New Zealand has raised short-term interest rates to one of the highest levels in the high-income world, yet housing prices have continued to rise at approximately the same rate (see Figure 8.3).[315] New Zealand's housing price escalation is largely immune to Reserve Bank interest movements. The problem is land rationing.

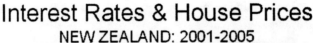

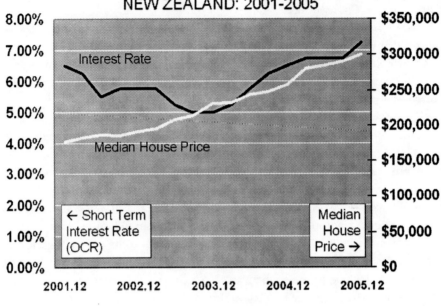

Figure 8.3

The Nexus between Densification and Housing-Affordability Losses

When the supply of new houses falls behind the demand, prices can be expected to rise. Scarcity increases prices, whether in the housing market or any other. Thus, where urban land-use policy creates scarcity, excessive housing-price escalation can be expected, as the Brookings report itself indicated. This has been the experience of urban areas adopting strong anti-suburban policies.

Leading New Urbanist architect Andres Duany was forcefully criticized colleagues who do not acknowledge the cost-increasing nature of land-rationing strategies. In a message to an anti-suburban e-mail list he responded:

> There is NO question that urban growth boundaries and that elaborate environmental studies and elaborate public processes increase the cost of housing by creating scarcity. (And don't tell me otherwise, because I am not stupid, nor am I inexperienced, nor do I have underdeveloped powers of observation).[316]

One of the principal goals of anti-suburban policy is to increase housing choices. However, when housing prices rise relative to income, housing choice is necessarily reduced. For some it will be reduced to the ultimate degree—by making home ownership impossible.

It thus appears that many of the present urban area housing-affordability crises are strongly associated with densification policies. In most such areas, densification policies have created scarcity and housing affordability has declined. Planners have been unable to structure policies that limit land development without creating scarcity, and there is no reason to believe that they will be able to in the future. The very nature of land restrictions loose enough to not force housing prices higher would nullify achievement of anti-suburban objectives.

Impacts on Low-Income and Minority Households

All home owning households begin by purchasing their first house. It is first homebuyers that are paying the ultimate price of anti-suburban policies, through unnecessarily higher house prices that can deny the opportunity of home ownership.

The planning-induced housing-cost increases are likely to disproportionately injure minority lower-income households most. The higher land prices can be expected to make home ownership more expensive, and could drive rental prices higher. Because they are more sensitive to housing-cost increases, low-income households can be expected to sustain disproportionate costs from urban growth boundaries. In the United States, because of their generally lower incomes, minorities, principally African Americans and Hispanics, will bear the burden, through denial of home ownership.

Indeed, there is already evidence that greater opportunity for minorities and suburbanization are associated. Matthew Kahn, at Tufts University in Massachusetts, found that more sprawling urban areas have higher rates of African American home ownership.[317] Moreover, in California, with its intense land regulation, an Hispanic research institute, the Tomas Rivera Foundation, has found anti-suburban growth controls and excessive development impact fees to be a principal barrier to greater Hispanic home ownership.[318]

Housing affordability in the Sydney area has become so much worse than the rest of the nation that Reserve Bank of Australia Governor Ian MacFarland advised young households to seek other urban areas.[319]

In Canada, recent immigrants and visible minorities tend to have lower incomes, and their income growth rates are less than those of their predecessors. Like American minorities, these Canadian cohorts will pay the highest economic price for policies such as the greenbelt legislation recently adopted in the Toronto area. Similar situations exist in other nations. Generally, as the price of housing artificially increases, it is those at the lower end of the income spectrum who pay the greatest price.

President Bush has established an objective, through his "ownership society" program, to increase minority home ownership by 5.5 million households by 2010. That objective will be far harder to achieve, and indeed may be precluded from achievement, by the policies of land rationing, which create scarcity and raise prices.

Platitudes about Housing Subsidies

Anti-suburbanites often express the view that subsidies and affordable-housing mandates on homebuilders can solve the problem. But, the extend of funding required to provide sufficient compensation to keep households in the home ownership market is far beyond anything but the slogans of the anti-suburbanites

If, for example, Southern California median multiples were to remain steady into the distant future and to spread statewide, the annual cost of a compensating mortgage subsidy could eventually double the level of all state and local taxation.[320] A mortgage subsidy program compensating for the lost affordability in just the Sydney area would eventually require more than the equivalent of 1.5 times the total state taxation in New South Wales.[321]

It is, of course, absurd to believe that subsidy programs can solve a financial problem that is so deep and widely spread throughout the economy. No economy has ever shown the capability of grandly subsidizing nearly everyone, whether in the United States or Nigeria. On a more fundamental level, however, low-income housing advocates note that the United States has never funded its housing programs at a level that would meet the needs of the presently statutorily eligible. To suggest that new or expanded housing subsidies are the answer to nullifying densification's affordability losses is both politically and economically naïve.

The idea of solving the problem by requiring homebuilders to include affordable housing units in their developments is similarly ineffective. The economically naïve often fail to realize that the cost of these units is not borne by home builders, but rather in higher prices charged to buyers of the other units. Even so, these "inclusionary zoning" policies can provide for only a small portion of the households driven out of the home ownership market. A review of California markets by Powell and Stringham found that affordable housing mandates are associated with house-price increases of more than $20,000 and a reduction in the supply of new housing.[322]

Allowing the market to deliver the lowest possible prices, so that home ownership, wealth creation, and social inclusion can be maximized, can solve the problem of housing affordability. This will also increase the effectiveness of low-income housing subsidies, which, by virtue of the lower market prices, will require less in financial resources.

Economic Impacts

Of course, rapidly falling housing affordability will hurt more than low-income households. Its impacts will, rather, be felt by virtually all households, whether by being denied home ownership and its economic advantages or by having to settle for less housing value where home ownership can be afforded.

Home ownership can continue to play its role in democratizing prosperity only if housing prices remain affordable. Moreover, should home ownership rates begin to decline materially, the broad middle-income category of households will decline with it.

Home ownership is approximately 70 percent in the United States, Canada, and Australia. In the longer run, structurally higher housing prices could substantially reduce this rate. It begins by denying access to first homebuyers. All home-owners were first-time homebuyers at one point. As prices rise to unaffordable levels, many would-be first-time homebuyers will be relegated to renting for longer, if not for their whole lives. The potential impacts can be estimated based upon mortgage approval requirements and median multiples (see Figure 8.4).[323]

- Oregon's median multiple, if reached at the U.S. national level, would have made the median-priced house unaffordable to approximately 15,000,000 more households in the United States. Ultimately, if this median multiple were maintained, it could be expected that the home-ownership rate would fall to approximately 50 percent.

- The highest median multiples from the California markets (and Sydney) would have made the median-priced house unaffordable to more than 50,000,000 households in the United States. Ultimately, if this median multiple were maintained, it could be expected that the home ownership rate would fall to under 20 percent.

Similar impacts can be expected in other nations. The decline in home ownership rates could be slowed by factors such as new financing mechanisms. However, a substantial decline seems inevitable where median multiples rise to the unprecedented levels now evident in many urban areas that have been captured by anti-suburban (smart growth) policies. Suffice it to say that lower home ownership must inevitably lead to less affluence and less economic growth than would occur in the absence of such policies.

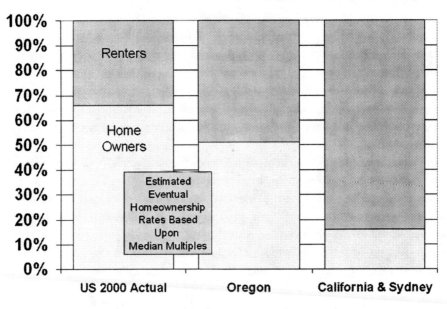

Home Ownership: Long-Term Implications
BASED UPON MEDIAN MULTIPLES

Figure 8.4

Rationing Opportunity

Housing on the urban fringe in high-income nations has provided lower prices and greater value. It is this very combination of low-cost land, efficient construction, and middle-income households that has led to the democratized prosperity that has only been achieved in these nations. Yet, there remain literally millions of households with insufficient incomes to enter even this affordable-housing market. To impose regulations that artificially raise the price of housing, unless there is some compelling requirement, is both inappropriate and unfair.

Indeed, the massive losses in housing affordability could lead to an economy in which inheritance could become a principal means of home ownership. Many households might attain home ownership only through inheritance. Most of those not so fortunate might never be able to afford homes. Overcrowding could return as households "double-up" so that they can afford houses.

In short, by rationing land, anti-suburban policies would ration economic growth, affluence, and opportunity. Anti-suburban policies would lead to a less-even distribution of wealth. They would skew wealth accumulation toward a declining share of land owners (land lords), while reducing the relative incomes of an expanding population of renters.

One of the most important historical economic advances was the replacement of economic systems based upon inheritance with those based broadly on equality of opportunity. Anti-suburban policies are already turning back the clock by taking the opportunity for home ownership away from many households. This is both a mistake and unnecessary.

9

The Cost of Neglecting Mobility

Anti-suburban policies seek to force people out of cars and into mass transit, which by slowing travel and making both mobility and access more difficult would lead to less productive urban areas.

Mobility and Opportunity

An urban area and its citizens require effective access and mobility to prosper. People must be able to access employment, shopping, and services. This requires that people are able to travel to such locations inexpensively, conveniently, and quickly. It can also mean that some goods or services are delivered to the consumer without the necessity of travel. In either case, the consumer or employee must be spatially matched with the good, the service, or the job.

Greater mobility improves employment opportunities, and, in turn, improves the economic performance of an urban area. A more prosperous urban area serves not only middle-income and more affluent households, but it improves the quality of life for low-income households as well. All of this occurs because larger, more mobile labor markets are more efficient. Employees have a greater selection of employers and employers have a greater selection of employees. The shorter amounts of time spent in commuting leave more time for people to engage in other productive activity.

The research cited previously (see Chapter 1) by Prud'homme and Lee makes this point. They find that as the percentage of jobs that can be reached increases in a particular period of time, urban economic production improves by a factor of 0.18. Thus, a 10 percent improvement in employment access would theoretically lead to an improvement in economic output of 1.8 percent.[324]

Our own research, covering urban areas from the high-, middle-, and low-income worlds, found that urban travel is strongly associated with higher urban income levels. This research suggests that mobility is more important than other factors, such as mass-transit market share, mass-transit service intensity, or population. Economic freedom, however, was found to be even more important.[325] This implies that the economic benefits of transportation cannot be optimized outside a system in which people are free to do what they want.

The London-Paris Contrast. Planning can retard economic development. This point is inherent in work commissioned by the Corporation of London.[326] Transportation and land use were found to be major contributors to the superior economic productivity of the Paris area in comparison to the London area. Generally, the report found that the labor market in Paris was more effective than in London, where the greenbelt has prevented continuous urbanization. This spatial arrangement, in and of itself, would have been of little consequence if the urban transport system had been effective enough in London to compensate for the longer travel distances. It is not.

The difference is urban planning. In London, interventionist policies sought to curb sprawl. In contrast, urban development was permitted to occur adjacent to the area of pre-existing urban development. In the London area, the greenbelt adds 10 miles or more to the commute of any resident from outside who works in London. Virtually no freeways have been provided for circulation outside the greenbelt, except for those that head toward London and generally end at the M-25 orbital highway. The result is that exurban residents have far fewer employment opportunities as a result of the artificially long commutes that have been required by the planning-induced disfiguration of the London urban form.

In Paris, on the other hand, nearby development was permitted to occur, and there was no need for commuters to travel through 10 miles of undeveloped greenbelt. In Paris, one of Europe's most comprehensive freeway systems provides mobility throughout most of the urban area. Thus, a suburban resident can access many more jobs by car, both in the core and in the suburbs. Mass transit is more efficient in Paris as well, because the suburban commuters heading toward the urban core start with a 10-mile advantage over their counterparts in exurban London, where the greenbelt forces longer work trips.

More high-income world urban areas are like Paris than like London. Suburbanization has occurred contiguous to the existing urban area, unlike the exurbanization and leapfrog development forced upon southeastern England by the London greenbelt.

It is beyond dispute that urban areas are more efficient and opportunities are greater if their residents are able to conveniently access a greater percentage of the employment and other activities. Urban areas have developed because of agglomeration economies, principally having to do with labor markets. If there were no advantage to larger labor markets, then a much less concentrated pattern of development would have evolved over the centuries.

However, anti-suburban transport policies would make urban labor markets less efficient. There would be more traffic congestion, travel speeds would be slower (see Chapter 6), and people would have fewer opportunities for employment, commercial, and personal access. Anti-suburbanites would do this by restricting automobile capacity and futilely attempting to transfer travel demand to mass transit.

The Urban Transportation Situation

The principal transportation problem facing urban areas in the high-income world is worsening urban traffic congestion. The traffic congestion analysis provided annually by the Texas Transportation Institute indicates the magnitude of the problem in the United States. In 1982, peak hour travel took 10 percent more time in urban areas with more than 1,000,000 residents than travel in uncongested periods. By 2002, the extra time required to travel during peak periods had more than tripled, to 33 percent. In another 25 years, if the same rate of increase continues, travel during peak hours will take 68 percent longer than during uncongested periods. A trip that would take 30 minutes in uncongested periods will take 50 minutes during peak periods. However, even this projection may be optimistic, because it seems unlikely that future road expansion will be as great as in the past.

Other factors could exacerbate traffic congestion. The rapidly growing commerce by truck makes expansion of roadways even more important. Large trucks consume a comparatively large share of roadway capacity. The average large truck on a U.S. urban freeway uses nearly four times the space of the average automobile. The Federal Highway Administration forecasts large truck volumes will increase more quickly than automobile volumes to 2020. The situation is even more serious outside the United States. Trucks represent a greater share of road volumes in Western Europe and Japan, because, unlike Canada and the United States, so little of the freight is carried on railroads.

It thus seems clear that future commuters are unlikely to be able to travel as far to work in the same amount of time as they do now. Moreover, densification, which would necessarily move jobs and residences closer together, would *increase* travel times because of the resulting greater traffic congestion and slower travel speeds.

Balkanizing Urban Areas: The Jobs-Housing Balance

Anti-suburbanites would seek to maintain or improve urban travel times by creating a jobs-housing balance. If people were to live closer to where they work, it is argued, travel distances and travel times could be reduced. This would be accomplished by densification and skillful urban design. It has been tried before, with little success.

In the United Kingdom, "self sufficient" new towns (such as Milton Keynes and Stevanage) were built in the exurbs with sufficient employment for the new residents. The jobs and the residents came, but the shorter travel distances did not. The 2001 census shows that residents of the new towns travel to work, on average, a distance twice the diameter (distance across) of the new towns they live in.[327] A large share of the residents work in other towns or in the large cities.

Urbanologist Peter Hall made similar findings with respect to Stockholm's satellite communities. Despite planning intentions similar to those in the U.K., the overwhelming majority of people work outside the communities in which they live.[328]

It might be expected that with its hyper-densities, Hong Kong would have achieved a jobs-housing balance that would minimize work trip travel distances. However, the average work trip in Hong Kong is nearly five miles. For whatever reason, Hong Kong residents, in effect, pass literally millions of potential jobs on their way to work.[329]

Proximity to work is not the principal consideration in choosing where to live. The 2003 U.S. Census Supplemental Survey found that one-fifth of households that have recently moved chose their neighborhood based upon employment proximity. Only 13 percent of purchasing households chose their neighborhoods principally due to employment proximity. Moreover, proximity to mass transit was the principal attraction of the new neighborhood for only 1.1 percent of movers and 0.4 percent of movers purchasing homes.

In making their case for a jobs-housing balance, anti-suburbanites suggest that people are forced to commute an hour or two to work. In fact, in 2000, only eight percent of U.S. commuters traveled more than one hour to work and a disproportionate share were on mass transit, rather than in cars. Mass transit, which accounts for less than five percent of the nation's commuting, accounts for more than 20 percent of the commuting that takes 60 minutes or more.

People choose where they live based upon many factors, of which employment location is just one. Factors such as proximity to relatives, the house itself, schools, the neighborhood, balancing the commuting requirements of more than one worker and others are considered in making the housing location decision. Closer jobs may not match the qualifications and preferences of the employee. The bottom line is that no one is forced to commute one or two hours to work—they choose to, based upon an array of preferences.

There have been attempts to force people to live near where they work. Even where such restrictions have been tolerated, they are being discontinued. The Chinese government, which had assigned factory workers to living units near their employment, is abandoning the practice. The problem is fundamental, and beyond the purview of urban planners. People are not prepared, as Patrick Troy puts it, to "accept a circumscribed range of interests by confining their travel to public transport (mass transit) or only to those activities within easy reach of their homes."[330]

Households have been abandoning small towns for decades. Generally, small towns are too small to contain the critical mass of employment opportunities that can sustain a high-quality, modern standard of living for a growing population. There are, of course, exceptions, such as university towns and towns along Interstate highways, motorways and autoroutes that depend upon traveler trade. However, more often than not, small-town economies are suffering, so much so that they can be desperate enough to seek facilities, such as new prisons, that are strongly opposed in the larger urban areas where opportunities abound.

Small towns, whether standing alone, or as enclaves within Balkanized larger urban areas simply do not have the agglomeration economies that would make them economically sustainable. No amount of urban planning will change that. The problem is that people have different preferences for themselves than planners have for others.

Ironically, the most favorable jobs-housing balances exist in the automobile oriented suburbs. For example, in the New York metropolitan area, the most favorable jobs-housing balances are in suburban counties, where, in most, the difference between the number of jobs and residential workers is less than 20 percent. None of the far more dense New York City boroughs achieve such a balance and by far the worst balance is in New York County (Manhattan). Manhattan, the most favored real estate of the smart growth and New Urbanist movement in the United States has 2.75 times as many jobs as residential residents.[331]

In fact, anti-suburban policies discourage people from living near where they work. For example, in urban areas such as Washington, DC, and New York, anti-suburban policies are driving people further away, with the fastest growing portions of the metropolitan areas located far from the core. Anti-suburban policies in closer areas have made them generally off-limits for development. As a result, people in the New York area are moving to northeastern Pennsylvania and those in the Washington area, to West Virginia or halfway to Richmond. The result is a significant increase in especially long commute trips. The hope of planners to force people back into the urban core remains as elusive as ever.

Thus, both the international experience and personal preferences render planning ineffectual in minimizing work trip distances or travel times. Herding cats might be easier.

Latest Fad: Demonizing Free Parking

The latest assault on suburban lifestyles comes from planners who would outlaw free parking under the guise of improving economic efficiency. The most important work on the subject[332] strongly bases its argument on the unsubstantiated assertion the less free parking would lead to less suburbanization and substantially more mass transit use. There is no attempt to explain how people making people pay for parking will induce them to use mass transit services that do not go where they need to go.

In fact, however, the impact of taking away free parking would likely *expand* suburbanization, as people would drive to peripheral areas where parking is free. Moreover, free parking bans would work to the advantage of larger retailers, and against smaller local retailers, as people would combine shopping trips to minimize parking expense. This would mean more large store and super center shopping.[333]

Unrealistic Expectations for Mass Transit

The key to the anti-suburban transportation agenda is mass transit. There is an implied general view that mass-transit use can be readily substituted for automobile use. Consistent with the belief that "mass transit is the answer," a 2004 national poll by the Associated Press found that approximately one-half of respondents believed that expanding mass transit should have a higher priority than expanding highway capacity. The public expects that mass transit will be able to make it possible to travel around the urban area more quickly and conveniently, as traffic congestion worsened. It should not be surprising that this faith has arisen in a populace that has for so long been exposed to "mass transit is virtuous" hyperbole.

The reality is not so promising. At the policy level, elected officials and mass-transit board members have sought funding for massive infusions of funding to expand mass transit, especially through urban-rail systems. Many, like those of us on the Los Angeles County Transportation Commission who approved plans for the Los Angeles rail system (1980), did so because they believed that these rail systems would reduce traffic congestion. A quarter century after we approved the Los Angeles plan and obtained voter approval, approximately 500 miles of rail lines have been opened—three light-rail lines, one subway line, and six commuter-rail lines. Los Angeles County's population has risen more than 2.5 million. Yet, automobile use is up 50 percent, average peak period travel delays are up 150 percent, and fewer people ride mass transit than in 1985, before the rail systems were opened.

Portland's Worsening Traffic Congestion. The results are not materially different in Portland, where densification and anti-highway policies have combined to seriously increase traffic congestion. Portland opened its first light-rail line in the mid-1980s and has since opened additional lines. Yet, Portland's mass-transit-based strategy has not been sufficient to keep traffic congestion under control. The transportation choice cited on Congressman Blumenauer's Web site is no different in Portland than anywhere else. People who are going downtown have a choice between cars and mass transit. People who are going elsewhere do not.

In fact, from 1985 to 2002, Portland's traffic congestion intensified at a rate exceeded only by Los Angeles, according to the Texas Transportation Institute's Travel Time Index. Highway use increased approximately 105 percent from 1985 to 2002.[334] Portland's traffic congestion is worse than that of any principal urban area under 2,000,000.[335] Traffic volume per square mile has increased more than 50 percent since before the first light-rail line was opened. The share of work trips on mass transit dropped 20 percent from 1980 (the last year with data before the first light-rail line opened) to 2000. Belatedly, regional officials have woken up to the fact that Portland's excessive traffic congestion is taking an economic toll. A report co-sponsored by Metro, the land-use planning agency, calls for significant highway expansion, which it justifies by Portland's loss of competitiveness and the fact that businesses are being driven away by the traffic congestion.[336] Vancouver's similar anti-highway policies have led to serious concerns about future competitiveness and a prestigious business alliance has called for significant highway expansion to alleviate the extensive traffic congestion.[337]

Mass Transit and Traffic Congestion—Unrelated Subjects. It may be surprising, but higher mass-transit market shares are associated with *greater* traffic congestion (see Figure 9.1).[338] This is not to suggest that mass transit increases traffic congestion. It is rather the result of the fact that urban areas with greater mass-transit market shares tend to have higher urban densities, which, as has been shown above, worsen traffic congestion.

The experience in Portland and elsewhere shows that present mass-transit strategies, even when lavishly funded, will not attract people out of their cars. Literally thousands of miles of new mass-transit routes have been constructed in the high-income world to attract drivers out of their cars. Yet, highway volumes continue to rise, and mass-transit market shares are stable or falling.

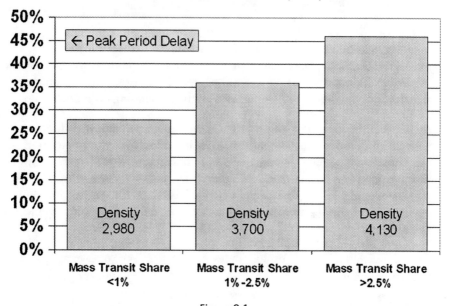

Figure 9.1

There have been no material successes in reducing traffic volumes. Only a few urban areas have managed to reduce the automobile share of travel. For example, during the 1980s and 1990s, Zurich, Boston, and Brussels managed to transfer approximately one percentage point of travel from automobiles to mass transit. However, in each case, automobile traffic volumes and congestion increased substantially.

The reality is reflected in long-term transportation plans that generally project no material reduction in automobile market share and increasing automobile travel volumes. A notable exception is Melbourne, where the long-term plan seeks an 11 percentage point transfer from cars to mass transit over 20 years. The plan contains no blueprint to accomplish the task. This is not surprising, since such a large shift of demand from cars to mass transit has never occurred and is probably impossible.

Funding Distortions. In a number of cases, metropolitan planning organizations have committed a substantial part of future funding to mass transit. However, in what should surprise both respondents to polls and mass-transit officials, these investments will, according to projections in the very same plans, do virtually nothing to reduce automobile use. Long-term (25-year) transportation plans are heavily weighted toward mass transit and away from highway capacity increases.[339] For example:

- In the San Francisco and Boston metropolitan areas, more than 70 percent of spending will be on mass transit, and less than 30 percent on highways. Yet, mass transit's market share is less than five percent in both areas. Automobile use, comprising more than 95 percent of travel, is not projected to be materially reduced, despite the disproportionately high spending on mass transit.

- Atlanta's 2000 adopted plan projected spending 55 percent of its funding on mass transit, despite the fact that mass transit has less than three percent of the travel market. The high spending levels on mass transit would have, according to the projections of the planning agency, reduced the share of travel by car only marginally, from 97.6 percent to 96.4 percent. Of course, automobile traffic volumes would continue to increase, and traffic congestion would get worse.

Overall, 17 large U.S. metropolitan areas plan to spend, on average, 50 percent of their financial resources on mass transit. Yet, mass transit's market share averaged less than two percent in these areas. Mass transit was to receive more than 25 times its share of funding (see Figure 9.2).[340] In addition, as in Atlanta, in virtually no case do the regional plans anticipate a substantial transfer of automobile use to mass transit in exchange for the funding lavished on mass transit.

This is apparently simply the continuation of a long-term trend, according to Alan Altshuler and David Luberoff of Harvard University's John F. Kennedy School of Government. They note that mass transit has received approximately one-half of all transportation public funding spent in urban areas since the 1970s.[341]

US Regional Spending & Travel Share
18 REGIONAL PLANS

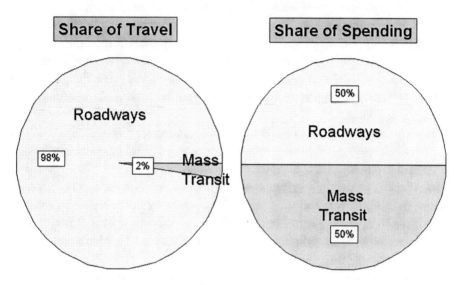

Figure 9.2

Regional transportation plans are filled with rhetoric that would lead the casual reader to imagine that there is a wholesale movement of drivers from cars to mass transit. For example, the Austin regional transportation plan indicates an intention of "reducing the vehicle miles traveled in the region."[342]

Nevertheless, the Austin plan, quite to the contrary, projects substantial increases in automobile use. This is consistent with virtually all other long-term transportation plans, whether in the United States, Western Europe, Japan, Canada, Australia, or New Zealand. Distortions such as these will lead, unnecessarily, to much greater traffic congestion in the future, as funding for the capacity improvements needed for highways is spent on hopeless attempts to attract people to mass transit. That very hopelessness is expressed in the same transportation plans, none of which anticipate a material movement of people from cars to mass transit.

The Key: Automobile Competitiveness

People like mass transit and will use it where it makes sense. The vast majority of workers commute by mass transit to the large central business districts of Tokyo,

Paris, London, and other large urban areas in Western Europe and Japan. Approximately 75 percent of New York (Manhattan) central business district employees commute by mass transit. The mass-transit market share is approximately 60 percent to the Chicago Loop central business district, and approximately 50 percent to the business districts of Boston, San Francisco, and Philadelphia. One-third of the transit commuters in the United States travel to these downtowns. This is an astonishing concentration of transit commuting activity. The combined land area of these downtown areas is less than 20 square miles, approximately the same size as the Disney New Urbanist community of Celebration (Florida).[343]

However, outside these core areas, mass transit usage is very limited, at a median market share of three percent. Mass transit's share of travel in the Paris suburbs is little more than one-fifth the share in the core city. The large downtown areas in other U.S. urban areas have much smaller mass transit market shares, typically 20 percent or less. Even in the New York metropolitan area, the mass transit work trip market share to the outer suburbs is only 2 percent, yet these outer suburbs contain 1.8 times as many jobs as the Manhattan central business district.[344]

It thus is a mistake to characterize the overwhelming use of automobiles in terms of choices or attraction (as in a "love affair with the automobile"). It is not that the people who commute to Manhattan or to the cores of Paris or Chicago like mass transit, while their neighbors, many more of whom commute to other areas, do not and are smitten by a "love affair" with the automobile. It is that automobile-competitive mass transit is available to the core and not to elsewhere. People do not use mass transit to commute to most areas of the United States, Canada, Western Europe or Australia simply because usable service doe not exist.

Mass transit to the large cores is successful because it competes well with the automobile. It is convenient and may take the same time or even less, door to door, as traveling by car. The key to attracting people out of cars into mass transit is automobile-competitive service. Downtowns and core areas have it; other places in the urban area do not. For example, commuting by transit to major suburban Chicago locations could average more than 2.5 hours, five times the average by car.[345] More than 95 percent of trips on Toronto's commuter-rail system either start or end at downtown's Union Station. A suburban Portland commuter can access 20 times as much of the urban area by car as by mass transit in 30 minutes. Now, most trips are not to the urban core, and suburb to suburb commuting has emerged as dominant. Even in Paris, 70 percent of trips are in the suburbs, never reaching the core

The disadvantages of mass transit relative to the car are fundamental. There is not enough of it, it does not go enough places, it is too slow, it is too infrequent, and it does not serve enough hours of the day. It often requires greater exposure to unpleasant weather, from the freezing winds and snow of Chicago or Stockholm to the oppressive heat and humidity of Hong Kong or Atlanta. There are simply not enough people traveling from the same place to the same place at the same time to make widespread automobile-competitive mass-transit service feasible.

Mass transit is not sufficiently close to the origin or destination of many urban trips. Studies indicate that people will generally walk only one-quarter mile (400 meters) or less to use mass-transit service.[346] Even where there is service, most trips in an urban area would require a time-consuming transfer from one bus or train route to another. The transfer times can, by themselves, exceed the amount of time it would take to complete the trip by car.

Finally, the local bus and light-rail lines that comprise most mass-transit services operate comparatively slowly, stopping frequently or being held up in traffic. Only express bus services and rapid-rail services (metro and commuter rail) can possibly compete with the automobile in travel time and then only for a small proportion of trips. Even light-rail systems are no faster than buses, unless operated in their own protected and grade-separated right of way, though they are much more costly. In Europe, "there is now little alternative to the car for a great majority of trips," according to Gerondeau, who further notes that no credible alternative exists for 80 percent of urban automobile travel.[347]

By contrast, the automobile makes it possible to travel from any point in the urban area to any other point, at any time. Gerondeau describes the car in Western Europe as providing "unprecedented freedom," because "it can leave from anywhere and go anywhere at any moment."[348] This is a reality evident throughout the high-income world. Some people use mass transit to get to destinations other than the urban core. However, generally, it is out of necessity rather than choice. Non-downtown transit commuters have lower incomes than average and often do not have a car available for their trip. 1990 U.S. census data indicate that outside-downtown mass-transit commuters had incomes 40 percent below average, while downtown mass transit commuters had incomes near average.

Mobility for Low-Income Households. There is a perception that low-income households depend substantially on mass transit for travel in the United States. However, the 2001 National Household Travel Survey indicates that 76 percent of low-income travel is by car and less than five percent by mass transit.

Attempts to provide reverse commute service for low-income workers seeking jobs in the suburbs have been a monumental failure. Mass-transit agencies establish a few routes into the suburbs, but most jobs are not within walking distance of the transit stops. In U.S. urban areas, low-income populations tend to be disproportionately concentrated in the urban cores, well away from the areas of high job growth in the suburbs. A reverse-commute bus or rail service can provide access to only a small portion of suburban jobs: the jobs that are within walking distance (one-quarter mile) of the transit route. This will be relatively few of the jobs available in the suburbs, which in many urban areas cover more than 1,000 square miles. A U.S. Federal Transit Administration study found that only 14 percent of jobs in the high-growth suburbs of Boston were within one hour's transit ride of inner-city low-income areas.[349] Of course, reverse-commute services are beneficial to the few people able to use them, but the sum of these benefits is small in relation to the need.

In fact, it is becoming increasingly clear that providing the mobility throughout the urban area to expand low-income employment opportunities requires cars. Raphael and Stoll, at the University of California, estimate that if automobiles were available to all African American households, the gap between non-Hispanic-white and African-American unemployment would be reduced by nearly one-half.[350] A Brookings Institution report concluded: "Given the strong connection between cars and employment outcomes, auto ownership programs may be one of the more promising options and one worthy of expansion."[351]

A study by the Progressive Policy Institute, a research organization affiliated with the Democratic Leadership Council (of the Democratic Party), noted:

> In most cases, the shortest distance between a poor person and a job is along a line driven in a car. Prosperity in America has always been strongly related to mobility and poor people work hard for access to opportunities. For both the rural and inner-city poor, access means being able to reach the prosperous suburbs of our booming metropolitan economies, and mobility means having the private automobile necessary for the trip. The most important response to the policy challenge of job access for those leaving welfare is the continued and expanded use of cars by low-income workers.[352]

This reality led President Clinton to propose reforms to encourage greater automobile ownership among welfare recipients.[353]

Urban Rail and Automobile Competitiveness. There is a view that mass transit will be more automobile competitive if new rail systems are provided. In recent decades, many billions of dollars have been spent to build or expand new urban-rail systems, especially in the United States, Western Europe, and Canada. Yet, these systems have done little to attract people from cars and the mass transit market share has continued to decline.

It is not, as is so often suggested, that the systems do not go to the right places. There are no right places. Trip patterns in the 21st century are far too dispersed to take advantage of the strength of mass transit—moving large numbers one place to another at the same time. The new rail systems are costly and can only be provided in relatively small parts of the urban area.

Anyone wishing to use mass transit for all of their mobility must work downtown and live in the urban core, because it is only in the urban core where service is frequent enough to minimize transfer times. However, those wishing to take advantage of the employment, attractions, activities, and quality of life amenities available outside downtown will need a car.

The substantial investments in new urban-rail systems have not been a part of any overall plan that would provide improved mass transit throughout urban areas. The rail lines and transit improvements are simply token, not a part of a grand vision being implemented.

In response to the emptiness of mass transit platitudes, we issued an Internet challenge in 2003 for a system design that would provide automobile competitive mass transit service throughout a major urban area.[354] No serious responses have been received. This is for good reason. Any such design would be too costly, as is outlined below.

However, the ineffectiveness of the token mass-transit expansions has not dawned upon the anti-suburbanites, who tend to thrive on individual narratives that add up to nothing of overall significance. They tell stories about this or that household whose trip to downtown has been made more pleasurable by this or that billion-dollar rail line. There is no doubt that extravagant government investments provide new advantages to a small number of people. However, these limited benefits cannot be extended to people in the rest of the urban area. Government resources are limited and should be used in a way that provides corresponding benefit to all of the targeted populations. A simple test should be applied to expensive tax financed mass-transit expansions:

> What government does for one it should do for all; What government does not do for all it should do for none.[355]

Hopeless Endeavor: Making Mass Transit Automobile Competitive

The automobile makes it possible for people to go wherever they want in an urban area whenever they want. To be automobile competitive, a mass-transit system would have to provide virtually the same mobility. This means that it must provide automobile-competitive service from within walking distance of virtually every point to within walking distance of every other point in the urban area. This is a practical impossibility.

Automobile-Competitive Mass Transit: Conventional Design. It would be exceedingly expensive to provide an automobile-competitive mass-transit system throughout a modern urban area using conventional designs. No-transfer (direct) service would need to be provided from within walking distance of each point in the urban area to within walking distance of each other point. Moreover, to be automobile competitive, each of the radial systems would need to provide at least much higher service frequency than today, and the hours of service would need to be substantially expanded. With the 0.25 square mile (400 meter) walking-distance requirement, this would mean that direct service would be needed in each of four "walking distance" zones per square mile. Thus, 2,000 radial mass-transit systems would be needed in an urban area covering 500 square miles (the approximate size of Portland). Obviously, service-design efficiencies could make it possible to provide the service for less than 2,000 times present costs, but an effective service design is likely to cost much more than an urban area can afford.

Automobile-Competitive Mass Transit: Walkable Grid. Some analysts have suggested "multi-nodal" mass-transit systems that would provide a grid, or mesh, of routes throughout an urban area. However, unless this mesh provides frequent and fast service to within walking distance of every point in the urban area, automobile competitiveness cannot be achieved.[356] *Nothing less could make mass transit competitive with the automobile.*

A dense grid of routes with stations within walking distance (one-quarter mile) of every point in the urban area would probably be the least expensive way to provide comprehensive, automobile-competitive mass-transit service. For example, an automated system might be constructed, using technology similar to the Vancouver Skytrain or the Lille (France) "VAL" metro. In addition to being automated, these systems also tend to use shorter trains and provide service that is more frequent. To be automobile competitive, the grid would need to be dense enough for rapid service to be available within walking distance of virtually all points in the urban area. This would require a grid of north-south and east-west routes one-half mile apart. The grid design would require transfers on most trips.

Transfers would be made more attractive by minimizing their time. This would require frequent service, such as every minute. Transfers would occur in covered stations and it is possible that average transfer times would be less than three minutes. The frequent service and rapid transfers would be required for the system to compete with the automobile for most trips. However, such a system would still be costly, but less costly than a traditional radial design. Based upon the discussion that follows, it is estimated that in an idealized urban area with Portland's population and density, the annual capital and operating expenditures would be more than 100 percent of gross annual personal income.

Automobile-Competitive Mass Transit: Balancing Density and Cost. If automobile-competitive mass transit cannot be designed for the modern urban area, then what about redesigning the urban area so that mass transit can provide automobile-competitive service?

The work of Pushkarev, Zupan, and Cumella[357] is often cited to suggest the population densities that would be required to make mass transit effective. This is useful research, but has been stretched far beyond its applicability by anti-suburbanites. The Pushkarev et al density conclusions relate to routes that serve downtowns, which are generally the largest employment centers in an urban area, and have the highest employment densities, but which generally contain a comparatively small share of urban area employment.

As was noted above, large pre-automobile, mass-transit urban areas had population densities of 50,000 per square mile (see Chapter 3). However, even that density would be insufficient to establish automobile-competitive mass transit in most urban areas. This is because as urban areas cover more land area, it is far more difficult to provide comprehensive mass-transit service. As urban areas expand geographically, the potential number of origins and destinations increases geometrically. An urban area covering 200 square miles will have four times as many potential origins and destinations as one covering 100 square miles. Today's urban areas, with exception of Hong Kong, cover much more land area than pre-automobile urban areas.

If an urban area were to spend as much of its gross income on mass transit as the highest spending, high-income world urban area (Berlin, at 2.6 percent[358]), it is estimated that densities would have to be radically increased to provide automobile competitive service throughout. At U.S. income levels, it is estimated that this would require urban population densities of 150,000 and more per square mile—higher than Hong Kong, Manhattan, and at least 40 times the present average U.S. urban density.[359] Because of lower incomes, the Berlin spending level would require even higher population densities in Western Europe and the rest of the high-income world.[360]

Of course, the Ceaucescuan option that would bulldoze the suburbs (see Chapter 11) and force people into hyper-density urban areas is absurd. The backlash in Portland and other areas has been over density increases that are trifling. Sieverts notes that the more dense, compact city can only be reached through undemocratic processes.[361] Undemocratic processes are, thankfully, becoming more of a thing of the past around the world.

Thus, even modest increases in density, of the extent already rejected by the people of Portland, will not provide the automobile-competitive services required to attract large numbers of drivers to mass transit. In a Portland that covered 250 square miles instead of the actual 500, the share of travel by car would be little different, because automobile-competitive mass transit would still be available for only a small portion of the trips. Such a Portland would, however, have even worse traffic congestion than it has today, and air pollution would be considerably more intense.

Thus, the anti-suburban prescription of transportation choice through mass transit simply cannot be achieved. Mass transit has made virtually no serious inroads against the automobile, because it *cannot*. The rhetorical transit microvision simply does not add up to anything that can be achieved at the macro level.

This reality was clearly stated by a seemingly unlikely source, the International Union of Public Transport, the international equivalent of the U.S. mass-transit lobbying organization, the American Public Transportation Association.

> In the United States, with the exception of New York, public transport is unable to compete with the automobile: its speed is half as fast, which means that door-to-door travel times, incorporating terminal distance times, waiting and transfer times, are 3 to 4 times longer on public transport.[362]

Rutgers University professor John Pucher, who is regarded as an advocate of mass transit, and Christian Lefevre have noted, "the extremely low-density suburbs that dominate metropolitan American development are almost impossible to serve effectively with public transport."[363]

Thomas Sieverts expressed a similar theme with respect to Europe, writing, "the diffuse character of urban areas does not lend itself to a conventional economic railway or bus operating offering a frequent enough service."[364] It is vain to hope that people will abandon their cars to get on mass-transit services that are not going where they need to go, or where they are available, take twice as long.

Highways: Malign Neglect

Despite their frequent claims that travel times are too long and that traffic congestion is too severe, there are indications that at least some anti-suburbanites would prefer for things to get worse. Portland's long-term land-use plan, for example, refers to the higher intensity of traffic congestion in Los Angeles as "something" to be replicated in Portland.[365] Portland's planners are not alone. There appears to be a naïve view that if traffic congestion becomes intense enough, then drivers will switch to mass transit. It is fair to wonder what level of traffic congestion will be required for drivers to abandon their cars in favor of mass-transit services that do not go where they are going.

A San Diego *North County Times* editorial referred to such views as "faith based gridlock."[366] The fundamental problem with the "congestion will force drivers to mass transit" line of reasoning is that, for the most part, the automobile remains the quickest way to make most urban trips, even where traffic congestion is severe. Indeed, a large proportion of urban trips cannot even be made by mass transit. People are simply not going to be driven by congestion out of their cars into buses and trains that are not going where they need to go.

Exaggerating Induced Traffic Effects. Planners justify not increasing highway capacity by the theory of "induced traffic." They trot out research demonstrating that new highways quickly fill up, and they claim that it is impossible to "build out of" traffic congestion. They paint a picture of a populace that would spend their whole lives "behind the wheel" if only enough roads were built. The research reports are fraught with difficulties, such as limiting the research to the new roads and not considering the overall road system volumes or the fact that the traffic on the new roads was transferred from older roads that now have lower volumes.

In fact, in the one urban area where an induced traffic effect could have been demonstrated, the evidence is lacking. In the early 1980s, Phoenix had a severely underdeveloped freeway system compared to other major urban areas in the United States. The view of local and state officials was that they did not want to "become another Los Angeles." However, increasing traffic congestion was to convince them that there was something worse—becoming Los Angeles without freeways. As a result, Phoenix undertook construction of new freeways. Phoenix has built more miles of new urban freeways than any other major urban area in the last two decades.

Based upon the induced traffic theory, it would be expected that residents of the Phoenix area would have rushed out to drive even more, and that overall travel volumes would have increased inordinately compared to other areas. In fact, the opposite occurred. Overall travel volumes in the Phoenix area increased 20 percent per capita from 1984 to 2002. This is well below the national urban average increase of 32 percent. Perhaps even more significant, Portland, with its adopted anti-freeway policies, experienced a 52 percent per capita increase in car use over the same period.

The story is similar in Houston, which had the nation's worst traffic congestion as late as 1985. Since then, major roadway expansions have been undertaken. In fact, average roadway travel increased only 10 percent from 1984 to 2002, less than one-third the national rate and less than one-fifth the rate of Portland, with its anti-highway policies. In Western Europe, Gerondeau indicates traffic can be improved except where urban areas have not invested sufficiently in roadways.[367]

U.S. Federal Highway Administration research does, in fact, demonstrate a small increase in traffic volumes due to better roads, averaging less than 8.6 percent across the entire roadway system. However, the increase is so small that it is more than cancelled out by the higher speeds, with a 4.6 percent average reduction in vehicle hours.[368] So-called induced demand might be better labeled "pent-up demand."

Anti-Suburban Transportation Policy: More Traffic Congestion

It is hard to imagine a less responsible public policy strategy than to limit roadway expansion in urban areas where traffic volumes continue to increase. The same philosophy applied to education would limit development of new schools, in the hope that people would stop having so many children. Hospitals might declare a moratorium on building new maternity wards to reduce the birth rate.

Some anti-suburbanites suggest that mobility is an outmoded goal, and change the subject to access—having destinations and services that are close by. However, this is just another way of expressing the concept of mobility. In the modern urban area, which draws millions of people because of the opportunities it provides, the very idea that access is any different from mobility lives only in the minds of planners, who all too often believe that they can predict the needs of those for whom they presume to plan.

In fact, greater mobility, which means more travel, is associated with more, not less economic output. People who spend less time traveling to work have more time for leisure activities. They may drive to a gymnasium or to a golf course. These leisure activities create employment for other people, and economic growth. If there were less leisure time, then there would be less employment in such activities.

There is sometimes an implication that drivers make all sorts of unnecessary trips. In fact, many of the additional trips have an economic purpose that contributes toward greater employment and thereby, the reduction of poverty. People can travel to shop at many locations in the urban area. If their only choice were mass transit, there would be fewer choices and they would often be captive to close by businesses, which would be able to charge higher prices. In core cities, where more people are captive to transit service, businesses often charge higher prices than the large retailers with large parking lots in the suburbs, both in the United States or Western Europe. They do so because they can. Where there is broad automobile ownership, businesses do not dare charge high prices, because their customers can drive elsewhere to shop.

Finally, as anti-suburban policies slow highway traffic, the public pays another price. Trucks are stuck in traffic along with commuters. Longer truck travel times mean higher costs, which are passed on to consumers in product prices.

Every year, the Texas Transportation Institute issues a report estimating the amount of travel delay suffered by commuters during peak periods in the United States. In 2002, travel delay during peak periods was estimated at more than 3.5 billion hours. If it were possible to switch all commuter automobile demand to transit, the additional travel time would amount to nearly 21 billion hours—or nearly 200 hours per commuter, the equivalent of nearly five workweeks per year. The economic loss, using the standard highway cost factor, would be approximately $275 billion—an amount that rivals the gross state product of Massachusetts or North Carolina.[369] In Canada, where the average mass transit commuter spends 41 more minutes traveling to and from work daily as the average automobile commuter, the economic loss would equal the gross provincial product of New Brunswick and Prince Edward Island combined.[370]

Mass transit cannot replace the automobile, because it does not do the same thing. As a result, there is no hope for mass transit to reduce traffic congestion. This is not only demonstrably true, but it is also indicated by the fact that virtually no long-term transportation plans project reduced levels of traffic congestion as the result of mass-transit strategies. The malign neglect must stop. Vibrant, growing urban areas need improved transportation capacity. Moreover, since there is no dispute that the overwhelming amount of future travel growth will be by car, additional transportation capacity means more highway capacity.

10

The High Price of Retail Restrictions

Big-Box Stores

The anti-suburban movement is particularly concerned about the retailing evolution being driven by the large, big-box retail stores. Wal-Mart has received most of the attention, which is understandable since it has achieved the highest annual sales volume of any company in the world. However, there are many other such retailers. These include general purpose and food retailers such as U.S.—based Target and K-Mart, European-based Carrefour and Auchan, and even firms outside the high-income world, such as Gigante in Mexico and Extra in Brazil. Other retailers have built big-box stores to provide a more limited range of goods, such as Toys-R-Us, Decathlon (Europe), Home-Depot, Texas (U.K.), Bauhaus (Europe), and a number of electronics and computer outlets.

Big-box stores tend to be far more efficient than the smaller and older stores. This is the result of such factors as greater labor productivity, more efficient management practices, and substantial improvements in distribution (logistics). As a result, they are able to charge lower prices. In addition, big-box stores tend to provide a larger range of merchandise for customers to choose from, whether in the general merchandise and grocery stores or in big-box stores that confine themselves to a smaller line of products (such as electronics).

The anti-suburban movement generally opposes the proliferation of big-box stores because of their perceived impact on existing smaller businesses, especially in downtown areas. The smaller, older, often downtown stores that anti-suburbanites see as threatened are crucial to their vision of the romanticized 1900 American small town. In 1900, downtown was the core of commercial activity. What might be characterized as a "cracker barrel" conception of downtown—where people are imagined sitting around a cracker barrel and talking—seems to be at the core of the view that downtown is crucial to community. This perceived loss of community is one of the principal concerns of the anti-suburban movement (see Chapter 7).

The romanticized downtowns that mass transit created have been declining for decades. Big-box stores were still years away when department stores started closing in downtown areas and the "dime" stores closed. Smaller retailers either moved or were replaced by stores that located in the enclosed malls that developed from the mid-1950s to the present. However, still additional innovations, principally the "strip" shopping centers and the big-box stores have imperiled the malls. From an aesthetic point of view, many might consider the downtown street of a small town more pleasing than the more modern innovations. Certainly, the architectural fraternity seems in no rush to offer design awards for strip malls. However, the principal function of retailing is not architecture; it is the broadest distribution of consumer goods.

To some degree, the characteristics of a suburb-free urbanization can be seen in the retail patterns that have, until very recently, been typical of large, dense inner cities. In many U.S. central cities, shopping is little different today than it was in the 1950s, and products are often considerably more expensive than in the larger retail establishments that have developed in the suburbs and even in the small towns of the American South. Generally, the Wal-Marts and Carrefour hypermarkets and other low-cost retailers, so important to minimizing product prices, have been absent, whether in Paris, New York, or St. Louis. The principal reason for this is the high cost of land, though planning regulations can also be to blame.

There are still households whose income is insufficient to afford a comfortable life. It is thus a mistake to block retail innovations that would improve their standard of living by lowering prices. This is what the anti-suburban movement would do.

Big-Box Store Regulation

The strategy of the anti-suburbanites is to outlaw or severely restrict development of big-box stores. In the United States, some communities have imposed bans on stores above a certain size. Similar bans will be found in the United Kingdom. The French have tended to limit the number of big-box stores that can be constructed, though allow larger stores.

In the United States, decentralized land-use responsibilities make it possible for big-box stores to locate in jurisdictions with less hostile commercial environments. Thus, Wal-Mart has built a large supercenter across the state line from anti-big-box Portland, in Vancouver, Washington. In the United Kingdom, restrictions on store sizes, and thus retail efficiency, have led to some of the highest food prices in Europe.[371]

In France, big-box stores are surrounded by parking lots generally larger than in the United States, and certainly much more crowded, with traffic directed by uniformed officers. Stores are not allowed to be open on Sundays and do not have the late weekday hours typical of the United States or Canada. This concentrates demand and creates substantial local traffic congestion in the area of the big-box stores, as well as the congestion that occurs in the large parking lots. Not only do people spend more time traveling from home to the more distant stores, but also the slower stop-and-go traffic increases the intensity of automobile-produced air pollution. Even worse, for consumers, Japan's arcane retail restrictions make large store development very difficult and have made both entry and expansion difficult.

Protecting the Haves

Much of the opposition to big-box stores is rooted in attempts to protect producers. This is not unusual, as businesses with a stake in the status quo have predictably sought legislative and regulator measures to keep competitors that are more efficient out of the market. Thus, during the 1920s and 1930s, there were attempts to outlaw the new, more efficient "five and dime" stores that were replacing the smaller general merchandise stores. These attempts on the part of a less efficient industry component to stop further progress were mercifully rejected and U.S. households have paid lower product prices and experienced a better quality of life as a result.

Economic history is rife with producer-protecting regulation. The guilds of Europe restricted competition and ensured that consumers would pay more than a competitive price for their goods, because there was little genuine competition. This kept prices in the older cities above market levels. In *The Wealth and Poverty of Nations*, John Landis notes that cost-saving commercial (price reducing) advances have come not from existing industry, but from new entrants who challenged them, "inventing and impoverishing new venues for encounter and exchange."[372]

Had the anti-suburbanites been active during the 19th century, they might have come to the aid of night soil removers, a profession that was, of course, made redundant by flush toilets. Foundations might have commissioned research documenting the loss of employment that would occur if flush toilets were allowed to proliferate. Researchers could have held congressional briefings and been given broad coverage in national news weekly magazines. They might have bemoaned the loss of community, the result of fewer interpersonal contacts that occurred because the night soil remover no longer visited houses and businesses.

The price, of course, would have been paid in negative health impacts due to the less sanitary conditions.

Cost-saving innovations have been a principal factor in economic growth and improving the quality of life for all households. This progress could have been stopped at any point. The lobbying efforts of the vested retail status quo could have succeeded in enacting legislation laws by which yesterday could "say no to tomorrow." This might have been good for entrenched businesses with weak competition, but consumers would have paid much higher prices.

Efficiency improvements have been changing the nature of communities, employment, and retailing for decades. The corner grocery stores of the pre-automobile age were replaced by the thousands of larger stores, many built by the A&P[373] chain. A&P was the nation's largest grocery retailer as late as the 1950s, when newer, larger stores (supermarkets) were built by Safeway, Kroger, Giant, and others. A&P chain stood by its smaller stores and became a shadow of its former self. Moreover, it was not just a matter of size. The newer supermarkets began providing larger product offerings, such as office supplies and over the counter medicines. Each of these developments provided incumbent competitors with serious challenges.

Further, smaller businesses are able to compete with the big-box stores. They compete by being entrepreneurial and providing goods and services that the big-box stores either cannot or choose not to provide. A report by the NRF Foundation notes that innovative small retailers can compete effectively with big-box stores and provides examples from around the nation.[374]

However, there is a broader issue that is missed by laws and regulations that protect companies from more efficient producers. As Lewis indicates, stronger economies develop where market incentives are skewed toward maximizing the benefits to consumers rather than producers.[375] There is a simple reason for this. Everyone is a consumer, but not everyone is a member of a producer class powerful enough to extract protection from government.

Producer protection comes at a price, as the experience of nations that have long had such policies indicates. Land use and market regulations have severely limited the development of modern, competitive retail sectors in Germany, France, the United Kingdom, and Japan, and households pay more than necessary as a result.

It is important to understand from whom these small businesses are being protected. It is not the big-box stores or their owners. It is rather the consumers. Regulations that limit productivity and innovation make it possible for retailers to charge more than the going rate for their goods. That means that the average household's income does not stretch as far, and therefore has a somewhat lower standard of living. The protected small business owners and employees are the beneficiaries of these policies, making what amount to windfall profits, wages, and benefits, at the expense of the community.

Big-Box Stores: Democratizing Prosperity

Big-box stores save households money. It has been estimated that Wal-Mart produces savings in food costs of nine percent in the United States.[376] The reality is that anti-big-box regulations, in reverse Robin Hood fashion, take from the less affluent and give to people who are more affluent. Lower prices are an important key to a democratized prosperity.

There is less innovation and this means that the retail sector is comparatively inefficient, not able to take full advantage of economies of scale and scope that are generally available in the United States. Consumer prices are higher than they would be if there were the "competitive intensity" precluded by the planning and market regulations. The price of protection in the retail sector is lower incomes and greater poverty.

The lower prices of retail innovation, like the lower prices of suburban housing and the lower prices of automobile-based transportation, have played an important role in democratizing prosperity. It should be no different in the future.

11

Anti-Suburban Dystopia

Case Dismissed

The anti-suburbanites have failed to make their case. The imperatives they propose to justify their destructive policies do not stand up to scrutiny.

There is no shortage of land for agriculture or open space, and urbanization poses no threat. The traffic congestion they claim to be a result of suburbanization is actually moderated by it. The big-box retail stores they claim destroy local economies improve the affluence of nearly all households by stretching what they can buy with their income.

Baseless Rhetoric. The anti-suburban "house of cards" is built on rhetoric and sloganeering. Urban planners induce politicians to blather on about replacing automobile use with mass transit. Yet, the planners themselves have not even been able to contort their computer models to project such a switch. Moreover, reality is much more problematic than models. Their solution to the housing affordability crises that has been created by their own policies is more rhetoric—subsidies to low-income and middle-income households. Yet, they have produced virtually no research that attempts to estimate the overwhelming costs that would be required to make whole all of those disadvantaged by the policies.

Faulty Research. Even when they take the trouble to do serious research, fatal flaws often appear. Suburbanization is blamed for obesity by research that excludes eating as a factor. Suburbanization is portrayed as destroying economic growth when some of the fastest growing large metropolitan areas in the high-income world are among the most suburbanized. Urban expansion is blamed for threatening agricultural production despite the fact that most retired land cannot be attributed to urbanization, while production has risen substantially. Suburbanization is blamed for reducing the amount of open space, when there is more of it now than five decades ago.

Selling the Trivial as Significant. An anti-suburban e-mail list contributor expressed the fear the movement was in danger of being dismissed as innumerate and romantic. Indeed, there is innumeracy in abundance. The small is sold as large. The anti-obesity publicity campaign, masked as university research, produces insignificant weight differences between areas it characterizes and more and less sprawling, yet trumps them up as of grave importance. Numbers are bandied about as if their significance is demonstrated by the number of digits to the left of the decimal point. So an imagined "costs of sprawl" less than $0.10 per day per day per capita is piled up far enough into the future to make the total $225 billion. Ten cents a day is not a significant amount in a nation with a per capita income of nearly $100 per day (approximately $35,000 per year).

Semantic Gymnastics. Language is twisted to give the impressions that are virtually the opposite of reality. They claim that suburbanization increases traffic. However, traffic is not the same thing as traffic congestion. In fact, suburbanization decreases traffic congestion by diluting it. Suburbanization is charged with increasing air pollution, yet the intensity of air pollution—which is the principal health hazard—is greater where there is less suburbanization. They claim their strategies increase housing and transportation choice, when they do the opposite. By raising housing prices, they take the choice of home ownership away from many households. By making urban travel slower and less convenient, they retard the quality of life and reduce employment opportunity.

Juvenile Claims. The characterization of consumers as lemmings lured over the cliff by house and car advertisements is absurd, arrogant, and juvenile. No profession, whether it is physicians, painters, or urban planners, has sufficient insight to second-guess the best interests of everyone else. No amount of advertising by homebuilders or car manufacturers will induce a material number of people to buy what they do not want. Gerondeau points to an accepted notion that Europeans have an irrational attachment to their cars. He concludes that Europeans, like Americans, Australians, and Japanese use cars for very rational reasons.[377]

Comedy Central. The other-worldliness of some anti-suburban characterizations should be relegated to late night comedy. Few of the thousands of U.S. suburbs have "gone broke" in the 40 years since Peter Blake so erroneously declared it already occurring. Few of the millions who grew up in American suburbs experienced the "near tenement" conditions of Blake's delusions. Kunstler's characterization of the American suburb as "a trashy and preposterous habitat" with "no future" is absurd. David Brooks was much more accurate in referring to American suburban life as living in the "future tense."

Demonization. Like so many political movements before it, anti-suburbanism attempts to advance its agenda by demonization and questioning motives.

For example, homebuilders, automobile manufacturers, and retailers are damned for seeking profits. Yet, profits drive an economy; profits are a prerequisite for a prosperous society. This is not just about business owners. Few people place the interests of the community or their neighbors first. People tend to serve their own interests first. This includes the car manufacturer, the homebuilder, the urban planner seeking a more prestigious position, the employee seeking a raise, the mayor seeking higher office and the clergyman hoping to be posted to a larger congregation. Demonization may have its place in theology, but it has no place in public policy.

No Road Map to the Future. Perhaps most surprising of all, the anti-suburbanites provide no road map to their purportedly more ideal world. They exhibit a childlike faith that anti-suburban strategies will make urban areas better places to live. But, anti-suburban literature provides no "bridge to tomorrow," much less the "bridge to yesterday" that would be required to return to the romantic past the New Urbanists envision. There are simply platitudes, rhetoric and, ultimately, images more rooted in hallucination than possibility. The romanticized 1900 American small town was far from ideal and cannot be restored except superficially, in the facades of retro-architecture. Yet, anti-suburbanism would invite people to live in the past tense, rather than the future tense they prefer.

Do *They* Even Believe Their Own Assessments? If suburbanization is half as destructive as Kunstler and Hayden contend, then indeed, we shall not only have to "give up mass automobile use," as Kunstler contends. We shall have to move back to the city and live in high-rise apartments at a density high enough to avoid building the hundred million solar houses that would be insufficient to avert Hayden's environmental catastrophe.

As politically unacceptable as such strategies would be, the extreme characterizations of suburban ills by, for example, Kunstler and Hayden, could require no less. It is for that reason that I published an article entitled, "Ceaucescu: Father of Smart Growth,"[378] making the point that achievement of the anti-suburban agenda would require all suburban development to be bulldozed and people to be resettled in dense cities, as was attempted by the late Romanian dictator.

If present patterns of urbanization are leading to such disaster, why are their anti-suburban solutions so timid? Why does Portland seek only to increase density by one-half when 15 times or more would be necessary to return to a pre-automobile urban form? Why does the Sierra Club incessantly use the city of San Francisco as a model, when its density would need to be increased by as much as 10 times to reverse automobile-oriented suburbanization in the Bay Area? If Apocalypse threatens, this would seem no time to propose half measures. If Kunstler, Hayden, and company were right, then nothing short of Ceaucescu-like bulldozing and hyper-dense urban resettlement would do. Fortunately, such extreme characterizations could not be more remote from reality.

The answer may be political. Perhaps the anti-suburbanites are realistic enough to see that strategies draconian enough to solve their imagined ills are so politically unacceptable as to threaten the movement itself.

Failing the Test. The bottom line is that the anti-suburban diagnosis does not add up. Patrick Troy characterized the policies of anti-suburbanism as "ill-informed" and having been presented in a "disingenuous way."[379] Amen.

Towards Dystopia

The anti-suburban movement is an attack on modern lifestyles. The threat comes from the policies proposed to right imagined wrongs. Anti-suburban policies will lead to a lower standard of living. The promise is not utopian; it is rather the opposite, dystopian.

In the anti-suburban dystopia, households would be less affluent, with millions driven out of the home ownership market and thereby out of the mainstream of economic life. Dystopia promises commuters longer travel times to fewer jobs, because traffic congestion would be so much worse. The slower traffic would intensify dystopia's air pollution, with negative health impacts. Dystopia's shoppers would pay more to shop, and their income would not go as far.

Perhaps the greatest irony is that continuation and expansion of anti-suburban policies could lead to environmental degradation. Rich economies are the cleanest. Less affluent societies would mean less environmental protection. If one thing is clear, it is that environmental protection is a product of economic growth and affluence. Environmental protection takes a back seat to more basic human needs, as the experience of the former communist world indicates.

Dystopian Economy. Dystopia's economic self-immolation could not come at a worse time. The high-income world nations face unprecedented economic challenges that require greater economic growth, not less. Government pension programs and other social welfare programs are nearly bankrupt in some nations, including in the United States. Slower economic growth would also mean slower technical progress, in crucial areas like medical research.

By no means can the results of anti-suburbanism—reduced housing affordability, lower home ownership rates, lower rates of wealth creation, greater traffic congestion, and higher product prices—mean a better life. It is not necessary for the future residents of Toronto, Sydney, or Brisbane to be huddled in the crowded, polluted, gridlocked confines of an arbitrary urban growth boundary, while all around them are vast expanses of land that could be developed to improve their quality of life, with virtually no material environmental impact.

What If There Had Been No Suburbanization?

In view of the negative effects promised by anti-suburban policies, it is appropriate to ask what life might be like if there had been no automobile-oriented suburbanization.

Suburbanization occurred principally because of consumer preferences—the operation of the market. In some cases, the results of those preferences were distorted by planning regulations, such as in the suburbs of Boston or the exurban areas outside London's greenbelt. However, whether in relatively unhampered markets or not, nearly all new development occurred on or near the fringe of urban areas. To keep this from happening would have required planning prohibitions even stronger than the heavy-handed policies in Sydney or pre-voter-revolt Portland. Greenfield development would have to have been prohibited.

Home Ownership. Before the start of World War II, home ownership was generally much lower in high-income nations than it is today. If the suburbs had not been permitted to develop, households seeking home ownership would have had to look in urban cores, where home ownership is far lower than in the suburbs (see Chapter 12). This would have rarified urban-core housing markets, leading to even higher prices. Home ownership rates would doubtfully have been much lower, and households less prosperous, being denied the wealth that they would have accumulated from buying a house rather than paying rent.

The larger number of renters would likely have paid a price as well. The higher property prices would have driven up the cost of rent. It is likely that more households would need housing subsidies, but with less in financial resources, such programs would have been even less effective than today.

Of course, in such a less affluent society, not only would there be more households in poverty, but there would have been far less opportunity for minorities and immigrants. In short, prosperity would have been less democratized.

Mobility. The story in mobility would have been little different. Car ownership would have remained beyond the means of many. The limited space for garaging cars in the dense urban area would raise the expense of ownership beyond today's levels. More people would be captive to mass transit, which cannot provide the comprehensive mobility throughout an urban area that the automobile affords.

The longer travel times and inconvenience of mass transit could have kept many women from joining the workforce. Mass transit simply cannot provide the convenient mobility necessary to deliver children to schools or day care centers. It is likely that many women who did enter the work force would have diminished career prospects because of transportation difficulties. It is likely that economic growth would have been less with fewer women with fewer good jobs. The situation for lower-income minorities would be even more difficult.

Traffic congestion would be worse. There would have been fewer automobiles, but they would be in operation many more hours, traveling slower, stopping more frequently in traffic, and emitting more pollution.

Infrastructure costs would have been higher as the already-overcrowded rail-transit systems in dense cores such as New York, London, Paris, and Tokyo would have required hugely expensive expansions far beyond anything ever seriously proposed. Water and sewer systems would have required extensive rebuilding in the most expensive of environments, to handle the additional demand.

Consumer prices would be higher, because the retail innovations that have occurred where land is cheap would have been precluded. Moreover, without broad automobile ownership, people would be captive to nearby retail outlets that would have the freedom from competition to charge higher prices.

As noted above (see Chapter 2), much of today's high-income world lived near or below present U.S. poverty levels at the start of World War II. Since that time, there has been an unprecedented expansion of income and widely dispersed prosperity. At the same time, there has been unprecedented expansion of automobile ownership and automobile-oriented suburban development. This has brought greater mobility and greater household wealth through home ownership. It seems unlikely that this prosperity would have been achieved without the underlying urban form of suburbanization.

Paying for Dystopia

Anti-suburbanism is already exacting a significant price in Portland, Sydney, London, San Diego, San Francisco, Christchurch, and elsewhere. Very real difficulties are being experienced by households that are being denied the opportunity to own their own homes and join the economic mainstream.

Not surprisingly, research is already indicating that anti-suburban land-use regulations are leading to lower levels of economic growth. A paper by Raven Saks of the Federal Reserve Board concluded, "metropolitan areas with stringent development regulations generate less employment growth than expected given their industrial bases"[380]

There is already evidence of migration from and slower growth in the highly restricted markets where housing affordability has substantially declined (see Chapter 8).

As is usual, losses in income will trickle down to people with lower incomes, who will find their housing choices and mobility more restricted, along with a less prosperous economy incapable of providing the subsidy assistance they would not need if anti-suburbanism's destructive policies had not been implemented. Anti-suburbanism is a matter of values. To the anti-suburbanite, a tidy urban area seems more important than one in which there is broad prosperity. The dreams of the anti-suburbanites can be achieved only by imposing the lowering of the standard of living for middle-and lower-income households. According to Lewis, "These measures distort markets severely and limit overall productivity growth, slow overall economic growth, and cause unemployment."[381]

There is an imperative for more, not less, economic growth in the future. There remains some prosperity to be democratized, even in the high-income world. Households still living in poverty will remain there unless further economic growth is allowed to produce the necessary opportunities. If economic growth should not be maintained, there will be less opportunity for lower-income households, and, indeed, their ranks are likely to increase, as lower-middle-income households see their quality of life decline. Prosperity needs to be expanded, not contracted.

Anti-Suburban Policy: The "Fatal Conceit" Revisited

Present urban planning suffers from the "fatal conceit" that Nobel Laureate Frederik Hayek identified in the now deceased Soviet Union—the belief that planners can reliably shape the world according to their wishes. Of course, the planners failed because the array of choices that constitute an economy cannot be foreseen or directed by even the most intelligent or perceptive. Similarly, the combinations of choices that people make in their lives, transport, and shopping are beyond the knowledge, much less the manipulation, of the planning elite.

Ceaucescu's urban planning bulldozed central Bucharest in the name of the people. U.S. urban planners used urban renewal to bulldoze low-income housing in the name of community. Those driven from their houses under the guise of democratic processes were no less victimized than those driven out by the dictator.

Because of their economic impacts, present trends in urban planning policy will lead to less obvious, but potentially more destructive, results, which will preclude households from owning their own homes and deny their participation in the mainstream of the economy. Anti-suburban policies are already transferring wealth and income from those with less to those with more. Now, throughout the high-income world, the policy bulldozers of the planners are poised to take the future away from millions of middle-income households.

PART IV
Sustainable Future Tense

12

The Universal Dream

Democratizing Prosperity

There is no reason for any other nation to turn its back on the economic prosperity and quality of life that has been associated with suburbanization. The dark picture painted by the anti-suburban movement resembles a negative of reality.

The high-income world, starting with the United States, enjoys unparalleled prosperity, which is experienced by nearly all households. The tale of woe is largely contained inside anti-suburbanite minds.

By most measures, the quality of life in the United States and the rest of the high-income world is better than it has ever been before. For example, in the United States:

- Home ownership is at record levels. From 1890 to World War II, less than 50 percent of U.S. households owned their own homes. On the eve of World War II, in 1950, the homeownership rate was 44 percent. Today the rate is just under 70 percent. African American and Hispanic home ownership are also at record high rates.

- Housing is less crowded than before. In 1950, the Census Bureau considered nearly 16 percent of households to be living in overcrowded conditions (more than one person per room). By 2000, the number had dropped to under six percent.

- Substantial progress has been made in reducing poverty. Since 1959[382] the nation has added more than 100 million new residents, yet the number of people living below the poverty line has dropped more than 3.5 million.

- The nation's housing is far more sanitary. In 1950, 35 percent of houses did not have complete indoor plumbing. By 1990, the figure had dropped to one percent.

- Communications have been greatly improved. In 1960, more than 20 percent of homes did not have a telephone. By 2000, telephones were in all but 2.5 percent of homes. This does not include the millions of mobile telephones—more than one for every two persons in the nation.

- People have far greater mobility than ever before. The car has made people able to travel quickly, conveniently, and inexpensively throughout the urban area. In 1950, 40 percent of households did not have cars. By 2000, the figure had dropped to 10 percent.

- Women have advanced into the mainstream of economic life. Women had to rely on men drivers to a substantial extent during the early 1950s, but no more. Today, women have achieved the independence that allows them to drive nearly as much as men. Without this mobility, it is inconceivable those women could have become such a large part of the workforce or that their contributions to the economy could have been as great.

- Air quality is substantially improved. As late as 1950, nearly one-half of the nation's houses were heated by highly polluting coal and wood. By 2000, this figure had dropped to less than two percent. Further, air pollution has been reduced despite a large increase in driving (see Chapter 6).

- Census data indicate that the average size of a new house has increased by a quarter since the early 1970s. With falling household sizes, this means that the space per person has increased 300 square feet (approximately 30 square meters), more than 60 percent. The New Urbanist architects Duany, Plater-Zyberk, and Speck concede "no other society approaches the United States in terms of the number of square feet per person, the number of baths per person, the number of appliances in the kitchen, the quality of the climate control, and the convenience of the garage."[383]

- All of this has occurred at the same time that the nation has remained a beacon of opportunity for immigrants. Since 1959, the nation has taken in more than 30 million immigrants, both legal and illegal. Many of these arrived with virtually no assets.[384]

- Immigrants have made rapid economic progress. In metropolitan areas, citizen immigrants have achieved nearly the same home ownership rates as citizens born in the United States.[385]

People work less time to pay for their goods and services. In *Myths of Rich and Poor,* Cox and Alm provide a number of estimates, including:[386]

- The price of a half-gallon of milk is earned in less than one-half the time at work as in 1950.

- The cost of a long coast-to-coast distance telephone call is earned in 98 percent less work time as in 1950.

- The cost of a kilowatt of electricity is earned in two-thirds less work time than in 1950.

- A three-pound chicken requires one-seventh the work time as in 1950.

- An hour of air travel requires 75 percent less work time than in 1950.

Earlier, Cox and Alm showed substantial reductions in the work-related costs of other products over the previous 40 years.[387] Home air conditioners require almost 90 percent less in labor time, refrigerators require 80 percent less, cars require 20 percent less, and new houses require 15 percent less labor time.

Of course, many products are in widespread use today that simply did not exist in 1950, such as home computers, video recorders, and microwave ovens. This is not to mention the substantial medical advances that could not have been afforded in a less prosperous economy.

The modern consumer has access to businesses and services that could only exist in a rich society, such as the exercise salons, dog bakeries, or other new business lines created by unparalleled affluence in pre—World War II America or the rest of the high-income world. Nor will many such businesses be found in middle-and low-income nations even today. These new ventures not only expanded consumer choice, but also employment opportunity. If all of this describes an economy in economic decline, then perhaps the sun will soon be observed rising in the west.

Poverty and Income Distribution. There has been a preoccupation in some circles about income distribution in the United States over the past 30 years. A number of reports have supported a "politics of envy" interpretation in which it is claimed that the "rich keep getting richer" and the "poor keep getting poorer." That is at least one-half true. The rich have become richer. However, the poor have made economic progress as well. From 1971 to 2001, the average income of least affluent quintile (20 percent) of households rose 26 percent (inflation adjusted).[388]

Progress has been so substantial that a report by the Swedish Research Institute of Trade found U.S. African American incomes comparable to the overall

Swedish incomes (average Swedish income is approximately the same as the Western European average).[389]

At the same time, annual compensation (wages and employer-paid benefits) per employee has increased. Data from the U.S. Department of Labor Bureau of Labor Statistics indicate that from 1971 to 2001, total compensation per full-time equivalent employee rose 22 percent—more than $7,500. This increase alone equals or exceeds the per capita income of most nations. Moreover, average hours worked declined, meaning that average compensation per work hour increased even more.[390]

It is thus true that the more affluent have gained more than the less affluent. However, the principal point is that all, including the poor, have gained. There is often a tendency to think of poverty in relative terms, such as the income of the lowest-income quintile compared to the highest. However, this is a mistake. If, for example, poverty is defined as having an income in the bottom 10 percent, the poverty can never be eradicated. Relative poverty indicators are as inappropriate as they are rooted in envy. What is important is not how much low-income households have in relation to rich households; it is whether they have enough to live a comfortable life.

Thus, for example, the United States defines poverty in terms of a standard of living, not in terms of envy. It would, of course, be desirable for all households to prosper to the same extent as the most affluent. However, despite considerable attempts under socialist, mixed, and free market economies, income equality has not been achieved.

No economic system has yet been identified that can substantially reduce income inequality without reducing even more the income of the lowest-income households. That is why policies that improve the absolute incomes of low-income households are preferable to envy-based relative measures. Joseph Schumpeter expressed the purpose of a free market economic system with respect to income distribution not in "providing more silk stockings for queens, but in bringing them within the reach of factory girls in return for steadily decreasing amounts of effort"[391]

High-income nations have different policies that seek to improve incomes among the least affluent. Western European nations tend to have larger social welfare systems and higher rates of long-term unemployment, which they accept in return for less economic growth and affluence. In the United States, the policy priority is employment and economic growth. Most people live well both in Western Europe and the United States. Further, low-income households in the United States and Western Europe live better than average households in most middle-income and virtually all low-income nations. The most reliable road to greater affluence for all, including low-income households, is strong economic growth.

Moreover, Harvard's Benjamin Friedman suggests in a recent book that economic growth is more than desirable, but also necessary for longer-term social cohesion.[392]

Suburbanization and Prosperity

Whether the modern pattern of urban development is called urban sprawl or suburbanization, it has been undeniably associated with unparalleled affluence and the democratization of prosperity.

This has led to home ownership increases in many countries. In the United States, homeownership was approximately 48 percent in 1890, a figure that hardly changed before the losses that occurred in the 1930s. By 2000, home ownership was approaching 70 percent. The story was similar in other high-income world nations. More households were able to own homes and build up equity.

Land was developed on the urban fringe for housing because it was less expensive, which lowered housing prices. Mel Weber, of the University of California, notes the relationship between lower-density suburban development and lower costs: "Persons and forms within a given urban settlement have long been adapting to the costs of density and congestion by moving to the outskirts of town."[393] As a result, home ownership rates tend to rise as the distance from the core increases.[394] For example:

- In the United States, core home ownership is 75 percent in the outer suburbs, and 49 percent in the cores of metropolitan areas with more than 1,000,000 population.[395]

- In Paris, outer suburban home-ownership is 54 percent, compared to 30 percent in the ville de Paris.[396]

- In the Tokyo-Yokohama area, outer suburban home ownership is 70 percent, while it is 41 percent in the core.[397]

- In the Toronto area, outer suburban home ownership is 80 percent, compared to 43 percent in the core.[398]

Automobile availability has increased substantially, travel speeds and travel times have been reduced, and people are able to inexpensively reach employment and shopping locations throughout urban areas. At the same time, a greater array of products has been brought within reach of all households due to strong retail competition.

The connection between suburbanization and prosperity is nothing new. As early as 1776, Adam Smith noted that to obtain quality workmanship, it was necessary to avoid the core city guilds and go to the suburbs.[399] In fact, it was in new towns and suburbs that much of the new wealth was created during (and since) the Industrial Revolution.

The Future: Land-Use Policy

Generally, there is no shortage of land for development adjacent to or nearby most of the high-income world's major urban areas. Even after preserving environmentally sensitive lands, plenty of land remains for future generations to build their houses, new businesses, and recreation facilities. For the most part, the land shortages that have reduced housing affordability are contrived, the result of urban-planning policies (see Chapter 8).

There is an ample supply of land for urban development to expand in the United States without materially reducing the amount of land available for agriculture or open space. The United States is one of the fastest growing high-income nations. From 2000 to 2030, it is projected that the population will increase approximately 80,000,000, an approximately 29 percent increase. If past trends continue, nearly all of the growth will be in urban areas. If the new urban growth continues at the densities of new development experienced in the 1990s, the total share of land covered by urbanization would increase from the present 2.6 percent to 3.5 percent in 2030. More than 96 percent of the land would still be rural—principally agricultural or open space. The overall human footprint would still be far smaller than it was in 1950, because the reduction in agricultural land due to improved productivity would remain far greater than the new urbanization. Yet, this small increase in urban land would house, in greater affluence, a population larger than that of France and the Netherlands combined. There is no reason why future generations should not share in the American Dream, and live better than people today. The same is true in the rest of the world.

Where governments allow people to buy the housing they want, where they want it, it will continue to be built for affordable prices. This can be accomplished while preserving environmentally sensitive lands. The continuing housing affordability of fast growing urban areas, including Atlanta, Dallas-Fort Worth, Houston, and others demonstrates that builders have no difficulty in supplying sufficient housing a strong market where permitted, because their governments have not adopted the land-use regulations of Portland, Sydney, or London that are so destructive to housing affordability.

In fact, the future tense of home ownership, shared by households around the world, is sustainable, if the anti-suburban policies rooted in the past tense are rejected.

The Future: Transportation Policy

Transportation can be improved in the urban area of the future. The first requirement is to accept the fact that the automobile and the truck are here to stay. Jane Holz Kay could not be more wrong in her characterization of the automobile as a source of poverty. Where there are cars in economies structured to serve consumers first, there is affluence, pure and simple. The democratization of mobility is crucial to the democratization of prosperity. Moreover, the car defines mobility.

With the automobile, virtually all of the urban area can be reached, and comparatively inexpensively. People can shop for the lowest prices and accept the best jobs. Indeed, the automobile is the most effective mass-transit system ever developed. It moves more people, it moves them quicker, it takes them to more places, and it is available virtually all of the time. The automobile's success is due to the fact that it effectively meets the needs and wants of people. In the modern urban area, mobility and the automobile are inseparable.

Future advances may improve upon the automobile or make it obsolete. However, these advances will not reduce mobility, force people to travel in groups, slow their travel times, or make it inconvenient to travel much of the day. That is why mass transit, though important in its comparatively small market niches, is not the future, but rather the past.

Urban areas can be designed to accommodate the automobile. The 1960s designers of Milton Keynes, the new town northwest of London, accommodated perhaps the highest automobile-oriented population densities in the world, by providing a high-capacity grid-based arterial street system. Traffic congestion has been held relatively in check.[400] Yet, the Milton Keynes urban area is nearly 20 percent more dense than Los Angeles (8,400 persons per square mile). Perhaps it is possible to expand urban areas of up to 10,000 per square mile densities and, with skillful design and sufficient capacity, keep traffic congestion from becoming severe.

However, for the social engineers who delude themselves into believing that densification can be used to force people out of their cars, a dose of reality is required. As was noted above, affordable mass transit that provides the automobile-competitive service required to attract people out of their cars would require population densities of between 100,000 to 150,000 per square mile or more, depending on the size of the urban area and the relative affluence. There is a vast no-man's land between densities of 10,000 and at least 100,000 per square mile. Within this area, sufficient roadway space cannot be reasonably provided to keep the traffic moving, and there is not a sufficient critical mass for an automobile-competitive transit system that can be afforded. Among high-income world urban areas, only Hong Kong approaches the necessary density. The required transit-oriented densities are simply beyond practical achievement. As Sieverts notes, higher densities are not achicvable.[401] Suburban households in Sydney, Paris, Los Angeles, or Portland will not stand by while governments force 50 additional people to crowd into their space.

In some higher-density U.S. urban areas, comparatively favorable traffic congestion conditions were maintained well into the 1980s. Even in Los Angeles, the most congested U.S. urban area, traffic congestion was less intense in 1982 than any urban area with more than 3,000,000 population today.

However, traffic congestion has worsened significantly since the early 1980s. This has principally occurred because roadway capacity has not been allowed to expand with growing traffic volumes, partially due to the doctrines of urban planning. Until the early 1980s, roadways were generally expanded consistent with demand. This is no longer the case, and for no reason.

As late as 1985, Houston had the worst traffic congestion in the United States. Efforts were undertaken, particularly under Texas Department of Transportation chairman and then mayor Robert Lanier, to expand urban roadway capacity, both freeways and non-freeway arterials. Houston's experience has demonstrated that sufficient capacity can be built to serve the demand. By 1993, traffic-congestion-related delays had declined 40 percent. In more recent years, the Lanier policies have not been continued, but traffic congestion remains below the 1986 peak and similar to far smaller Portland (which had less than one-fifth Houston's traffic intensity in 1986).

The reality is beginning to dawn in a number of places. The Labour government in the United Kingdom, after having pursued anti-automobile policies initiatives by the previous Conservative government has come to announce that its role in transportation is facilitation of mobility, not to reduce their travel. Secretary of State for Transport Alistair Darling told the House of Commons, "Our job is to help people travel, not to stop them."[402]

Solving the traffic-congestion problem requires resolute action. The starting point is to establish traffic-congestion objectives and to allocate scarce funding to the most effective projects so that the objectives can be achieved.

Texas provides an example. If current trends are allowed to continue, traffic congestion can be expected to worsen considerably, which will have serious negative economic impacts. Unlike some urban areas in the nation, the political leadership in Texas has recognized that the mass-transit-favoring rhetoric of planners does not translate into reality, even on the projection pages of regional plans.

The Governor's Business Council report[403] provided Governor Rick Perry with a plan that would establish long-term goals to reduce traffic congestion. The governor was quick to instruct the State Department of Transportation to proceed with the Texas Metropolitan Mobility Plan (TMMP), and regional planning agencies are in the process of developing plans and adopting objectives in Dallas-Fort Worth, Houston, San Antonio, Austin, and smaller urban areas. It is expected that the finally adopted objectives will be in a range of from a 15 to 25 percent maximum-peak-hour delay.[404] One of the methods proposed for project evaluation standard is the cost per reduced delay hour. Application of this standard would generally ensure that expenditures are best used, improving the chances of achieving the traffic congestion reduction objective. It would be best for such standards to be applied to mass-transit projects and highway projects alike, so that the greatest improvement could be achieved. However, this would be opposed by mass-transit interests, whose share of receipts from the public purse exceed by many times their contribution to urban mobility.

The Texas urban areas, which are already among the world's most competitive housing markets, can be expected to improve their competitiveness in transportation as this program is implemented and other urban areas follow the Portland model that aims for exactly the opposite, more traffic congestion.

In 2005, Atlanta followed the lead of Texas, adopting goals to reduce traffic congestion, at the direction of Governor Sonny Perdue.[405]

As in the case of land use, the future tense of transportation is sustainable. There is no reason to turn back the clock.

The Future: Retailing

Innovation in retailing, if it is allowed, will continue and consumers will pay still lower prices. Like the corner grocery stores, and the Woolworth's, Kresge's and Sears' that preceded them, Wal-Mart and other big-box chains will face stiff competition in the future. Big-box stores may survive for decades or may find themselves threatened by new retail innovations. However, whether there is a Woolworth, Sears, Wal-Mart, Target, LeRoy Merlin, or Circuit City in the future is not of concern to public policy. The issue is to serve consumers with the lowest possible prices, which requires the competitive intensity and innovation cited by Lewis.

Urban Areas of Opportunity (Urban Areas of Refuge)

In 2000, I was invited to debate Congressman Blumenauer on land use and transportation at the annual "Railvolution" conference in San Francisco. Late in the debate, the Congressman challenged me to name a metropolitan area whose planning really excited me. I was taken aback. I answered the question in an analytical and not terribly effective manner, not with the succinct response that might have jarred the polite audience, most of which favored the Congressman's position. Later that afternoon, the answer struck me, albeit too late—"Kansas City, which if it were on the west coast, we would call San Francisco."

Kansas City. Kansas City is both an urban area of opportunity and an "urban area of refuge."[406] It is an area of opportunity for middle households seeking the best quality of life for their money. It is an urban area of opportunity for businesses seeking the low-cost environments that are crucial to competitiveness. It is not surprising that research is beginning to indicate that overly restrictive land-use regulation stunts economic growth.

However, it is also an urban area of refuge. Here, laws and regulations do not stand in the way of broad home ownership, effective mobility throughout the area, and low product prices. This creates greater opportunities for households to enjoy a higher quality of life and achieve greater affluence.

What makes Kansas City the San Francisco of the American Midwest is its central city monuments and public buildings that clearly indicate the historic leadership of Kansas City believed that their city was every bit as important as San Francisco. Kansas City has not become as important as San Francisco, at least partly because its location was less fortunate with respect to weather and the demographic migrations that would take place in the second half of the 20th century.

Urban planning works well in Kansas City. Housing is affordable, travel times are superior, and there is little traffic congestion. This success is not because the anti-suburban disease is absent among local urban planners. It is rather that the political structure is such that the planners have little opportunity to intrude into areas that are not their business. The urban area stretches across the state line, so that it encompasses not only the historic cores of Kansas City, Missouri, but also those of smaller Kansas City, Kansas, and extensive suburbs in both states. In Kansas City,[407] urban planning is largely the amalgam of households' plans, as people are generally left alone to do as they like.

Like virtually all urban areas, Kansas City has long since expanded beyond the early 20th century core, which is in the state of Missouri. Some of the suburbs are in Missouri and others are in the adjacent state of Kansas. Kansas City is a metropolitan area of opportunity largely because it has avoided the types of densification strategies that have taken the hope of home ownership away from perhaps millions of households from Portland to Sydney and London. Further, the metropolitan area has large, efficient retailers who serve consumer interests by the lowest prices competition can currently produce. Finally, Kansas City has one of the world's best urban transportation systems. There is a high quality, high capacity, near-grid freeway system, which provides access throughout the urban area. Mass transit's market share, rounded to the nearest percentage point, is zero.

Just as important, an effective grid of major arterial streets serves the area, so that when there are difficulties on the freeways, drivers can find acceptable alternate routes. Like so many other historic U.S. core cities, there is substantial new residential and mixed-use development in the core.

There are other urban areas of opportunity and urban areas of refuge. Among the largest urban areas in the high-income world, at least four stand out as potential urban areas of refuge, Houston, Dallas-Fort Worth, Atlanta, and Montreal.

Houston. Houston may be the metropolitan area of greatest opportunity, because its land-use policies have the least restrictions. The core city of Houston, with a larger population than any U.S. city other than New York, Los Angeles, or Chicago, has no government-imposed zoning. This has a competitive effect on suburban areas, and perhaps even on other close by metropolitan areas, especially Dallas-Fort Worth. Houston, as was noted above, is the fourth fastest growing large urban area in the high-income world, yet continues to have superior housing affordability. At the same time, retailers are free to build in Houston. And, to complete its high rating, the statewide Texas Metropolitan Mobility Program will make Houston, like Dallas-Fort Worth and other metropolitan areas in the state, even more competitive in the decades to come. Already, the area has an effective freeway system that has been expanded to accommodate new demand, and this is complemented by a strong arterial grid system that has also seen significant improvements.

Dallas-Fort Worth. Dallas-Fort Worth mirrors Houston's advantages, except for the lack of government-imposed zoning. Housing affordability is superior, despite the high housing demand in this, the third fastest growing major urban area in the high-income world. Dallas-Fort Worth has an effective freeway system, with major grid elements. A strong grid of high-capacity-surface arterial streets supports this system. These systems will be expanded to reduce traffic congestion under the Texas Metropolitan Mobility Program. Dallas-Fort Worth starts with the advantage of having the least intense traffic congestion of any U.S. urban area with a population of more than 3,000,000. In addition, for the most part, retailers are allowed to build the facilities that they need to sell their goods at the competitive prices that do so much to improve the living standards of all, and particularly low-income households.

Atlanta. For some years, travel agents have done a "land office" business in arranging trips for fawning public officials and business leaders to see, first hand, the Potemkin Village that Portland has created. The first class cabins of Portland flight have often been occupied by business leaders from Atlanta. However, the wrong people have been visiting the wrong urban area. What is it that Atlanta can learn from Portland, which has managed, through its anti-suburban policies to dreadfully worsen traffic congestion and destroy housing affordability? Would the large African American population that is buying homes in suburban Atlanta be better off if housing prices were to escalate and they were forced to continue renting (as would be the case based upon the Portland experience)? It is inappropriate to pursue policies that negate the decades-long effort to reduce the income gap between African Americans and non-Hispanic whites. Would it be better if Atlanta's residents had to travel across a state line to shop at a Wal-Mart Supercenter to get the best prices? Of course not. For the most part, few urban areas have been as successful as Atlanta. Portland does not even come close.

Atlanta's most pressing problem may be its transportation system. Atlanta has built more new Metro than any urban area in the United States outside the Washington, DC, area and has been among the top 10 in metro construction in the world over the past quarter century. Of course, this made little or no difference, because all of these expensive miles provide automobile-competitive mass-transit service to little more than downtown. However, Atlanta's extravagant spending on urban rail is "neither here nor there," because such a small share of travel is on mass transit. Atlanta's problem is an inferior roadway system.

Atlanta's freeway system has not been designed to serve the entire urban area, and there is virtually no major arterial street grid, which means drivers have no reasonable alternatives when there are difficulties on the freeway system. Among the thirty largest urban areas in the high-income world, Atlanta ranks 26th in its density of freeways, and last among large U.S. urban areas.[408] Fortunately, regional authorities have recently adopted a plan to develop an arterial grid, something I proposed in 2000.[409] Atlanta will need to act resolutely to improve its roadway system, or it could see future growth diverted to the other urban areas of the American South that have thus far been bypassed by spectacular growth.

Montreal. In some respects, Montreal contains elements that could position it as an urban area of opportunity. The most important advantage is its highway system. Montreal has the most dense freeway system in North America, ranking sixth out of the top 30 metropolitan areas in the high-income world.[410] Montreal's freeway density is a full one-third greater than that of Los Angeles, which has the most dense freeway system in the United States. The Montreal freeway system extends well into the suburbs and exurbs and there is plenty of attractive land that could be developed for new housing and businesses. Just as importantly, the Quebec government is expanding many of the existing freeways and building new routes. If Montreal can remain immune from the destructive land-use policies now being implemented in neighboring Ontario, some of the area's decades-long competitive loss could be restored. The language barrier could be a deterrent, but if Montreal's cost advantages become greater, growth could well increase. Montreal's improved prospects for competitiveness are analyzed further in our report for the Economic Institute of Montreal.[411]

Smaller Metropolitan Areas: There are a number of smaller metropolitan areas that could be added to the urban areas of refuge list. Most of them are in the United States. With 50 states, instead of Australia's six or even Canada's 10 provinces, the chances of a public policy fad sweeping them, as has occurred with urban consolidation in Australia, is less remote. Kansas City has already been mentioned. The most promising additional urban areas of refuge would include Cincinnati, Columbus, Grand Rapids, Greensboro, Greenville-Spartanburg, Indianapolis, Oklahoma City, San Antonio, Tulsa, and Virginia Beach (Norfolk). Other, still smaller areas could well begin to grow by capturing growth being driven away from the metropolitan areas with policies that destroy housing affordability and malignly neglect the transportation improvements needed to forestall intense traffic congestion.

Other Metropolitan Areas. Metropolitan areas in emerging nations have a substantial opportunity. If they can afford the temptation to impose restrictive land-use policies, greater economic growth can be expected because of the greater mobility, economic growth, and wealth creation associated with lower-density development. For example, metropolitan areas in the Eastern European nations added to the European Union in the last enlargement are likely to experience faster economic growth and greater competitiveness if they allow land and retail markets to operate and facilitate greater mobility. Similar prosperity can be expected in other rapidly emerging urban areas, such as in China, or Cairo, which has surprisingly wise urban planning policies.[412]

"Virtual" Urban Areas. But people are in the process of developing their own urban areas. The concept of core-city-based metropolitan areas may be nearing obsolescence. Labor markets are no longer constrained by the boundaries of municipalities, states, or provinces. Thomas Sieverts sees an urban network structure (which he calls the "zwischenstadt") developing that "enables inhabitants with a car to compose their personal metropolis *à la carte* in the form of highly specialized islands of activity."[413] James Heartfield seems to suggest that this has already occurred, noting, "Today there is no London, as such," further suggesting that there has been an "end of the boundary" between urban and rural areas.[414]

Urbanization might better be understood in terms of the individual household and the area that can be reached in a particular period of time rather than in terms of a downtown core owing its importance to little more than history. A world of variety in people yields variety in mobility desires. For some, the virtual urban area may extend just a few blocks or a few miles, and be only a small part of the metropolitan area. For others, the virtual urban area may be literally thousands of square miles, with travel to work or other locations many miles away. There is no reason why it should not be so.

An Urban Planning Reformation

Assemblyman Ray Haynes of California once told me that the urban areas of that state actually worked much better before there was a state requirement for comprehensive urban planning. Until the 1970s, California built the roadways that were required, following a blueprint that was the vision of Governor Edmund G. (Pat) Brown,[415] who served from 1957 to 1965, Since comprehensive planning was adopted, traffic congestion has become much worse, and housing is much less affordable. Before comprehensive planning, the state experienced its greatest growth, approximately 100 percent from 1950 to 1975, yet was more successful in handling its problems. From 1975 to 2000, growth was barely 50 percent, yet traffic has gotten much worse and housing affordability has plummeted.

It is legitimate to ask whether urban planning should follow the "command and control" model currently in vogue. People tend to make their own plans and do what they prefer to do. Planners may well tell people where they cannot live or where they cannot work. However, democratic governments cannot tell people where they *must* live or work. Where the plans of government are not in sufficient accord with the preferences of people, distortions occur. In some cases, they are minor, such as the "under the table" household improvements contracted for by Canadians seeking to avoid payment of the Goods and Services Tax (GST). In other cases, they can be very destructive, such as such as urban-planning-accelerated blockbusting that destroyed wealth and neighborhoods and made the transition to racial equality so much more difficult in the United States. Peter Gordon rightly points out that "preferences trump policies," which is why, in the final analysis, even dictatorships have to be concerned about public opinion.

Urban planning was not always as it is today. Pre-urban-renewal planners seemed content to facilitate the growth that they expected and the travel patterns that would be preferred by the growing community. There was a time that planners lived in the future tense. Many 19th century maps of U.S. cities show future street networks laid out well beyond the actual area of urbanization. There are the exemplary grid arterial systems that exist in so many large urban areas, such as Los Angeles, Phoenix, Chicago, Milton Keynes, and elsewhere. Highway planners sought to develop high-capacity freeways to move people from wherever they started in the urban area to wherever they were going. The freeway planners of 1940s Los Angeles appear to have been better prepared to meet the travel patterns of the early 21st century than their contemporaries. Had their plans been fully implemented, traffic conditions in Los Angeles would be far better than they are today.

Sieverts objects to the popular view that urban areas are not planned unless the job is done by urban planners. Rather, the modern urban area is the amalgamation of planning by the households and businesses in the area.[416]

Urban planning should be restored as a facilitative, supportive discipline, stripping it of the inappropriate social engineering component. Figure 12.1[417] provides a vivid example of appropriate and inappropriate urban planning. The wide, paved path was chosen for the people by planners in Evry, a suburb of Paris. The people, themselves, have chosen a less formal path across the grass. Good planning provides for the preferences of people, rather than attempting to steer them.

Figure 12.1

None of this is intended to suggest that suburbanization or urban sprawl is inherently good. It is rather to reaffirm the truth that where people are allowed to pursue their preferences without unnecessary restrictions, the results tend to be superior. So long as this can be accomplished without "material threat to others and the community," as the Lone Mountain Compact suggests, then there is no harm worthy of regulation.

The Universal Dream

The Montreal audience of urban planners and mass-transit officials could not have been more shocked at hearing a presentation by my colleague Jean-Claude Ziv, chair of the Transport, Tourism, and Logistics Department at the Conservatoire National des Arts et Metiers in Paris. Doubtless, they had come expecting another anti-sprawl cleric to rail against the evils of the automobile, or at least to offer the obligatory burnt offerings at the altar of sustainability, consistent with urban-planning doctrine.

However, the message of Professor Ziv was surprisingly different. He noted that much of what was called sustainable was simply not being accepted by the people, and that to force unwanted mandates on the public was both inappropriate and dictatorial, even "Stalinist." His message that sustainability must be acceptable violated the most revered beliefs of anti-suburbanism, and rightly so. A sustainability that is not sustainable itself cannot achieve its objectives.

The media is filled with self-righteous condemnation of an urban sprawl they rarely define or understand. Urban planners drive to public meetings in their cars or SUVs to rail against automobiles, to public hearing congregations that are usually small and never representative. Yet, people in the high-income world drive more every year, while people in the middle-income and low-income nations purchase cars even before they can afford them. The media trumpets the ills of suburbanization and urban sprawl, yet people clamor for more housing on larger lots in the suburbs, whether in the United States, Portugal, China, or Romania. The anti-consumerists damn the Wal-Marts and Carrefours, but people, affluent and poor, flock to big-box stores to get the best prices and improve their standard of living.

For genuine environmentalists, there is no alternative to a sustainability that is acceptable and thus sustainable itself. There is room for justifiable regulation. Water needs to be clean. Air must be clean. In addition, all of this can be accomplished without huddling people into overcrowded cities surrounded by land that could much better accommodate them without threatening the environment, and in greater affluence.

However, the quality of life of the high-income world is sustainable. The air and water is cleaner than ever before, and more substantial advances are ahead. In fact, by far the best environments are to be found in the high-income nations, all of which have seen nearly all of their new urban development to consist of suburbanization—that dreaded word *sprawl*.

Unlike the myopic, poorly researched, incomplete, and ill-conceived anti-suburban view, a world in which people are allowed to do what they want, subject to necessary regulation adds up to an achievable reality. Indeed, it has been happening for decades. A future in which people are allowed to live, work, and shop where they want, unless there is good reason why not, will be more prosperous. It will better be able to meet the daunting government fiscal challenges ahead.

The Canadian Broadcasting Company reporter mentioned in the beginning of the book had it right. Land-use policy is a subject much larger than urban planning. It is about the future and the quality of life itself.

On a campaign stop during the 1952 U.S. presidential election, the ultimately defeated Democratic Party candidate, Governor Adlai E. Stevenson of Illinois expressed the determination that the future requires:

> Our people have had more happiness and prosperity, over a wider area, for a longer time than men have ever had since they began to live in ordered societies 4,000 years ago. Since we have come so far, who shall be rash enough to set limits on our future progress? Who shall say that since we have gone so far, we can go no farther? Who shall say that the American dream is ended?[418]

Doubtless, the governor would have been shocked had the dean of an urban planning seminary risen in objection, to claim that the American Dream has ended, or at least it needed substantial redefinition.

It is doubtful, however, that Governor Stevenson would have been deterred from his faith in the American Dream, which is also the European Dream, the Japanese Dream, the Canadian Dream, the Great Australian Dream, the Kiwi Dream, and the Universal Dream. The Universal Dream has been the result of the unprecedented economic growth that has occurred in the last five decades, itself the product of the human ingenuity that flourishes where people are allowed to plan their own lives. The democratization of prosperity must be expanded. There should be more middle-income households, not less.

The Dream must be expanded to include the Hungarian Dream, the Chinese Dream, the Nigerian Dream, the Mexican Dream, the Brazilian Dream, and the Indian Dream. It cannot happen too soon.

Afterword

The Universal Dream, in its American, Australian, New Zealand, Canadian, European and other forms around the world has been associated with an unprecedented improvement in the quality of life for hundreds of millions of people.

Yet, there is a "War on the Dream, the result of policies that seek to control urban sprawl or suburbanization. The campaign operates under various names, such as "smart growth" or "urban consolidation." The proponents and governments that implement anti-suburban policies do so with little debate. Ideological dogma provides the foundation of much of the foundation of these initiatives, rather than rational, objective analysis. There is rarely any serious analysis of consequences. However, anti-suburban policies do have consequences, what are called "negative externalities" in economics. The most important consequences are:

- **Substantially higher housing costs relative to incomes.** Anti-suburban policies outlaw development on large swaths of land, creating scarcity and increasing housing prices. This must inevitably reduce home ownership and thereby the creation of wealth among millions of middle-and lower-income households.

- **Less productive urban areas.** Anti-suburban policies seek to force people to use mass-transit services that simply do not go where they are going, by failing to provide the roadway capacity necessary to accommodate rising demand. This increases the intensity of both traffic congestion and air pollution. Beyond the health and quality of life consequences, greater traffic congestion leads to lower levels of economic growth in urban areas.

- **Higher consumer prices**. Anti-suburban policies seek to limit or ban expansion of the big-box retail stores. This will lead to more strained budgets, with the greatest negative effects on low-income households.

All of this may sound somewhat abstract. However, it is very serious. Urban planning has already destroyed housing affordability in many urban areas and the intense traffic congestion it generates is driving businesses and economic growth away. Less economic growth means fewer jobs. Less productive urban areas are likely to lead to lower wages and more unemployment. All of this, when combined with higher product prices means that many households are likely to be less well off in the future. In short, the anti-suburban agenda aims economies toward fewer middle-income households and greater concentration of wealth. The pity is that the Dream is being threatened for virtually no reason. Virtually all of the justifications offered for anti-suburban policies are without foundation.

The supreme accomplishment of the high-income economies has been the democratization of prosperity that has occurred since World War II. With most of the world still living in comparative poverty, it is clear that neither economic growth nor wealth creation can be taken for granted. Moreover, economic growth is not a luxury; it is, as Benjamin Friedman has shown, crucial for social cohesion.

Thus, the imperative is to:

- Restore good planning that facilitates the preferences of people, rather than attempting to command and control them.

- Reject anti-suburban policies where they have not been implemented.

- Repeal anti-suburban policies where they have been enacted.

Only by such actions will economies and their urban areas be positioned to ensure that future generations live better than ours.

APPENDIX

Definition of Urban Terms

There is considerable confusion about terms used to describe urbanization, especially the term *city*. The city might be simply the historical core municipality, such as the city of Chicago or the ville de Paris. Often the term *city* is used to denote the urban area or agglomeration, which includes the historical core municipality and the continuously developed suburbs. Finally, the term *city* is sometimes used to describe an entire metropolitan area or labor market, which includes the historical core municipality, continuously developed suburbs and exurbs, which are not connected by continuous development to the urban area or agglomeration.

This lack of clarity can be noted in press reports that often use the term *city* to denote any of the three potential meanings above. For most overall urban analysis, either the urban area (agglomeration) or the metropolitan area (labor market) is most appropriate. The following urban terms are used frequently, and are defined as follows.

City generally means a municipality, which would typically have locally elected administration, such as a city council and a mayor. In some cases a city can also be a higher-level region, such as the ville de Paris, which is also a department; San Francisco, which is also a county; or the city of Shanghai, which is also a provincial level administrative district.

Central City: The central city or core city is the municipality in an urban area or metropolitan area that emerged historically as the most prominent in the urban area. Almost without exception, the name of the core city is also shared with the urban area and the metropolitan area. For example, the metropolitan area that includes and surrounds the city of New York is the New York metropolitan area or the New York urban area.

Usually the core city will be the largest in the urban area or metropolitan area. However, this is not always so. San Jose, not a core city, is now the largest city in the San Francisco metropolitan area. Usually an urban area or metropolitan area

will have many cities (the Paris metropolitan area has more than 1,000 municipalities or communes). The core city of Chicago, with nearly 3,000,000 residents, is just one of many cities in the Chicago metropolitan area or the Chicago
urban area. It is, however, possible for the city to be larger than either the urban
area or the metropolitan area. Examples are Anchorage, Alaska, and the Chinese
cities of Chongqing, Shanghai, Beijing, and Tianjin.

At the same time, a central city may be relatively small in relation to the corresponding urban area or metropolitan area. For example, according to the most
recent census, the city of Sydney had a population of less than 50,000, out of an
urban area with 3.5 million residents, while Adelaide had a population of under
20,000, out of an urban area of approximately 1.0 million.

A core municipality usually includes the historical core. However, through
annexation and consolidation, a central city can absorb areas that are suburban in
character. This has occurred in cities such as Portland, Los Angeles, San Antonio,
Toronto, and Rome.

The Urban Core: Generally the urban core or the *inner city* is in the central
city. Sometimes the urban core includes adjacent municipalities that developed
during the same period as the core city. For example, Frederiksburg is a part of
the core of the Copenhagen urban area, L'Hospitalet is a part of the core of the
Barcelona urban area, and Cambridge is a part of the core of the Boston urban
area core.

Suburb: Collectively, the *suburbs* are all of the continuous urbanization that
extends beyond the core city (all of the urban area except the historical core
municipality and other adjacent historical municipalities). A specific suburb can
be an individual municipality or community in the suburbs. For example, the cities of Evanston and Oak Park are suburbs of Chicago. In the London area,
municipalities that are outside the Greater London Authority, but inside the
greenbelt are suburbs, such as Epsom and Ottershaw.

Exurb: An *exurb* is a municipality (or a community) or urban area in a metropolitan area that is separated by rural territory from the principal urban area. For
example, DeKalb and Kankakee are exurbs of Chicago. The urban areas that are
within the London metropolitan area, but outside the greenbelt, are exurbs, such
as St. Albans and Milton Keynes.

Urban Area means an area of continuous urban development. An urban area
will virtually never be the same as a municipality. Usually it will include many
municipalities, though in the case of many geographically large municipalities,
such as Anchorage or Shanghai, the urban area will be smaller than the core city.
For example, the Chicago urban area (population over 8,000,000) includes the

city of Chicago and many other cities. An urban area might be thought of as defined by the lights seen from an airplane on a clear night. Some nations formally designate urban areas, which are called "urbanized areas" in the United States, "unites urbaines" in France, urban areas in the United Kingdom and Canada, "urban centers" in Australia and "urban agglomerations" in India. An urban area is also an *agglomeration*. A *conurbation* is an urban area that forms when two or more urban areas grow together, as has occurred in Osaka-Kobe-Kyoto, Essen-Dusseldorf (the "Rhine-Ruhr-Wupper"), Katowice-Gliwice (Poland), or the Washington and Baltimore urban areas, which are converging into a single urban area. Demographia has developed the only comprehensive list of world urban areas over 500,000 population with land area and densities.[419]

Metropolitan area means a labor market, or the area from which the urban area draws its employees. For example, the Chicago metropolitan area (population nearly 10 million) includes the city of Chicago, the Chicago urban area, and adjacent rural areas from which many people travel to work in the urban area. A metropolitan area will nearly always be larger than the urban area, because urban areas routinely draw a large number of workers from surrounding rural territory. A metropolitan area may include more than one urban area. For example, the Washington urban area and the Baltimore urban area are in the Washington-Baltimore metropolitan area, while the Los Angeles metropolitan area includes a number of urban areas, such as Los Angeles, Riverside-San Bernardino, Mission Viejo, Santa Clarita, Simi Valley, Oxnard-Ventura, and Palm Springs. The United States designates consolidated metropolitan areas, which are routinely used where they exist, as opposed to their metropolitan statistical area (MSA) components. A metropolitan area will usually include many cities, but, as noted above, in rare cases the core city may be larger than the metropolitan area. Many nations, such as the United States, France, Brazil, India, Argentina, and Canada formally designate metropolitan areas.

About the Author

Wendell Cox is an international public policy consultant and principal of Wendell Cox Consultancy (Demographia), in the St. Louis, Missouri-Illinois, metropolitan area. He has consulted for government and private sector clients around the world on issues of urban policy, transport, and housing. He maintains three Internet Web sites, including www.demographia.com, www.rentalcartours.net, and www.publicpurpose.com. The *National Journal* honored the latter as one of the best transport Web sites in the United States. He has lectured internationally.

Wendell Cox has conducted substantial research that has led to the development of unique products. Examples include:

- The *Demographia International Housing Affordability Survey* (co-authored with Hugh Pavletich, of Pavletich Properties in Christchurch, New Zealand), which provides comparisons between markets in the United States, the United Kingdom, Canada, Australia, Ireland, and New Zealand).

- *Demographia World Urban Areas*, which represents the first estimates of land areas and densities for all world urban areas with more than 500,000 residents.

Wendell Cox serves as a visiting professor at the Conservatoire National des Arts and Metiers (a national university) in Paris. He is a vice-president of CODATU, an international organization dedicated to improving urban transport in the developing world. He is also a member of the steering committee of the International Conference on Competition and Ownership in Land Passenger Transport.

Mayor Tom Bradley appointed Wendell Cox to three terms on the Los Angeles County Transportation Commission (1977–1985), where he served as a principal member, along with the five county supervisors, the Mayor, the city council president, and mayors from smaller cities. In connection with these responsibilities, he was elected as chair of two American Public Transit Association committees (Governing Boards, and Policy and Planning). He was the author of the amendment to the Proposition A tax referendum that provided the funding and impetus for the urban-rail system in Los Angeles.

Speaker of the United States House of Representatives Newt Gingrich appointed Wendell Cox to the Amtrak Reform Council (ARC) in 1999, to complete the unexpired term of New Jersey Governor Christine Todd Whitman. He served until 2002, when ARC completed its congressional mandate.

He is a visiting fellow at the Heritage Foundation (Washington), a senior fellow at the Institut économique de Montréal, the Heartland Institute (Chicago), the Frontier Centre for Public Policy (Winnipeg) and senior fellow for urban policy at the Independence Institute (Denver). He holds titles at a number of other research organizations. Wendell Cox also served three years as director of public policy for the American Legislative Exchange Council, a Washington-based organization of state legislators.

Endnotes

1. See Irving L. Janis, *Victims of Groupthink*, New York: Houghton Mifflin Company, 1972.

2. As used herein, the "high-income world" includes the United States, Western Europe, Japan, Canada, Australia, Hong Kong, Singapore and New Zealand.

3. Peter Blake, *God's Own Junkyard: The Planned Deterioration of America's Landscape*, New York: Holt Rinehart and Winston, 1979, p. 34.

4. Dolores Hayden, *Building Suburbia: Green Fields and Urban Growth*, New York: Pantheon Books, 2003, p. 229.

5. Rober Earle Howells, "The Anti-Burb," *Smithsonian*, July 2004.

6. Neal R. Pearce, *Littleton's Legacy: Our Suburban Dream Shattered.* www.postwritersgroup.com/archives (June 6, 1999).

7. James Howard Kuntsler, *The Geography of Nowhere: The Rise and Decline of America's Man-Made Landscape*, New York: Simon & Schuster, 1999, pp. 108, 168, 200.

8. *The Eye*, "The Suburbs are Killing Us" (editorial). Toronto, ON: February 19, 2004.

9. Jane Holz Kay, *Asphalt Nation: How the Automobile Took over American an How We Can Take it Back*, Berkeley, CA: University of California Press, 1997, p. 39.

10. Kunstler, p. 248.

11. Jeremy Rifkin, *The European Dream: How Europe's Future Is Quietly Eclipsing the American Dream*, New York: Jeremy P. Tarcher/Penguin, 2004, p. 178.

12. Peter Callithorpe, *The Next American Metropolis: Ecology, Community, and the American Dream*, New York: Princeton Architectural Press, 1993, p. 15.

13. Hayden, p. 201.

14. Blake, p. 34.

15. Rifkin, pp.16–17.

16. Bert Sperling and Peter Sandler, *Cities Ranked and Rated,* Hoboken, NJ: Wiley Publishing, Inc., 2004, p. 58.

17. Merriam-Webster Dictionary, http://www.m-w.com.

18. Internet Web site of Congressman Earl Blumenauer, http://blumenauer.house.gov/Issues/Issue.aspx?SubIssueID=76, accessed February 1, 2005.

19. *USA: Urban Transport Market Shares by Mode,* http://www.publicpurpose.com/ut-scbpm2004.htm (www.publicpurpose.com is a Web site of Wendell Cox Consultancy).

20. Callithorpe, p. 16.

21. Callithorpe, p. 10.

22. Hayden, p. 18.

23. Wolfgang Zuckerman, *End of the Road: The World Car Crisis and How We Can Solve It,* Post Mills, VT: Chelsea Green Publishing Company, 1991, pp. xiii, 92.

24. David Gurin, *Understanding Sprawl: A Citizen's Guide.* Vancouver, BC: The David Suzuki Foundation, 2003.

25. Angus Maddison, *The World Economy: Historical Statistics*, Paris: Organization for Economic Cooperation and Development, 2003.

26. Poverty threshold for a family of three, per capita.

27. Estimated based upon Maddison OECD data, using a 0.858 relationship between gross domestic product and gross personal income (the 2000 rate in the United States).

28. Bernard Salt, "Our New Neighbourhoods Can't Be Built on Nostalgia," *The Australian,* June 1, 2006.

29. Richard Pipes, *Property and Freedom,* New York: Vintage Books, 2000, p. 8.

30. Terry L. Anderson and Laura E. Huggins, *Property Rights: A Practical Guide to Freedom and Prosperity*, Stanford, CA: Hoover Institution Press, 2003, p. 4.

31. Hernando DeSoto, *The Mystery of Capital: Why Capitalism Triumphs in the West and Fails Everywhere Else*, New York: Basic Books, 2000.

32. DeSoto, p. 228.

33. DeSoto, p. 210.

34. North and Thomas, *The Rise of the Western World: A New Economic History*, Cambridge, UK: Cambridge University Press, 1973, p. 127, 131.

35. Richard Florida, *The Rise of the Creative Class*, New York: Basic Books, 2002.

36. Kotkin refers to the quest for the "Creative Class" as offering "only poor returns." See Joel Kotkin, "Uncool Cities," *Prospect*, October 25, 2005: http://www.prospect-magazine.co.uk/article_details.php?id=7072), accessed July 12, 2006.

37. North and Thomas, p. 8.

38. Pipes, p. 286.

39. James Gwartney and Robert Lawson, *Economic Freedom of the World: 2004 Annual Report*, Vancouver, BC: Fraser Institute, 2004; Marc A. Miles, Edwin J. Fuelner, and Mary Anastasia O'Grady, *2005 Index of Economic Freedom*, Washington: Heritage Foundation, 2005.

40. World Bank, *Doing Business in 2005: Removing Obstacles to Growth*, Washington, 2005, p. 5.

41. Based upon gross domestic product per capita, adjusted for purchasing power (purchasing power parity). This is different than comparisons based upon monetary exchange rates. The United States is a low-cost economy, while Western European countries and Japan tend to be higher-cost economies. For example, the Swiss gross domestic product per capita is greater than in the United States. However, the lower cost of living in the United States means that more can be purchased, and thus, at purchasing power parity, the gross domestic product per capita in the United States is higher.

42. Calculated from Maddison.

43. William W. Lewis, *The Power of Productivity: Wealth, Poverty, and the Threat to Global Stability.* Chicago, IL: University of Chicago Press, 2004.

44. Lewis, p. 13.

45. The Australian research was completed before wide adoption of urban consolidation policies.

46. Lewis, p. 13.

47. Heritage Foundation Center for Data Analysis calculations from U.S. Federal Reserve Board, Survey of Consumer Finance, 1998 as cited in Wendell Cox and Ronald D. Utt, *Smart Growth, Housing Costs and Home Ownership,* Washington: Heritage Foundation, April 6, 2001.

48. As cited in Wendell Cox and Ronald D. Utt, *Smart Growth, Housing Costs, and Home Ownership,* Washington: Heritage Foundation, April 6, 2001.

49. David Brooks, *On Paradise Drive: How We Live Now (And Always Have) in the Future Tense,* New York: Simon & Schuster, 2004.

50. Pew Research Center, *Global Gender Gaps: Women Like Their Lives Better.* : http://people-press.org/commentary/display.php3?AnalysisID=71, October 29, 2003. Accessed June 14, 2004.

51. Rifkin, p. 8.

52. Paul H. Douglas, *Building the American City: Report of the National Commission on Urban Problems to the Congress and to the President of the United States,* Washington: U.S. Government Printing Office, 1968, p. 2.

53. Thomas A Kean (Chairman) and Thomas Ludlow Ashley (Vice-Chairman), *Not in My Back Yard: Report to President Bush and Secretary Kemp by the Advisory Commission on Regulatory Barriers to Affordable Housing,* Washington: U.S. Department of Housing and Urban Development, 1991, "Mandate to the Commission" (page unnumbered).

54. Alan E. Pisarski, *Cars, Wome,n and Minorities: The Democratization of Mobility in America,* Washington: Competitive Enterprise Institute, 1999.

55. Remy Prud'homme and Chang-Woon Lee (1998), "Size, Sprawl, Speed, and the Efficiency of Cities," Paris, France: Obervatoire de l'Économic et des Institutions Locals.

56. http://www.perc.org/publications/articles/lone_mountain_full.php, accessed February 28, 2005.

57. Thomas Sieverts, Cities without Cities: An Interpretation of the Zwischenstadt, London, U.K.: Spon Press, 2003, p. vii.

58. www.pbs.org/pov/hongkong/livingcity. accessed 1 January 2002.

59. See *Sierra Club Promotes Black Hole of Calcutta Densities, Then Retreats,* www.demographia.com/db-sierraclub500.htm and *Unsustainable Densities: Environmental Impacts II Pulled from Sierra Club Web site* www.demographia.com/db-sierra3.htm. (www.demographia.com is a Web site of Wendell Cox Consultancy).

60. The Smart Growth America report uses sub-metropolitan areas (primary metropolitan statistical areas) as its principal analysis base. Primary metropolitan areas often do not include entire urban areas and are thus less than ideal for many measures, perhaps none more inappropriate than suburbanization. The U.S. Bureau of the Census, in its new metropolitan definitions, has discontinued the use of primary metropolitan statistical areas. Among complete metropolitan areas (metropolitan statistical areas or consolidated metropolitan statistical areas), Providence is rated by Smart Growth America as least sprawling.

61. Gurin, p. 3.

62. Karen A. Danielsen, Robert E. Lang, and William Fulton, "What Does Smart Growth Mean for Housing?, *Housing Facts and Findings,* Fall 1999, Volume 1 Issue 3 http://www.fanniemaefoundation.org/programs/hff/v1i3-smart_growth.shtml, accessed January 4, 2005.

63. Email from the Sierra Club, June 18, 2001, reproduced at http://www.demographia.com/db-sierraclub500.htm.

64. Calculated from Jesse H. Ausubel and Cesare Marchetti, *The Evolution of Transport,* http://www.aip.org/tip/INPHFA/vol-7/iss-2/p20.pdf.

65. *Ville de Paris Population & Density from 1365,* http://www.demographia.com/dm-par90.htm.

66. Calculated from information in Danielle Chadych and Dominique Leborgne, *Atlas de Paris: Evolution d'un Paysage Urbain,* Paris: Parigramme, 1999, p. 62.

67. *London Urban Area: Historical Estimated Population & Density:* http://www.demographia.com/db-lonuza1680.htm.

68. Jesse H. Ausubel and Cesare Marchetti, *The Evolution of Transport,* http://www.aip.org/tip/INPHFA/vol-7/iss-2/p20.pdf.

69. *Paris Urbanized Area: Population and Density from 1807,* http://www.demographia.com/db-parisua.htm, *New York Urban Area: Population and Density from 1800 (Provisional)* http://www.demographia.com/db-nyuza1800.htm, and *London Urban Area: Historical Estimated Population & Density* http://www.demographia.com/db-lonuza1680.htm. 1900 Los Angeles estimate based upon street map analysis.

70. *Demographia World Urban Areas,* http://www.demographia.com/db-worldua.pdf.

71. *Suburban, Core & Urban Densities by Area: Western Europe, Japan, United States, Canada, Australia & New Zealand,* http://www.demographia.com/db-intlsub.htm.

72. As used herein, the New World is the United States, Canada, Australia and New Zealand.

73. Lincoln Institute of Land Policy, *Alternatives to* Sprawl, 1995, p. 7.

74. The suburbs of Dallas-Fort Worth cover less than 800 square miles. This compares to the 1,000 square miles of suburban Paris. Calculated from 2000 U.S. census data and 1999 France census data.

75. Calculated from 1999 census data.

76. *Brussels: Suburban and Suburbanizing,* http://www.rentalcartours.net/rac-bruxelles.pdf. (www.rentalcartours.net is a Web site of Wendell Cox Consultancy).

77. *Zurich Urbanization and Suburbanization from 1930,* http://www.demographia.com/db-zur.htm and *Zurich: Spilling into the Mountains,* http://www.demographia.com/rac-zurich.pdf.

78. *Milan: Transport Potential,* http://www.rentalcartours.net/rac-milano.pdf.

79. *Barcelona: More than Meets the Eye,* http://www.demographia.com/rac-barcelona.pdf.

80. In response to the tendency of planners to "miss" the suburban areas of urban areas, we developed a series of travelogues under the title, "Urban Tours by Rental Car," www.rentalcartours.net.

81. http://www.demographia.com/db-metro-we1965.htm.

82. See Robert M. Fogelson, *Downtown: Its Rise and Fall, 1880–1950,* New Haven, CT: Yale, 2001.

83. For example, the Chicago Loop, the second largest downtown area in the United States, covers barely one square mile of the urban area's more than 2,100 square miles.

84. *Employment Density in International Central Business Districts,* http://www.demographia.com/db-intlcbddens.htm.

85. Central business districts with more than 750,000 jobs.

86. See Joel Garreau, *Edge Cities: Life on the New Frontier,* New York: Doubleday, 1991.

87. Gross domestic product per capita exceeding $15,000 in 1995.

88. These estimates of population and urban land area are for continuously built up urban areas. They are not based upon jurisdictions, such as cities or counties. In the United States, France, the United Kingdom, and Canada, the data is from national census authorities and is based upon census divisions (such as census tracts). Other estimates have been made by the author based upon examination of satellite maps and road maps and include only the urban "footprints," generally following U.S. Census Bureau urbanized area criteria.

89. *Demographia World Urban Areas.*

90. All urban areas over 2,500 population.

91. All U.S. data is from the 2000 census unless otherwise indicated.

92. *USA Urbanized Areas: Density of New Development: 1950–2000,* http://www.demographia.com/db-uza19502000incre.htm

93. San Jose is not included in the overall analysis because its population is less than 3,000,000.

94. The U.S. Bureau of the Census classifies San Jose and San Francisco as separate urban areas. Yet, the two areas are adjacent and represent continuous development. It is the author's view that these two urban areas are in

fact one. But, for simplicity, the U.S. census urban area definitions are used.

95. *Boston: Atlanta Style Suburban Sprawl*, http://www.rentalcartours.net/rac-boston.pdf.

96. Paris suburbs have a density of 7,400 persons per square mile, compared to the Los Angeles figure of 6,750.

97. The twenty-three wards of the former municipality, which was abolished in the 1940s.

98. Over 2,500 population.

99. The U.S. figure is 2,400.

100. The former municipality of Toronto, which was consolidated with five other municipalities in 1997.

101. *Sydney Urbanized Area: Statistical Local Areas by Population Density: 1999*, http://www.demographia.com/db-sydney-dense.htm.

102. *U.S. Urban Personal Vehicle & Public Transport Market Share from 1900*, http://www.publicpurpose.com/ut-usptshare45.htm and *USA: Urban Transport Market Shares by Mode*, http://www.publicpurpose.com/ut-scbpm2004.htm.

103. Estimated from national population data and American Automobile Manufacturers Association, *World Motor Vehicle Data*, 1993.

104. Calculated from U.S. census data.

105. Calculated from Census of Japan data.

106. *High-Income World Metropolitan Areas: Core City & Suburban Population Trends*, http://www.demographia.com/db-highmetro.htm.

107. *Urbanization in the United States from 1945*, http://www.demographia.com/db-1945uza.htm.

108. Calculated from U.S. Bureau of the Census and Department of Labor data.

109. *Commercial Land Use Per Job: Paris Metropolitan Area (Ile-de-France): 1999*, http://www.demographia.com/db-paris-comml.htm.

110. *USA, Canada, Western Europe, Asia: 14 Nations: Gross Domestic Product Per Capita from 1960 at Purchasing Power Parity,* http://www.demographia.com/db-ppp60+.htm.

111. Christian Gerondeau, *Transport in Europe,* Boston, MA: Artech House, 1997, p. 233.

112. Kenneth T. Jackson, *Crabgrass Frontier: The Suburbanization of the United States,* New York: Oxford University Press, 1985, 318.

113. *Core Population Trends: International Cities:* http://www.demographia.com/db-intlcitycores.htm.

114. Pre-1997 amalgamation city.

115. *High-Income World: Core Cities and Densification,* http://www.demographia.com/db-worldcore400.htm.

116. *Share of Suburban Growth from Central Cities: 1950–2000,* http://www.demographia.com/db-subccshare.htm.

117. *Paris Urban Area: 1921–1999,* http://www.demographia.com/db-paris-seine-pc.htm.

118. *Japan: Metropolitan Areas and Core Cities: 1965–2000,* http://www.demographia.com/db-metro-japan1965.htm.

119. *High-Income World Metropolitan Areas: Core City & Suburban Population Trends,* www.demographia.com/db-highmetro.htm.

120. David Brooks, *On Paradise Drive: How We Live Now (And Always Have) in the Future Tense,* New York: Simon & Schuster, 2004.

Chapter 4: Planning and the Post-war American City

121. Since 1950.

122. Since the 2000 census, Louisville has combined with its suburbs that are in Jefferson County.

123. See David Rusk, *Cities Without Suburbs,* Washington: Woodrow Wilson Center Press, 1995.

124. Wendell Cox, *Growth, Economic Development, and Local Government Structure in Pennsylvania,* Harrisburg, PA: Pennsylvania State Association of Township Supervisors, 2005.

125. Edward L. Glaeser and Jacob L. Vigdor, *Racial Segregation in the 2000 Census: Promising News,* Washington: The Brookings Institution, http://www.brookings.edu/es/urban/census/glaeser.pdf, accessed June 1, 2006.

126. Alan Berube and Thacher Tiffany, "The Shape of the Curve: Household Income Distributions in U.S. Cities: 1979–1999," *Living Cities Census Series,* Washington: The Brookings Institution, August 2004, p. 7.

127. Statistics Canada classifies whites and aboriginals (native North Americans) as non-visible and all other racial groupings as "visible minorities."

128. Catherine Wyatt, "France Forming Ethnic Ghettos," London:

British Broadcasting Corporation, July 6, 2004 (http://news.bbc.co.uk/2/hi/europe/3871447.stm, accessed December 8, 2004).

129. Third largest building in the world.

130. Bernard J. Friedan and Lynn B. Sagalyn, *Downtown, Inc.,* Cambridge, England: MIT Press, 1990, pp. 20–22.

131. Friedan and Sagalyn, pp. 25–27.

132. Quoted in Marc A. Weiss, "The Origins and Legacy of Urban Renewal," *Federal Housing Policy & Programs: Past and Present,* Edited by J. Paul Mitchell, Piscataway, NJ: The Center for Urban Policy Research/Rutgers, 1985, p. 259.

133. , Wiess, p. 254, 269.

134. The devastation of urban planning is not limited to the United States. Romanian dictator Nicolai Ceaucescu condemned thousands of homes and churches in the core of Bucharest to construct a new governmental center, the core of which is the "Palace of the People," the third largest building in the world.

135. Mindy Thompson Fullilove, M.D., *Root Shock: How Tearing Up City Neighborhoods Hurts America and What We Can Do About It,* New York: Ballantine Books, 2004, p. 24.

136. Fullilove, p. 24.

137. Douglas, pp. 80–87.

138. Based upon 1950 average household size.

139. Fullilove, p. 59.

140. Quoted in Weiss, p. 257.

141. Personal e-mail from Cook County Sheriff Deputy (Retired) Walter A. Schwalm, October 8, 2004.

142. For a comprehensive description of blockbusting, see W. Edward Orser, *Blockbusting in Baltimore,* Lexington, KY: University Press of Kentucky, 1994, p. 102.

143. Fullilove, p. 68.

144. Jane Jacobs became a virtual icon of urban policy. After her 2006 death, articles appeared describing views as consistent with the anti-suburban movement. This revisionist history is untrue and is answered in Leonard Gilroy, "What Jane Jacobs Really Saw," *Opinion Journal,* May 2, 2006: http://www.opinionjournal.com/la/?id=110008319.

145. Jane Jacobs, *The Death and Life of Great American Cities,* New York: Vintage Books, 1961.

146. Chicago Housing Authority, *Robert Taylor Homes,* http://www.thecha.org/housingdev/robert_taylor.html, accessed November 22, 2004.

147. See: *Urban Tours by Rental Car: St. Louis: From Carthage to the Future,* http://www.rentalcartours.net/rac-stl.pdf. The city of New Orleans has experienced a greater loss than St. Louis, due to the flooding that resulted from levee failures and the design of the Intercoastal Waterway in connection with Hurricane Katrina in 2005. See: *Urban Tours by Rental Car: New Orleans: Destroyed by Government Floods,* http://www.rentalcartours.net/rac-no.pdf. The permanent population loss may or may not ultimately exceed that of St. Louis.

148. See Paul S. Grogan and Tony Proscio, *Comeback Cities: A Blueprint for Urban Neighborhood Revival,* Boulder, CO: Westview Press, 2000, pp. 11–30.

149. Thomas J. Nechyba and Randall P. Walsh, "Urban Sprawl," *Journal of Economic Perspectives,* Fall 2004, p. 186. http://www.ingentaconnect.com/content/aea/jep/2004/00000018/00000004/art00009, accessed February 1, 2005.

150. A higher figure, approximately 5 percent, is often cited from the U.S. Department of Agriculture National Resources Inventory. This figure,

however, includes urban *and* rural development. See also United States Department of Agriculture, Economic Research Service, "Land Use, Value, and Management: Urbanization and Agricultural Land," (http://www.ers.usda.gov/briefing/LandUse/urbanchapter.htm, accessed May 2, 2006.

151. Calculated on a province basis. Historical data on geographical extent of urban areas is not readily available.

152. Calculated from Statistics Canada data, 2001.

153. *Estimated   Urban   Land   Area: Selected   Nation,* http://www.demographia.com/db-intlualand.htm.

154. Also called "domesticated" land or the "cultura."

155. Estimated from U.S. Bureau of the Census, U.S. Department of Agriculture Economic Research Service, and National Resources Inventory data.

156. Japan Land Information Division/Land and Water Bureau, Ministry of Land, Infrastructure, and Transport, http://tochi.mlit.go.jp/h14hakusho/setsu_1-2-1_eng.html, accessed March 2, 2005.

157. Based upon data in U.S. Census Bureau American Housing Survey reports for Portland (2002) and Atlanta (2004). http://www.census.gov/hhes/www/housing/ahs/metropolitandata.html,

158. Robert Burchell, Naveed A. Shad, David Listokin, Hilary Phillips, Anthony Downs, Samuel Seskin, Judy Davis, Terry Moore, David Helton, and Michelle Gall, *The Costs of Sprawl—Revisited,* Washington: Transportation Research Board, 1998, p. 6.

159. Urban areas over 2,500 population. Calculated from Statistics Canada data.

160. Internet Kowloon Walled City (2004). "Miscellaneous Numbers of the Kowloon Walled City." Digital document: http://www.flex.co.jp/kowloon/restore/statis_e.html, accessed June 14, 2004.

161. Calculated from Jeffrey Kenworthy, Felix B. Laube, and Peter Newman, *An International Sourcebook of Automobile Dependence in Cities, 1960–1990.* Boulder CO: University of Colorado Press, 1999 (latest comprehensive data available).

162. Calculated from Jeffrey Kenworthy, Felix B. Laube, and Peter Newman, 1999.

163. Calculated from Kenworthy and, Laube, and Newman, 1999.

164. *Journey to Work Travel Times: International by Urban Area Size,* http:// www.publicpurpose.com/ut-intljtwtimesize.htm and *Japan and USA: Work Trip Travel Times in Large Metropolitan Areas,* http://www. publicpurpose.com/ut-jtw-japanusa.htm.

165. Data from Kenworthy, Laube, and Newman, 1999, Millennium Cities Database and U.S. Bureau of the Census.

166. Derived from Catherine Ross and Anne E. Dunning (1997). "Land Use and Transportation Interaction: An Examination of the 1995 NPTS Data," *Searching for Solutions: Nationwide Personal Transportation Survey Symposium.* Washington, DC: U.S. Federal Highway Administration.

167. Even the anti-suburban Sierra Club agrees that higher densities increase traffic volumes. Dr. John Holtzclaw has said that driving cost per capita is 20 to 30 percent less per capita in a neighborhood that is double the density of another. http://www.sierraclub.org/sprawl/articles/designing.asp, accessed January 5, 2005.

168. Peak hour travel delay is measured by the Travel Time Index, developed and annually reported by the Texas Transportation Institute at Texas A&M University. A Travel Time Index means that travel during peak periods requires 1.20 times as much time as during uncongested periods, which adds a 20 percent delay to a trip.

169. Peter Gordon and Harry W. Richardson, "Prove It: The Costs and Benefits of Sprawl," *Brookings Review,* Fall 1998.

170. Adelaide's only freeway is a one-way roadway operating in different directions in the morning and evening peak periods.

171. *High-Income World Urban Areas: Freeway Access and Capacity,* http:// www.publicpurpose.com/ut-worldfwy.htm.

172. David Hartgen and Daniel O. Curley, *Beltways: Boon, Bane, or Blip? Factors Influencing Changes in Urbanized Area Traffic: 1990–1997.* Charlotte, NC: Center for Interdisciplinary Transportation Studies, University of North Carolina—Charlotte, 1999.

173. Calculated from data in Stacy C. Davis and Susan W. Diegel, *Transportation Energy Data Book: Edition 24,* Oak Ridge, TN: Center for Transportation Analysis, Oak Ridge National Laboratory, 2004, Table 2–13.

174. Bjorn Lormborg, *The Skeptical Environmentalist: Measuring the Real State of the World*, Cambridge, UK: Cambridge University Press, 2001, p. 165.

175. Per capita pollution levels declined even more.

176. U.S. Environmental Protection Agency, *Air Emission Trends*, http://www.epa.gov/airtrends/econ-emissions.html, accessed March 3, 2005.

177. Mobile 5 model (U.S. Environmental Protection Agency).

178. Randall O'Toole, "Dense Thinking," *Reason*, January 1999.

179. Calculated from Kenworthy, Laube, and Newman, http://www.demographia.com/db-intlapdens.htm.

180. *Air Pollution Variation in International Cities*, http://www.demographia.com/db-intlpollu-avepct.htm.

181. Joel Schwartz, *No Way Back: Why Air Pollution Will Continue to Decline*, Washington, DC: AEI Press, 2003, pp. 19, 21.

182. Calculated from Environment Canada, *Canada's 2003 Greenhouse Gas Inventory: Summary*, http://www.ec.gc.ca/pdb/ghg/inventory_report/2003summary/2003summary_e.cfm. Accessed May 5, 2006.

183. Canada's Kyoto target is to reduce greenhouse gas emissions to a level 6 percent below 1990. In 2003, light gasoline and diesel vehicles (cars, SUVs, trucks, and motorcycles) produced 93,000 kilotons of greenhouse gases, compared to the 180,000-kiloton reduction that would be required to achieve the Kyoto target. http://www.climatechange.gc.ca/cop/cop6_hague/english/overview_e.html.

184. David L. Greene and Andreas Schafer, *Reducing Greenhouse Gas Emissions from U.S. Transportation*, Arlington (VA), Pew Center on Global Climate Change, May 2003, http://www.pewclimate.org/docUploads/ustransp%2Epdf, accessed June 1, 2006.

185. The terms "person mile" and "passenger mile" are equivalents. "Person mile" is used to denote the total number of miles traveled by all people in personal vehicles (such as cars and SUVs). "Passenger mile" is used for mass transit. Passenger miles do not include the on-duty travel, of bus or train operators or personnel.

186. This is considerably below the figures often quoted based upon American Automobile Association figures or other sources. These sources do not use actual data for the entire automobile and sport utility vehicle fleet, but

rather tend to use vehicles five years old or less. The average age of the vehicle fleet in the United States is nearly double that number. The $0.21 figure is calculated from actual spending on cars as reported in the National Income and Product Accounts.

187. *U.S. Cost of Automobiles/SUVs and Public Transport per Passenger Mile from 1960,* http://www.publicpurpose.com/ut-drvg1960.htm.

188. This excludes the increase in expenditures that has been required to provide demand responsive (door-to-door) service for the elderly and the physically handicapped, which is approximately 5 percent of spending.

189. *US Public Transport Expenditure Escalation above Inflation: 1970-,* http://www.publicpurpose.com/ut-trexpesc.htm and Wendell Cox, *Transit: Half A Trillion for Nothing,* From the Heartland web log, http://www.fromtheheartland.org/blog/2006/07/transit_halfatrillion_dollars.php.

190. *USA Mass Transit: New Value 1970-2004:* http://www.publicpurpose.com/ut-value2004.htm

191. I drafted legislation sponsored by Colorado State Senator Terry Considine and Representative (now Governor) Bill Owens to require Denver's mass-transit system to competitively tender 20 percent of its service. The mandate has now been increased to 50 percent. During the first 10 years (1988–1998), savings exceeded $100 million and substantial service expansions were financed.

192. See Wendell Cox, *Competitive Tendering of Public Transport,* Presentation to the Road and Public Transit Symposium, Centre Jacques Cartier, Montreal, 2004 (http://www.publicpurpose.com/ut-ct-mon2004.pdf).

193. This has been documented in a number of sources. A more recent publication is a Federal Reserve Bank of St. Louis publication by Thomas A. Garrett (*Light Rail Transit in America* http://www.stlouisfed.org/community/assets/pdf/light_rail.pdf, 2004).

194. Bent Flyvbjerg, *Megaprojects and Risk: An Anatomy of Ambition,* Cambridge, UK: Cambridge University Press, p. 16.

195. Flyvbjerg, p. 31.

196. Calculated from http://www.publicpurpose.com/ut-2003hwytr.htm.

197. A detailed description of the problems with social costs is found in Steven N. S. Cheung, *The Myth of Social Cost,* San Francisco, CA: Cato Institute, 1980.

198. Calculated from Mark Delucci, "Should We Try to Get the Prices Right," http://www.uctc.net/access/access16.pdf, accessed December 14, 2004. Also see *Automobile and Transport Externalities: USA:* http://www.publicpurpose.com/ut-external.htm.

199. Author's estimate, using Eurostat data for urban areas in the EU-15 (1998–2001), weighted by urban area size and using an assumption that the relationship between work trip market share and overall market share is similar to the United States.

200. The automobile share in Nagoya, the third largest metropolitan area, is approximately 75 percent and lower in the many smaller urban areas.

201. Calculated from *US Urban Personal Vehicle & Public Transport Market Share from 1900* http://www.publicpurpose.com/ut-usptshare45.htm. The market share is 2.4 percent including school buses and private shuttles *USA: Urban Transport Market Shares by Mode,* http://www.publicpurpose.com/ut-scbpm2004.htm.

202. Calculated from U.S. census data.

203. Calculated from Kenworthy. Laube, and Newman, 1999, and International Union of Public Transport, Millennium Cities Database, 2001.

204. Calculated from Kenworthy. Laube, and Newman, 1999.

205. Remy Prud'homme, Richard Darbara, David Newbury, Achim Diekman, and Bert Elbeck, *Is Our Present Transport System Sustainable?* Paris: Presses de L'ecole National Pontes et Chaussees, 1999.

206. *Change in Travel: Tokyo-Yokohama, Osaka-Kobe-Kyoto & Nagoya: 1990–2002,* http://www.publicpurpose.com/ut-japan3fr1990.htm.

207. *Public Transport Market Share Trends: International Urban Areas from 1980,* http://www.publicpurpose.com/ut-intlmkt95.htm

208. Calculated from *US Urban Personal Vehicle & Public Transport Market Share from 1900,* http://www.publicpurpose.com/ut-usptshare45.htm

209. Blake, p. 34.

210. Burchell et al (1998), p. 4.

211. Patrick N. Troy, *The Perils of Urban Consolidation*, Annandale, NSW, Australia: The Federation Press, 1996, pp. 55–76.

212. Robert W. Burchell, George Lowenstein, William R. Dolphin, Catherine C. Galley, Anthony Downs, Samuel Seskin, and Terry Moore, *Costs of Sprawl—2000*. Washington, DC: Transportation Research Board, 2002.

213. Wendell Cox and Joshua Utt, *The Costs of Sprawl Reconsidered: What Does the Actual Data Show?* Washington, DC: Heritage Foundation (http://www.heritage.org/Research/SmartGrowth/bg1770.cfm), 2004.

214. Municipal sewer and water utilities tend to be organized as self-financing government enterprises, funded by user fees and receiving little or no general government subsidy.

215. Cox and Utt, 2004.

216. Wendell Cox, *Growth, Economic Development, and Local Government Structure in Pennsylvania*, Harrisburg, PA: Pennsylvania State Association of Township Supervisors, 2005.

217. Cox and Utt, 2004.

218. Troy, p. 71.

219. Adam Smith, *The Wealth of Nations* (New York: Modern Library, 1957), p. 129.

220. Such a theory is developed by Mancur Olson, for example, in *The Rise and Decline of Nations: Economic Growth, Stagflation, and Social Rigidities* (New Haven and London: Yale University Press, 1982).

221. This is also the case in mass transit. See Wendell Cox, *Performance Measures in Urban Public Transport,* paper presented to the 8th International Conference on Competitive and Ownership in Public Transport, Rio de Janeiro, www.publicpurpose.com/t8-gbc.pdf.

222. Charles M. Tiebout, "A Pure Theory of Local Government Expenditures," *Journal of Political Economy* (1956) 64.

223. Center for Rural Pennsylvania, July 2000, *Differences in the Cost of Living Across Pennsylvania's 67 Counties,* http://www.ruralpa.org/clr2000.pdf, accessed February 15, 2005.

224. Reid Ewing, Rolf Pendall, and Don Chen, *Measuring Sprawl and Its Impact.* www.smartgrowthamerica.com.

225. Calculated from www.accra.org data.

226. Urbanized areas with more than 1,000,000 population.

227. U.S. Government Accounting Office, *Community Development: Extent of Federal Influence on 'Urban Sprawl' is Unclear,"* April 1999, http://www.gao.gov/archive/1999/rc99087.pdf, accessed February 5, 2005.

228. Burchell, et al (2000), pp. 126–127.

229. Central ownership is not dealt with here, given that it has now been rejected by nearly all world economies.

230. European Union policy refers to this concept as "subsidiarity."

231. Cox and Utt, 2004.

232. Wendell Cox, *Growth, Economic Development, and Local Government Structure in Pennsylvania,* Harrisburg, PA: Pennsylvania State Association of Township Supervisors, 2005.

233. Pietro S. Nivola, *Laws of the Landscape: How Politics Shape Cities in Europe and America,* Washington, DC, Brookings Institution Press, 1999.

234. *USA: Number of General Purpose Governments in Metropolitan Areas over 500,000* (http://www.demographia.com/db-metgovts2002.htm).

235. Andrew Sanction, *Merger Mania: The Assault on Local Government,* Montreal, QC: McGill-Queen's University Press, 2000.

236. Cox, 2005.

237. *Chicago Area Local Government Wages & Salaries: Core and Suburbs: 1997,* http://www.publicpurpose.com/ge-1997chi.htm. This analysis includes only wages and excludes employer-paid benefits, which are related to the wage level and are probably also higher in the city of Chicago than in the suburbs.

238. *Diseconomies of Scale in U.S. Public Transport Bus Operations: 1997,* http://www.publicpurpose.com/ut-us97mbecsc.htm.

239. Virtually all of the major competitive tendering programs in the world have had their beginning outside the mass transit agencies themselves. More often than not the impetus will be legislative, as in Colorado, or in some cases, units of general government (not mass-transit authorities or districts) or policy organizations (such as the Los Angeles County Trans-

portation Commission in the late 1980s or the San Diego Metropolitan Transit Development Board).

240. "Back to Prosperity: A Competitive Agenda for Renewing Pennsylvania," Washington, DC: Brookings Institution, 2003. http://www.brookings.edu/es/urban/publications/pa.htm, accessed January 31, 2005.

241. Cox, 2005.

242. *High-Income World Urbanized Areas: Growth and Population Density,* http://www.demographia.com/db-econ-uaintl.htm.

243. Robert D. Putnam, *Bowling Alone: The Collapse and Revival of American Community,* New York: Simon & Schuster, 2000.

244. Troy, p. 38.

245. Kay, p. 274.

246. Sieverts, p. 32.

247. Barbara A. McCann and Reid Ewing, *Measuring the Health Effects of Sprawl.* Washington, DC: Smart Growth America and the Surface Transportation Policy Project, 2003, http://www.smartgrowthamerica.org/healthreport.html, accessed February 15, 2005.

248. New York City is composed of five counties, or boroughs. No other city in the United States is composed of more than one complete county.

249. Among the many misled publications were *The Eye* (*The Eye,* 2004) and Gurin.

250. Six percent of the sample drove five hours or more daily. This is four times the national rate, based upon National Household Travel Survey information.

251. Ross C. Brownson and Tegan K. Boehmer, "Patterns and Trends in Physical Activity, Occupation, Transportation, Land Use and Sedentary Behaviors" (draft). Washington, DC: Paper prepared for the Transportation Research Board,(2003) 14.

252. Committee on Physical Activity, Health, Transportation, and Land Use, *Does the Built Environment Influence Physical Activity: Examining the Evidence* (Washington, DC: Transportation Research Board Institute of Medicine, 2005), p. 7–2.

253. Marion Nestle and Michael F. Jacobson, "Halting the Obesity Epidemic: A Public Health Policy Approach," *Public Health Reports,* January/February 2002.

254. Ronald D. Utt, PhD, *Obesity and Lifestyle: Is it Your Hamburger or Your House?* Washington, DC: Heritage Foundation, http://www.heritage.org/Research/SmartGrowth/wm343.cfm, accessed February 5, 2005.

255. Riina Bray, BASc, MSc, MD, CCFP; Catherine Vakil, MD, CCFP, and David Elliot, PhD, *Report on Public Health and Urban Sprawl in Ontario.,* Toronto, ON: Ontario College of Family Physicians, January 2005.

256. Lewis, pp. 38–42, 239.

257. *State of the Nation's Housing,* Joint Center for Housing Studies of Harvard University,   http://www.jchs.harvard.edu/publications/markets/son2004.pdf, and Mark Vitner, "Are there Storm Clouds Ahead for the Nation's Housing Market? Wachovia Economic Research, http://www.wachovia.com/ws/econ/view/0,2513,00.pdf.

258. *Second Annual Demographia International Housing Affordability Survey,* Demographia and Pavletich Properties, Ltd., http://www.demographia.com/dhi-ix2005q3.pdf.

259. See, for example, *Housing Affordability Calculations: What You Get is not What You Want,* http://propbd.co.nz/afa.asp?idWebPage=9504&idBobDeyProperty Articles=4654&SID=482 962420, May 28, 2005, accessed July 11, 2006.

260. Dr. Timothy Leunig, "Turning NIMBYs into IMBYs", *The Guardian,* September 2, 2004. http://society.guardian.co.uk/housingdemand/0,14488,1192601,00.html, accessed September 3, 2004. The article noted that a 220-acre (90 hectare) farm released for development would rise in value from £500,000 to £250,000,000.

261. Kate Barker (2004). *Review of Housing Supply: Delivering Stability: Securing Our Future Housing Needs: Final Report—Recommendations.* Norwich, England: Her Majesty's Stationery Office. http://www.hm-treasury.gov.uk/consultations and legislation/barker/consult barker index.cfm, accessed March 8, 2005, p. 77

262. Testimony by Paul Pollard. *Productivity Commission, Inquiry into First Home Ownership, Transcript of Proceedings,* February 3, 2004 http://

www.pc.gov.au/inquiry/housing/trans/sydney040203.rtf, accessed February 7, 2005.

263. Proffers are used extensively in the northern Virginia suburbs of Washington, DC.

264. John Landis, Michael Larice, Deva Dawson, and Lan Deng, *Pay to Play: Residential Development Fees in California Cities and Counties, 1999* (Sacramento, CA: State of California Business, Transportation and Housing Agency, August 2001).

265. Landis, Larice, Dawson, and Deng, 2001.

266. Brett M. Braden and Don L. Coursey, "Effects of Impact Fees on the Suburban Chicago Housing Market," *Heartland Policy Study #93*, (Chicago: Heartland Institute, 1999).

267. Development impact fees in the Chicago area are considerably lower than in California. The reviewed sample ranged from $2,200 to $8,900.

268. Donghuan An, Peter Gordon, and Harry Richardson, *The Continuing Decentralization of People and Jobs in the United States*, presentation to the 41st Annual Meeting of the Western Regional Science Association, Monterey, CA, February 17–20, 2002, http://www-rcfuscedu/~pgordon/pdf/wrsa_2002Apdf.

269. Yan Song and Gerrit-Jan Knapp (undated). "New Urbanism and Housing Values: A Disaggregate Assessment," p. 6, http://www.smartgrowth.umd.edu/research/pdf/Jue_paper.pdf, accessed July 2, 2004.

270. Ronald D. Utt, *Review of HUD's 1991 Report: Not in My Back Yard: Removing Barriers to Affordable Housing*, prepared for Aspen Systems and the U.S. Department of Housing and Urban Development, November 8, 2002, p. 1 http://www.demographia.com/db-nimbyreview.pdf.

271. *Not in My Back Yard.*

272. Pipes, p. 246

273. In Las Vegas and Phoenix, governments seem to be seeking to maximize their financial return by sales at well below the rate of demand. No indication was found to indicate that the housing affordability consequences have been seriously considered.

274. Robert Bruegmann, *Sprawl: A Compact History*(Chicago: University of Chicago Press, 2005).

275. Paul Krugman, "About that Hissing Sound in the Zoned Zone," *The New York Times,* 8 August 2005.

276. Edward L. Glaeser and Joseph Gyourko, *The Impact of Zoning on Housing Affordability,* (Cambridge, MA: Harvard Institute of Economic Research, 2002).

277. National Association of Realtors data, www.realtor.org, 2nd quarter 2004.

278. Edward L. Gleaser and Joseph Gyourko, *The Impact of Building Restrictions on Housing Affordability,* http://www.newyorkfed.org/research/epr/03v09n2/0306glae.pdf, 20041212 p. 35.

279. U.S. Department of Housing and Urban Development, *Why Not in Our Backyard: Removing Barriers to Affordable Housing: An Update to the Report of the Advisory Commission on Regulatory Barriers to Affordable Housing,* Washington, 2005, p.5. http://www.huduser.org/Publications/pdf/wnioc.pdf, accessed March 7, 2005.

280. *Second Annual Demographia International Housing Affordability Survey.*

281. *Housing Affordability: USA States: 1970 to 2000,* http://www.demographia.com/db-usafford1970.htm.

282. *Major Market Housing Affordability: United States: 1995–2005,* http://www.demographia.com/db-haff19952005us.htm.

283. People who move from elsewhere in the nation.

284. *Domestic Migration & Land Rationing: U.S. Metropolitan Areas over 1,000,000: 2000–2005,* http://www.demographia.com/db-metmigrasmg.htm.

285. *Second Annual Demographia International Housing Affordability Survey.*

286. *Demographia United States Metropolitan Areas: 2005,* http://www.demographia.com/db-metmic2004.pdf.

287. U.S. Census Bureau estimate, 2000 to 2005.

288. *Demographia United States Metropolitan Area Internal (Domestic) Migration Report: 2000–2005,* http://www.demographia.com/db-2005migdom.pdf,

289. Based upon analysis of 1990 and 2000 census data by Randal O'Toole, "Did Smart Growth Make Portland Affordable," *Vanishing Automobile*

Update #52, March 2005. http://ti.org/vaupdate52.html, accessed March 13, 2005.

290. Calculated from U.S. Bureau of the Census data and Portland Metro data in http://www.metro-region.org/article.cfm?articleid=857, accessed January 7, 2004.

291. Andres Duany, "Punching Holes in Portland," op-ed in *The Oregonian*, December 19, 1999.

292. Jane M. Swift, *Overcoming Barriers to Housing Development in Massachusetts* (Boston: The Pioneer Institute, 2001).

293. Chapter 40B Task Force, *Report to Governor Mitt Romney*, May 31, 2003, http://www.mass.gov/dhcd/Ch40Btf/report/report.pdf.

294. Edward L. Glaeser, Jenny Schuetz, and Bryce Ward, *Regulation and the Rise of Housing Prices in Greater Boston* (Pioneer Institute for Public Policy Research and Rappaport Institute for Greater Boston, Kennedey School of Government, Harvard University, 2005). http://www.ksg.harvard.edu/ rappaport/downloads/housing_regulations/regulation_housingprices.pdf.

295. *Second Annual Demographia International Housing Affordability Survey*.

296. Andrew Sum, Ishwar Khadiwada, Mykhaylo Trub'skyy, with Sheila Palma and Jacqui Matroni, *Home Ownership in Massachusetts: A New Assessment* The Massachusetts Institute for a New Commonwealth, http://www.massinc.org/publications/reports/PolicyBrief3/ policy_brief3.html. Accessed February 7, 2005.

297. Bonnie Huedorfer, Barry Bluestone, and Stan Helmich, *The Greater Boston Housing Report Card 2003: An Assessment of Progress on Housing in the Boston Area*, Center for Regional and Urban Policy of Northeastern University   http://www.curp.neu.edu/pdfs/FinalHousingReportCard.pdf, accessed January 5, 2005.

298. http://www.realtor.org/research.nsf/Pages/MetroPrice, accessed February 7, 2005.

299. Doug French, *Feds Drive Up Nevada Home Prices*, http://www.npri.org/ issues/issues02/i_b081202.htm, accessed February 7, 2005.

300. Mark Latham, quoted in *What's Happening in the Suburbs: Two Views*, Evatt Foundation, http://evatt.labor.net.au/news/17.html, accessed June 1, 2006.

301. Bernard Salt, "LA Likeness Lingers in La-La Land," *The Australian*, July 28, 2005.

302. *Calculated from Summary of Terrestrial Protected Areas in NSW by Type,* Australian Government: Department of the Environment and Heritage, http://www.deh.gov.au/parks/nrs/capad/2002/nsw/nsw-type02.html.

303. *Second Annual Demographia International Housing Affordability Survey.*

304. Marion Powell, *National Summit on Housing Affordability: Resource Paper,* Canberra, Australia, June 2004, p. 23.

305. *Second Annual Demographia International Housing Affordability Survey.*

306. Assumes urban density at outside greenbelt densities and growth from 1931. At Los Angeles suburban densities, only one-third of the greenbelt would have been developed. See: *London: What If there had been No Green Belt? A Development Estimate,* http://www.demographia. com/db-longrbelt.htm.

307. Center for Economics and Business Research, Ltd and Observatoire de l'Economie et des Instiutuions Locales University of Paris XII, 1997. *Two Great Cities: A Comparison of the Economics of London and Paris.*

308. *Second Annual Demographia International Housing Affordability Survey.*

309. See Wendell Cox, *Myths About Urban Growth and the Toronto "Greenbelt,"* Fraser Institute, Vancouver: 2004, http://www.fraserinstitute.ca/ admin/books/files/UrbanGrowth&TorontoGreenbelt.pdf, accessed July 13, 2006.

310. Quebec metropolitan area.

311. Nelson et al.

312. Nelson et al, p. 24 (emphasis in original).

313. J. Phillips and E. Goodstein, "Growth Management and Housing Prices: The Case of Portland, Oregon." *Contemporary Economic Policy* 18:3, 2000 (Cited in Nelson et al.)

314. Nico Calavita, Kenneth Grimes, and Allah Malach, "Inclusionary Housing in California and New Jersey: A Comparative Analysis, *Housing Policy Debate,* Volume 8 Issue 1, 1997, http://www.fanniemaefoundation.org/ programs/hpd/pdf/hpd_0801_calavita.pdf, p. 5.

315. *Second Annual Demographia International Housing Affordability Survey.*

316. E-mail from Andres Duany to a Congress of New Urbanism mailing list (CNU@LSV.UKY.EDU), Subject: Affordable Housing and New Urbanist Principles, July 15, 2004. Emphasis in original

317. Matthew E. Kahn, "Does Sprawl Reduce the Black/White Housing Consumption Gap?" *Housing Policy Debate*, Volume 12, Issue 1.

318. Waldo Lopez-Aqueres, Joelle Skaga, and Tadeusz Kugler (2002). *Housing California's Latino Population in the 21st Century: The Challenge Ahead.* Los Angeles, CA: The Tomas Rivera Policy Institute.

319. Commonwealth of Australia, *Official Committee Hansard House of Representatives Standing Committee on Economics, Finance and Public Administration: Reference: Reserve Bank of Australia Annual Report 2004* Melbourne: August 12, 2005, http://www.aph.gov.au/hansard/reps/commttee/R8516.pdf.

320. Assumes a housing price multiple of 10.0 and a mortgage interest rate of 6.0 percent.

321. Mortgage subsidies required based upon the estimated excess of housing prices (compared to a housing price multiple of 3.0), a 6.0 percent interest rate, and a 30-year mortgage.

322. Benjamin Powell and Edward Stringham, *Housing Supply and Affordability: Do Affordability Mandates Work?* Los Angeles, CA: Reason Foundation, 2004.

323. Assumes mortgage affordability at 29 percent of income and average mortgage interest rate from 2000 to 2004.

324. Remy Prud'homme and Chang-Woon Lee, 1998.

325. Wendell Cox, "Public Transport Performance Indicators: Implications for Emerging Urban Areas", presentation to the CODATU X Congress, Bucharest, Romania, May 2004, http://www.publicpurpose.com/c11-icators.pdf.

326. Center for Economics and Business Research, Ltd and Observatoire de l'Economie et des Instiutuions Locales University of Paris XII, 1997. *Two Great Cities: A Comparison of the Economics of London and Paris.*

327. *Southeast England New Towns Commuting Distance and Urban Area Geographical Size,* http://www.demographia.com/db-seuknewtowns.htm.

328. Peter Hall, *Cities in Civilization* (New York, NY: Pantheon Books, year), pp. 842–887.

329. Millennium Cities Database.

330. Troy, p. 113

331. *Demographia New York Employment and Commuting,* http://www.demographia.com/db-nyc-employ.pdf.

332. Donald Shoup, *The High Cost of Free Parking,* Chicago: Planners Press, 2005.

333. A detailed analysis of the issue will be found in a forthcoming American Highway Users Alliance policy report by the author, which will be posted at http://www.demographia.com/db-freepark.pdf.

334. Calculated from Texas Transportation Institute data.

335. A principal urban area is the largest urban area in a metropolitan area (For example, Los Angeles is the principal urban area in the Los Angeles metropolitan area. Other urban areas in the Los Angeles metropolitan area, such as Riverside-San Bernardino and Simi Valley are smaller and are thus secondary urban areas.

336. Economic Development Research Group, *The Cost of Congestion to the Economy of the Portland Region,* December 5, 2005: http://www.metro-region.org/library_docs/trans/coc_exec_summary_final_4pg.pdf.

337. Delcan and Economic Development Research Group, *Economic Impact Analysis of Investment in a Major Commercial Transportation System for the Greater Vancouver Region,* July 2003: http://www.gvgc.org/pdfs/SW1040_FinalReport_Revised2.pdf.

338. Estimated from U.S. Bureau of the Census, U.S. Federal Transit Administration, and U.S. Federal Highway Administration data for 2000.

339. Based upon transportation plans in effect in 2002. Information from C. Kenneth Orski, "The Myth of Underfunded Mass Transit," *Innovation Briefs,* July-August 2002.

340. Based upon Orski, 2002.

341. Alan Altshuler and David Luberoff, *Mega-Projects: The Changing Politics of Urban Public Investment,* (Washington, DC: Brookings Institution Press, 2003), p. 176.

342. *CAMPO 2030 Mobility Plan*, Austin, TX: Capital Area Metropolitan Planning Organization, 2004 http://www.campotexas.org/.

343. *Demographia Central Business Districts,* http://www.demographia.com/db-cbd2000.pdf.

344. *Demographia New York Employment and Commuting.*

345. *Chicago Suburban Rail Summary,* http://www.publicpurpose.com/ut-cr-chicago.pdf.

346. In recent years, the U.S. Federal Transit Administration has begun to use a one-half (800 meter) radius for planning. This expansion, of course, increases the theoretical number of people served by a mass-transit system. But in fact, there has been no behavioral change that would justify this longer distance. People with cars are not likely to walk one-half mile to access mass transit. Western Europe continues to use the quarter-mile (400 meter) standard.

347. Gerondeau, pp. 221, 223.

348. Gerondeau, p. 221.

349. Annalynn Lacombe, *Welfare Reform and Access to Jobs in Boston* (Washington, D.C.: U.S. Department of Transportation, Bureau of Transportation Statistics, 1998).

350. Steven Raphael and Michael Stoll, *Can Boosting Minority Car-Ownership Rates Narrow Inter-Racial Employment Gaps?* (National Science Foundation, June 2000).

351. Evelyn Blumenberg and Margy Waller, "The Long Journey to Work: A Federal Transportation Policy for Working Families," Center for Urban and Metropolitan Policy, Brookings Institution, July 2003, p. 2.

352. Margy Waller and Mark Alan Hughes, "Working Far from Home: Transportation and Welfare Reform in the Ten Big States," Progressive Policy Institute, August 1, 1999. See also Anne Kim, "Why People Need Affordable Cars," Blueprint: Ideas for a New Century, February 11, 2003, at www.ndol.org/ndol_ci.cfm?contentid=251220&kaid=114&subid=143.

353. Press release, "President Clinton Announces Transportation Grants to Help Low-Income Families," White House, October 16, 2000.

354. *Demographia,* http://www.demographia.com/db-challenge-choice.htm.

355. This is the "guiding principle" of the Demographia websites (http://www.demographia.com/r-msn.htm).

356. Arnadlo Bagnaso and Patrick Le Gales (1997). *Villes en Europe*. Paris, France: La Decouverte.

357. Boris Pushkarev, Jeffrey Zupan, and Robert Cumella, *Urban Rail in America*. (Bloomington, IN: University of Indiana Press, 1982).

358. Calculated from Millennium Cities database.

359. "Illusion of Transit Choice" model output (http://www.publicpurpose.com/ut-mtautocomp.htm)

360. All of these estimates assume that an automobile-competitive mass transit system would be in a subway (underground) configuration. The system would cost less if it were built as an elevated railway, though it would still be far from affordable. Even so, most neighborhoods would not accept being hemmed in by elevated rail viaducts within an average of one-quarter mile in every direction. Automobile-competitive mass-transit service is simply beyond the financial means of any modern, automobile-oriented urban area. Output from model developed in Wendell Cox, "The Illusion of Transit Choice," *Veritas*, March 2002, http://www.publicpurpose.com/illusion.pdf.

361. Sieverts, p. 123

362. Jean Vivier, *Millennium Cities Database for Sustainable Mobility: Analyses and Recommendations* (Brussels, Belgium: International Union of Public Transport, 2001), p. 33–34.

363. John Pucher and Christian Lefevre, *the Urban Transport Crisis in Europe and North America* (Chippenham, UK: Antony Rowe, Ltd, 1996), p. 199.

364. Sieverts, p. 78.

365. Metro, *Metro Measured*, May 1994, p. 7.

366. North County Times, "Our Faith-Based Gridlock Plan," January 9, 2005. http://www.nctimes.com/articles/2005/01/10/opinion/editorials/1_9_0519_20_48.txt. Accessed May 2, 2006.

367. Gerondeau, p. 266.

368. *FHWA Research on Induced Traffic Little Effect*, http://www.publicpurpose.com/hwy-induced.htm.

369. Data for 2001, calculated using National Household Transportation Survey data and assumes that all automobile demand would be transferred to mass transit at average mass-transit commuting speeds. Of course, such a transfer is impossible, because many commute trips simply cannot be made by mass transit.

370. Calculated from Statistics Canada data for 2005 (Martin Turcotte, *The Time it Takes to Get to Work and Back: 2005,* Ottawa: Statistics Canada, 2006, http://www.statcan.ca/english/research/89-622-XIE/89-622-XIE2006001.pdf) .

371. See Competition Commission, *Supermarkets: A Report on the Supply of Groceries from Multiple Stores in the United Kingdom,* http://www.competition-commission.org.uk/reports/446super.htm, accessed December 14, 2004.

372. John Landis, *The Wealth and Poverty of Nations: Why Some Are So Rich and Some are So Poor* (New York: W. W. Norton & Company, year), p. 44.

373. Great Atlantic and Pacific Tea Company.

374. Jack Stanyon, *Challenges of the Future: The Rebirth of Small Independent Retail in America,* NRF Foundation, http://www.morriscommunityfoundation.com/page02challenges.htm, accessed March 6, 2005.

375. Lewis, p. 299.

376. Global Insights, *The Economic Impact of Wal-Mart,* http://www.globalinsight.com/publicDownload/genericContent/11-03-05_walmart.pdf, accessed May 1, 2006.

377. Gerondeau, p. 220.

378. Wendell Cox, *Ceaucescu: Father of Smart Growth,* http://www.heartland.org/Article.cfm?artId=13577, accessed February 28, 2005.

379. Troy, in "Acknowledgment."

380. Raven E. Saks, *Job Creation and Housing Construction: Constraints on Metropolitan Area Employment Growth,* http://www.federalreserve.gov/pubs/feds/2005/200549/200549pap.pdf.

381. Lewis, p. 14.

382. Earliest year for which data are available.

383. Andres Duany, Elizabeth Plater-Zyberk, and Jeff Speck, *Suburban Nation: The Rise of Sprawl and the Decline of the American Dream* (New York: North Point Press, 2000).

384. According to federal immigration data, more than 25 million legal immigrants were admitted from 1959 to 2003, while the number of illegal immigrants in the nation was estimated at 7,000,000 in 2000.

385. Sherrie A. Kossoudji and Stan Sedo, *Immigrants, Natives and Home Ownership*, http://www.chicagofed.org/news_and_conferences/ conferences_and_events/files/ financial_access_for_immigrants_kossoudji.pdf.

386. W. Michael Cox and Richard Alm, *Myths of Rich and Poor: Why We're Better off than We Think* (New York: Basic Books, 1999), pp. 43–44.

387. W. Michael Cox and Richard Alm, "Time Well Spent: The Declining Real Cost of Living in America," *1997 Annual Report: Federal Reserve Bank of Dallas.*

388. Calculated from U.S. Bureau of the Census data.

389. Fredrik Bergström, VD, and Robert Gidehag, *Tänk om Sverige varit en amerikansk delstat: En diskussion och analys av hushållsinkomster i Sverige och USA och betydelsen av ekonomisk tillväxt*, Stockholm, Sweden: The Swedish Research Institute of Trade (HUI), 2002.

390. Calculated from U.S. Department of Commerce Gross Domestic Product data and U.S. Bureau of Labor Statistics data.

391. Joseph A. Schumpeter, *Capitalism, Socialism and Democracy* (New York: Harper and Row, 1950), p. 67 (quoted in Cox and Alm, 1997).

392. Benjamin M. Friedman, *The Moral Consequences of Economic Growth* (New York: Alfed A. Knopf, 2005).

393. Mel Weber, "The Joys of "Spread City," *Urban Design*, 1998: 3(4), pp. 201–226.

394. Calculated from national census data.

395. Calculated from U.S. Bureau of the Census data.

396. Calculated from INSEE data.

397. Calculated from Japan Statistics Bureau data.

398. Calculated from Statistics Canada data.

399. Adam Smith, *The Wealth of Nations* (New York: The Modern Library, 1937), p. 129.

400. Anti-suburbanites indicate a preference for local street grids, claiming that they reduce traffic congestion compared to cul-de-sacs and loop designs. In fact, local street traffic volumes are small and where they become large, neighborhoods often seek traffic restraint measures or the development of "virtual" cul-de-sacs by blocking entry at some intersections. In fact, cul-de-sacs and loops are safer than local street grids, while they consume considerably less space. See Julie Tasker Brown and Sevag Pogharian, *Learning from Suburbia: Residential Street Pattern Design* (Ottawa, ON: Canada Mortgage and Housing Corporation, March 2000).

401. Sieverts, p. 33.

402. Department for Transport (United Kingdom), *The Future of Transport White Paper—6234*, http://www.dft.gov.uk/strategy/futureoftransport/statement.htm, (July 26, 2004).

403. Michael Stevens, Tim Lomax, Tim, David Ellis, Alan E. Pisarski, and Wendell Cox, *Texas' Roadways—Texas' Future: A Look at the Next 25 Years of Roadway Supply, Demand, Cost, and Benefits* (Austin, TX: Governor's Business Council, 2003).

404. Travel Time Index of 1.15 to 1.25.

405. Our 2004 report proposed this strategy, See Wendell Cox and Alan Pisarski, *Blueprint 2030: Affordable Mobility and Access for All of Atlanta and Georgia* (Atlanta: Georgians for Better Transportation, 2004). http://ciprg.com/ul/gbt/atl-report-20040621.pdf, accessed May 5, 2006.

406. This issue is further discussed in *Urban Tours by Rental Car: The Kansas City Advantage: Livability,* http://www.rentalcartours.net/rac-kc.pdf.

407. The Kansas City urban area has 1,361,000 residents and a population density of 2,330 per square mile (2000).

408. *Major High-Income World Urban Areas: Freeway Access and Capacity,* www.publicpurpose.com/ut-worldfwy.htm.

409. Wendell Cox, *A Common Sense Approach to Transportation in Atlanta* (Atlanta, GA: Georgia Public Policy Foundation, June 2000), http://www.publicpurpose.com/ut-atl2000.pdf.

410. *Major High-Income World Urban Areas: Freeway Access and Capacity*, www.publicpurpose.com/ut-worldfwy.htm.

411. Demographia, *Housing and Transport in Montreal: How Suburbanization is Improving the Region's Competitiveness*, Montreal, QC: Institut économique de Montréal, 2006. http://www.iedm.org/uploaded/pdf/juillet06_en.pdf (in French: http://www.iedm.org/uploaded/pdf/juillet06_fr.pdf), accessed July 8, 2006.

412. *Cairo: Urban Planning Model* (http://www.rentalcartours.net/rac-cairo.pdf).

413. Sieverts p. 78.

414. James Heartfield, *Farewell to the City?*, http://www.spiked-online.com/Articles/0000000CAFFC.htm, accessed May 7, 2006.

415. His son, Jerry, did not share this optimism and popularized the term "era of limits" as governor two decades later.

416. Sieverts, p. 3.

417. Photograph by author.

418. September 1952 speech, transcribed by author from *Great Speeches of the 20t^{b} Century*, (CD), Rhine Records, 1991.

419. *Demographia World Urban Areas*, http://www.demographia.com/db-worldua.pdf.

Index

A&P, 173
Adelaide, 37, 138, 139, 140
advertising, 10
Africa, 12, 13
African Americans
  in the 1960s, 64
  move to the suburbs, 66
  population distribution, 57–58
  prejudice, 58
  and property values, 63
  and World War II, 57–58
agriculture
  amount of land used for, 71
  Australia, 71, 73
  Canada, 71, 73
  Japan, 73
  threat to, 78
  U.S., 71
air pollution, 186
  health effects of, 87
  and population density, 86–87
  reduction of, 186
  from transportation, 85
Alm, R., 186, 187
Altshuler, A., 158
amalgamation, 104–107
American democracy, 109
American Dream, the, 5, 20–21, 202
American Planning Association, the, 103
anti-automobile movement, 28
anti-sprawl activists
  beliefs of, 7
  fervor of, 4
  inventiveness of, 4
anti-sprawl movement, 5, 6
anti-suburban movement

acceptable sprawls, 28
affordable-housing mandates, 146
automobile use and, 24
beliefs of, 8
cause of suburbanization, 102
and central planning, 102–103
and community, 112
definition of, 8
and the development of big-box stores, 171
failure of, 115, 175–178
favoritism, 130
housing affordability and, 142
jobs-housing balance, 153–155
land-use regulations, 180
mass transit, 155
new urbanism, 111
and obesity, 113–115
and open spaces, 73
plan for the future, 177
price of, 180–181
priorities of, 181
research by, 175
and retail, 170
and semantics, 8
serial land development, 76
speculation, 125–126
subsidies and, 146
transportation, 155
vision of, 8–9
anti-suburban policies
  broader context, 12
  consequences of, 119
  densification, 121
  distribution of wealth, 149
  and dystopia, 178

978-0-595-39948-2
0-595-39948-7

Printed in the United States
64249LVS00010B/103